The Complete Air Fryer Cookbook Beginners

Master the Art of Air Frying with Quick, Delicious, and Effortless Recipes for Every Meal—From Breakfasts to Dinners and Sweet Treats

Weldon Frederick

Copyright© 2025 By Weldon Frederick

All rights reserved worldwide.

No part of this book may be reproduced or transmitted in any form or by any means, electronic or mechanical, including photo- copying, recording or by any information storage and retrieval system, without written permission from the publisher, except for the inclusion of brief quotations in a review.

Warning-Disclaimer

The purpose of this book is to educate and entertain. The author or publisher does not guarantee that anyone following the techniques, suggestions, tips, ideas, or strategies will become successful. The author and publisher shall have neither liability or responsibility to anyone with respect to any loss or damage caused, or alleged to be caused, directly or indirectly by the information contained in this book.

Table of Contents

INTRODUCTION ……………………………………………………………… 2
Chapter 1   Breakfasts ……………………………………………………… 5
Chapter 2   Family Favorites …………………………………………… 17
Chapter 3   Fast and Easy Everyday Favorites ……………………… 23
Chapter 4   Snacks and Appetizers ……………………………………… 28
Chapter 5   Poultry ………………………………………………………… 40
Chapter 6   Beef, Pork, and Lamb ……………………………………… 53
Chapter 7   Fish and Seafood …………………………………………… 66
Chapter 8   Vegetables and Sides ……………………………………… 78
Chapter 9   Vegetarian Mains …………………………………………… 89
Chapter 10   Desserts ……………………………………………………… 94
Appendix 1   Air Fryer Cooking Chart …………………………………… 101
Appendix 2   Index …………………………………………………………… 103

INTRODUCTION

The Complete Air Fryer Cookbook for Beginners is more than just a recipe collection—it's a gateway to a healthier, more efficient, and delicious cooking experience. Featuring over 300 recipes that span every meal, snack, and dessert, this book is your ultimate guide to mastering the art of air frying. Whether you're preparing breakfast for one, dinner for the family, or hosting a party, this cookbook will help you create mouthwatering dishes with ease.

Why Choose Air Frying?

Air frying has revolutionized modern cooking by providing a healthier alternative to traditional frying methods. Using rapid air circulation, air fryers create a crispy, golden finish with minimal oil, preserving the natural flavors and textures of your ingredients. This means you can indulge in your favorite meals—crispy fries, juicy chicken, or decadent desserts—without the guilt. With the help of this cookbook, you'll learn how to achieve perfectly cooked results while prioritizing your health. Benefits of air frying include:

1. Reduced Fat Content. Air fryers use up to 85% less oil than traditional deep-frying methods, making your meals lighter and heart-healthier.

2. Preserved Nutrients. By cooking with less oil and shorter cooking times, air fryers retain the essential vitamins and minerals in your food.

3. Quick and Convenient. Air fryers are perfect for busy lifestyles, offering fast cooking times and easy cleanup.

A Recipe for Every Occasion

This cookbook caters to every meal of the day and every taste preference, ensuring you never run out of ideas for your air fryer. Here's a glimpse of the variety you'll find:

1. Breakfast Delights to Start Your Day Right. Why settle for a rushed morning meal when you can prepare wholesome, satisfying breakfasts in your air fryer? Recipes like Creamy Avocado Bacon Eggs, Sweet Potato Breakfast Hash, and Maple Glazed Doughnuts will energize your mornings with minimal effort.

2. Family Favorites Everyone Will Love. Bring the family together over crowd-pleasing dishes such as Cheesy Roasted Sweet Potatoes, Steak and Vegetable Kebabs, and Berry Cheesecake. These recipes are easy to prepare and guaranteed to satisfy even the pickiest eaters.

3. Quick and Easy Snacks and Appetizers. Whether you're hosting a party or craving a midday snack, this cookbook has you covered with options like Buffalo Bites, Crispy Breaded Beef Cubes, and Parmesan French Fries. These bite-sized treats are perfect for sharing—or keeping all to yourself.

4. Decadent Desserts to Satisfy Your Sweet Tooth. Indulge in guilt-free sweets made in your air fryer, such as Blackberry Peach Cobbler, Bourbon Bread Pudding, and Double Chocolate Brownies. These recipes prove that healthy eating can still be deliciously indulgent.

Simplicity Meets Versatility: The Air Fryer Advantage

The air fryer is not just a tool—it's a game-changer. This book includes detailed instructions to help beginners and seasoned cooks alike unlock its full potential. From basic tips like preheating to advanced techniques like baking and dehydrating, you'll learn how to use your air fryer for a wide range of culinary tasks.

1. Mastering the Basics. Even if you're

new to cooking, this book makes it easy to get started. Each recipe comes with step-by-step instructions, cooking times, and portion sizes, so you can confidently prepare meals without guesswork.

2. Beyond Frying. The air fryer's capabilities go far beyond frying. With recipes for roasting, grilling, baking, and even steaming, you can create diverse dishes like Lemon Garlic Shrimp with Zucchini Ribbons, Roasted Snapper with Shallots and Fresh Tomatoes, and Classic Fish Burgers with Tartar Sauce.

3. Time-Saving Techniques. For busy individuals, the air fryer is a lifesaver. With most recipes requiring under 30 minutes of cooking time, you'll spend less time in the kitchen and more time enjoying your meals. Plus, the easy cleanup ensures that cooking remains a stress-free activity.

Healthy Eating Made Easy and Enjoyable

The Complete Air Fryer Cookbook for Beginners is designed with health-conscious cooks in mind. From vegetarian mains like Creamy Russet Potato Au Gratin and Greek-Style Eggplant Boats to low-fat poultry dishes like Herb-Roasted Thanksgiving Turkey Breast, this book offers recipes that align with your dietary goals.

It also includes nutritional information for every recipe, empowering you to make informed choices about what you eat. Whether you're watching your calorie intake, reducing carbs, or increasing your protein consumption, there's a recipe to suit your needs.

A Lifelong Companion in Your Kitchen

This cookbook isn't just for beginners—it's a resource you'll return to time and again. With its extensive range of recipes and easy-to-follow guidance, it's perfect for anyone who wants to explore the endless possibilities of air frying. Whether you're preparing a quick weeknight dinner or hosting a lavish holiday feast, this book ensures that every dish turns out perfectly.

Ready to Transform Your Cooking?

The Complete Air Fryer Cookbook for Beginners is more than a recipe collection—it's an invitation to embrace a healthier, more delicious way of cooking. With 2000+ days of diverse, easy-to-make recipes, this book will inspire you to get creative in the kitchen and enjoy every meal you prepare.

Dive in and discover how the air fryer can revolutionize your cooking, one dish at a time. Start your journey to effortless, healthy, and flavorful meals today!

Chapter 1

Breakfasts

Creamy Bacon Cheese Quiche

Prep time: 5 minutes | Cook time: 12 minutes | Serves 2

3 large eggs
2 tablespoons heavy whipping cream
¼ teaspoon salt
4 slices cooked sugar-free bacon, crumbled
½ cup shredded mild Cheddar cheese

1. In a large bowl, whisk eggs, cream, and salt together until combined. Mix in bacon and Cheddar. 2. Pour mixture evenly into two ungreased ramekins. Place into air fryer basket. Adjust the temperature to 320ºF (160ºC) and bake for 12 minutes. Quiche will be fluffy and set in the middle when done. 3. Let quiche cool in ramekins 5 minutes. Serve warm.

Twice-Dipped Cinnamon Biscuits

Prep time: 15 minutes | Cook time: 13 minutes | Makes 8 biscuits

2 cups blanched almond flour
½ cup Swerve confectioners'-style sweetener or equivalent amount of liquid or powdered sweetener
1 teaspoon baking powder
½ teaspoon fine sea salt
Glaze:
½ cup Swerve confectioners'-style sweetener or equivalent amount of powdered
¼ cup plus 2 tablespoons (¾ stick) very cold unsalted butter
¼ cup unsweetened, unflavored almond milk
1 large egg
1 teaspoon vanilla extract
3 teaspoons ground cinnamon

sweetener
¼ cup heavy cream or unsweetened, unflavored almond milk

1. Preheat the air fryer to 350ºF (177ºC). Line a pie pan that fits into your air fryer with parchment paper. 2. In a medium-sized bowl, mix together the almond flour, sweetener (if powdered; do not add liquid sweetener), baking powder, and salt. Cut the butter into ½-inch squares, then use a hand mixer to work the butter into the dry ingredients. When you are done, the mixture should still have chunks of butter. 3. In a small bowl, whisk together the almond milk, egg, and vanilla extract (if using liquid sweetener, add it as well) until blended. Using a fork, stir the wet ingredients into the dry ingredients until large clumps form. Add the cinnamon and use your hands to swirl it into the dough. 4. Form the dough into sixteen 1-inch balls and place them on the prepared pan, spacing them about ½ inch apart. (If you're using a smaller air fryer, work in batches if necessary.) Bake in the air fryer until golden, 10 to 13 minutes. Remove from the air fryer and let cool on the pan for at least 5 minutes. 5. While the biscuits bake, make the glaze: Place the powdered sweetener in a small bowl and slowly stir in the heavy cream with a fork. 6. When the biscuits have cooled somewhat, dip the tops into the glaze, allow it to dry a bit, and then dip again for a thick glaze. 7. Serve warm or at room temperature. Store unglazed biscuits in an airtight container in the refrigerator for up to 3 days or in the freezer for up to a month. Reheat in a preheated 350ºF (177ºC) air fryer for 5 minutes, or until warmed through, and dip in the glaze as instructed above.

Sweet Potato Breakfast Hash

Prep time: 15 minutes | Cook time: 18 minutes | Serves 6

2 medium sweet potatoes, peeled and cut into 1-inch cubes
½ green bell pepper, diced
½ red onion, diced
4 ounces (113 g) baby bella mushrooms, diced
2 tablespoons olive oil
1 garlic clove, minced
½ teaspoon salt
½ teaspoon black pepper
½ tablespoon chopped fresh rosemary

1. Preheat the air fryer to 380ºF (193ºC). 2. In a large bowl, toss all ingredients together until the vegetables are well coated and seasonings distributed. 3. Pour the vegetables into the air fryer basket, making sure they are in a single even layer. (If using a smaller air fryer, you may need to do this in two batches.) 4. Roast for 9 minutes, then toss or flip the vegetables. Roast for 9 minutes more. 5. Transfer to a serving bowl or individual plates and enjoy.

Cheesy Jalapeño Egg Cups

Prep time: 10 minutes | Cook time: 10 minutes | Serves 2

4 large eggs
¼ cup chopped pickled jalapeños
2 ounces (57 g) full-fat
cream cheese
½ cup shredded sharp Cheddar cheese

1. In a medium bowl, beat the eggs, then pour into four silicone muffin cups. 2. In a large microwave-safe bowl, place jalapeños, cream cheese, and Cheddar. Microwave for 30 seconds and stir. Take a spoonful, approximately ¼ of the mixture, and place it in the center of one of the egg cups. Repeat with remaining mixture. 3. Place egg cups into the air fryer basket. 4. Adjust the temperature to 320ºF (160ºC) and bake for 10 minutes. 5. Serve warm.

Crunchy Nut Granola

Prep time: 5 minutes | Cook time: 1 hour | Serves 4

½ cup pecans, coarsely chopped
½ cup walnuts or almonds, coarsely chopped
¼ cup unsweetened flaked coconut
¼ cup almond flour
¼ cup ground flaxseed or chia seeds
2 tablespoons sunflower seeds
2 tablespoons melted butter
¼ cup Swerve
½ teaspoon ground cinnamon
½ teaspoon vanilla extract
¼ teaspoon ground nutmeg
¼ teaspoon salt
2 tablespoons water

1. Preheat the air fryer to 250ºF (121ºC). Cut a piece of parchment paper to fit inside the air fryer basket. 2. In a large bowl, toss the nuts, coconut, almond flour, ground flaxseed or chia seeds, sunflower seeds, butter, Swerve, cinnamon, vanilla, nutmeg, salt, and water until thoroughly combined. 3. Spread the granola on the parchment paper and flatten to an even thickness. 4. Air fry for about an hour, or until golden throughout. Remove from the air fryer and allow to fully cool. Break the granola into bite-size pieces and store in a covered container for up to a week.

Maple Crunch Granola

Prep time: 5 minutes | Cook time: 40 minutes | Makes 2 cups

1 cup rolled oats
3 tablespoons pure maple syrup
1 tablespoon sugar
1 tablespoon neutral-flavored oil, such as refined coconut, sunflower, or safflower
¼ teaspoon sea salt
¼ teaspoon ground cinnamon
¼ teaspoon vanilla extract

1. Insert the crisper plate into the basket and the basket into the unit. Preheat the unit by selecting BAKE, setting the temperature to 250ºF (121ºC), and setting the time to 3 minutes. Select START/STOP to begin. 2. In a medium bowl, stir together the oats, maple syrup, sugar, oil, salt, cinnamon, and vanilla until thoroughly combined. Transfer the granola to a 6-by-2-inch round baking pan. 3. Once the unit is preheated, place the pan into the basket. 4. Select BAKE, set the temperature to 250ºF (121ºC) and set the time to 40 minutes. Select START/STOP to begin. 5. After 10 minutes, stir the granola well. Resume cooking, stirring the granola every 10 minutes, for a total of 40 minutes, or until the granola is lightly browned and mostly dry. 6. When the cooking is complete, place the granola on a plate to cool. It will become crisp as it cools. Store the completely cooled granola in an airtight container in a cool, dry place for 1 to 2 weeks.

Creamy Avocado Bacon Egg

Prep time: 15 minutes | Cook time: 20 minutes | Serves 4

6 large eggs
¼ cup heavy whipping cream
1½ cups chopped cauliflower
1 cup shredded medium Cheddar cheese
1 medium avocado, peeled and pitted
8 tablespoons full-fat sour cream
2 scallions, sliced on the bias
12 slices sugar-free bacon, cooked and crumbled

1. In a medium bowl, whisk eggs and cream together. Pour into a round baking dish. 2. Add cauliflower and mix, then top with Cheddar. Place dish into the air fryer basket. 3. Adjust the temperature to 320ºF (160ºC) and set the timer for 20 minutes. 4. When completely cooked, eggs will be firm and cheese will be browned. Slice into four pieces. 5. Slice avocado and divide evenly among pieces. Top each piece with 2 tablespoons sour cream, sliced scallions, and crumbled bacon.

Spiced Raisin Bagels

Prep time: 30 minutes | Cook time: 10 minutes | Makes 4 bagels

Oil, for spraying
¼ cup raisins
1 cup self-rising flour, plus more for dusting
1 cup plain Greek yogurt
1 teaspoon ground cinnamon
1 large egg

1. Line the air fryer basket with parchment and spray lightly with oil. 2. Place the raisins in a bowl of hot water and let sit for 10 to 15 minutes, until they have plumped. This will make them extra juicy. 3. In a large bowl, mix together the flour, yogurt, and cinnamon with your hands or a large silicone spatula until a ball is formed. It will be quite sticky for a while. 4. Drain the raisins and gently work them into the ball of dough. 5. Place the dough on a lightly floured work surface and divide into 4 equal pieces. Roll each piece into an 8- or 9-inch-long rope and shape it into a circle, pinching the ends together to seal. 6. In a small bowl, whisk the egg. Brush the egg onto the tops of the dough. 7. Place the dough in the prepared basket. 8. Air fry at 350ºF (177ºC) for 10 minutes. Serve immediately.

Breakfasts

Stuffed Hash Browns with Mushrooms and Tomatoes

Prep time: 10 minutes | Cook time: 20 minutes | Serves 4

Olive oil cooking spray
1 tablespoon plus 2 teaspoons olive oil, divided
4 ounces (113 g) baby bella mushrooms, diced
1 scallion, white parts and green parts, diced
1 garlic clove, minced
2 cups shredded potatoes
½ teaspoon salt
¼ teaspoon black pepper
1 Roma tomato, diced
½ cup shredded mozzarella

1. Preheat the air fryer to 380°F(193°C). Lightly coat the inside of a 6-inch cake pan with olive oil cooking spray. 2. In a small skillet, heat 2 teaspoons olive oil over medium heat. Add the mushrooms, scallion, and garlic, and cook for 4 to 5 minutes, or until they have softened and are beginning to show some color. Remove from heat. 3. Meanwhile, in a large bowl, combine the potatoes, salt, pepper, and the remaining tablespoon olive oil. Toss until all potatoes are well coated. 4. Pour half of the potatoes into the bottom of the cake pan. Top with the mushroom mixture, tomato, and mozzarella. Spread the remaining potatoes over the top. 5. Bake in the air fryer for 12 to 15 minutes, or until the top is golden brown. 6. Remove from the air fryer and allow to cool for 5 minutes before slicing and serving.

Healthy Oat Bran Muffins

Prep time: 10 minutes | Cook time: 10 to 12 minutes per batch | Makes 8 muffins

⅔ cup oat bran
½ cup flour
¼ cup brown sugar
1 teaspoon baking powder
½ teaspoon baking soda
⅛ teaspoon salt
½ cup buttermilk
1 egg
2 tablespoons canola oil
½ cup chopped dates, raisins, or dried cranberries
24 paper muffin cups
Cooking spray

1. Preheat the air fryer to 330°F (166°C). 2. In a large bowl, combine the oat bran, flour, brown sugar, baking powder, baking soda, and salt. 3. In a small bowl, beat together the buttermilk, egg, and oil. 4. Pour buttermilk mixture into bowl with dry ingredients and stir just until moistened. Do not beat. 5. Gently stir in dried fruit. 6. Use triple baking cups to help muffins hold shape during baking. Spray them with cooking spray, place 4 sets of cups in air fryer basket at a time, and fill each one ¾ full of batter. 7. Cook for 10 to 12 minutes, until top springs back when lightly touched and toothpick inserted in center comes out clean. 8. Repeat for remaining muffins.

Shrimp Bite-Sized Frittata

Prep time: 15 minutes | Cook time: 20 minutes | Serves 4

1 teaspoon olive oil, plus more for spraying
½ small red bell pepper, finely diced
1 teaspoon minced garlic
1 (4-ounce / 113-g) can of tiny shrimp, drained
Salt and freshly ground black pepper, to taste
4 eggs, beaten
4 teaspoons ricotta cheese

1. Spray four ramekins with olive oil. 2. In a medium skillet over medium-low heat, heat 1 teaspoon of olive oil. Add the bell pepper and garlic and sauté until the pepper is soft, about 5 minutes 3. Add the shrimp, season with salt and pepper, and cook until warm, 1 to 2 minutes. Remove from the heat. 4. Add the eggs and stir to combine. 5. Pour one quarter of the mixture into each ramekin. 6. Place 2 ramekins in the air fryer basket and bake at 350°F (177°C) for 6 minutes. 7. Remove the air fryer basket from the air fryer and stir the mixture in each ramekin. Top each frittata with 1 teaspoon of ricotta cheese. Return the air fryer basket to the air fryer and cook until eggs are set and the top is lightly browned, 4 to 5 minutes. 8. Repeat with the remaining two ramekins.

Triple-Berry Oven Pancake

Prep time: 10 minutes | Cook time: 12 to 16 minutes | Serves 4

2 egg whites
1 egg
½ cup whole-wheat pastry flour
½ cup 2% milk
1 teaspoon pure vanilla extract
1 tablespoon unsalted butter, melted
1 cup sliced fresh strawberries
½ cup fresh blueberries
½ cup fresh raspberries

1. In a medium bowl, use an eggbeater or hand mixer to quickly mix the egg whites, egg, pastry flour, milk, and vanilla until well combined. 2. Use a pastry brush to grease the bottom of a baking pan with the melted butter. Immediately pour in the batter and put the basket back in the fryer. Bake at 330°F (166°C) for 12 to 16 minutes, or until the pancake is puffed and golden brown. 3. Remove the pan from the air fryer; the pancake will fall. Top with the strawberries, blueberries, and raspberries. Serve immediately.

Spiced Apple Cider Donut Holes

Prep time: 10 minutes | Cook time: 6 minutes | Makes 10 mini doughnuts

Doughnut Holes:
1½ cups all-purpose flour
2 tablespoons granulated sugar
2 teaspoons baking powder
1 teaspoon baking soda
½ teaspoon kosher salt
Pinch of freshly grated nutmeg
¼ cup plus 2 tablespoons buttermilk, chilled
2 tablespoons apple cider (hard or nonalcoholic), chilled
1 large egg, lightly beaten
Vegetable oil, for brushing

Glaze:
½ cup powdered sugar
2 tablespoons unsweetened applesauce
¼ teaspoon vanilla extract
Pinch of kosher salt

1. Make the doughnut holes: In a bowl, whisk together the flour, granulated sugar, baking powder, baking soda, salt, and nutmeg until smooth. Add the buttermilk, cider, and egg and stir with a small rubber spatula or spoon until the dough just comes together. 2. Using a 1 ounce (28 g) ice cream scoop or 2 tablespoons, scoop and drop 10 balls of dough into the air fryer basket, spaced evenly apart, and brush the tops lightly with oil. Air fry at 350°F (177°C) until the doughnut holes are golden brown and fluffy, about 6 minutes. Transfer the doughnut holes to a wire rack to cool completely. 3. Make the glaze: In a small bowl, stir together the powdered sugar, applesauce, vanilla, and salt until smooth. 4. Dip the tops of the doughnuts holes in the glaze, then let stand until the glaze sets before serving. If you're impatient and want warm doughnuts, have the glaze ready to go while the doughnuts cook, then use the glaze as a dipping sauce for the warm doughnuts, fresh out of the air fryer.

Fully Loaded Breakfast Toast

Prep time: 10 minutes | Cook time: 10 minutes | Serves 1

1 strip bacon, diced
1 slice 1-inch thick bread
1 egg
Salt and freshly ground black pepper, to taste
¼ cup grated Colby cheese

1. Preheat the air fryer to 400°F (204°C). 2. Air fry the bacon for 3 minutes, shaking the basket once or twice while it cooks. Remove the bacon to a paper towel lined plate and set aside. 3. Use a sharp paring knife to score a large circle in the middle of the slice of bread, cutting halfway through, but not all the way through to the cutting board. Press down on the circle in the center of the bread slice to create an indentation. 4. Transfer the slice of bread, hole side up, to the air fryer basket. Crack the egg into the center of the bread, and season with salt and pepper. 5. Adjust the air fryer temperature to 380°F (193°C) and air fry for 5 minutes. Sprinkle the grated cheese around the edges of the bread, leaving the center of the yolk uncovered, and top with the cooked bacon. Press the cheese and bacon into the bread lightly to help anchor it to the bread and prevent it from blowing around in the air fryer. 6. Air fry for one or two more minutes, just to melt the cheese and finish cooking the egg. Serve immediately.

Ultimate Everything Bagels

Prep time: 15 minutes | Cook time: 14 minutes | Makes 6 bagels

1¾ cups shredded Mozzarella cheese or goat cheese Mozzarella
2 tablespoons unsalted butter or coconut oil
1 large egg, beaten
1 tablespoon apple cider vinegar
1 cup blanched almond flour
1 tablespoon baking powder
⅛ teaspoon fine sea salt
1½ teaspoons everything bagel seasoning

1. Make the dough: Put the Mozzarella and butter in a large microwave-safe bowl and microwave for 1 to 2 minutes, until the cheese is entirely melted. Stir well. Add the egg and vinegar. Using a hand mixer on medium, combine well. Add the almond flour, baking powder, and salt and, using the mixer, combine well. 2. Lay a piece of parchment paper on the countertop and place the dough on it. Knead it for about 3 minutes. The dough should be a little sticky but pliable. (If the dough is too sticky, chill it in the refrigerator for an hour or overnight.) 3. Preheat the air fryer to 350°F (177°C). Spray a baking sheet or pie pan that will fit into your air fryer with avocado oil. 4. Divide the dough into 6 equal portions. Roll 1 portion into a log that is 6 inches long and about ½ inch thick. Form the log into a circle and seal the edges together, making a bagel shape. Repeat with the remaining portions of dough, making 6 bagels. 5. Place the bagels on the greased baking sheet. Spray the bagels with avocado oil and top with everything bagel seasoning, pressing the seasoning into the dough with your hands. 6. Place the bagels in the air fryer and bake for 14 minutes, or until cooked through and golden brown, flipping after 6 minutes. 7. Remove the bagels from the air fryer and allow them to cool slightly before slicing them in half and serving. Store leftovers in an airtight container in the fridge for up to 4 days or in the freezer for up to a month.

Maple Glazed Doughnuts

Prep time: 10 minutes | Cook time: 14 minutes | Makes 8 doughnuts

1 (8-count) can jumbo flaky refrigerator biscuits	2 cups confectioners' sugar, plus more for dusting (optional)
Cooking oil spray	2 teaspoons pure maple syrup
½ cup light brown sugar	
¼ cup butter	
3 tablespoons milk	

1. Insert the crisper plate into the basket and the basket into the unit. Preheat the unit by selecting AIR FRY, setting the temperature to 350°F (177°C), and setting the time to 3 minutes. Select START/STOP to begin. 2. Remove the biscuits from the tube and cut out the center of each biscuit with a small, round cookie cutter. 3. Once the unit is preheated, spray the crisper plate with cooking oil. Working in batches, place 4 doughnuts into the basket. 4. Select AIR FRY, set the temperature to 350°F (177°C), and set the time to 5 minutes. Select START/STOP to begin. 5. When the cooking is complete, place the doughnuts on a plate. Repeat steps 3 and 4 with the remaining doughnuts. 6. In a small saucepan over medium heat, combine the brown sugar, butter, and milk. Heat until the butter is melted and the sugar is dissolved, about 4 minutes. 7. Remove the pan from the heat and whisk in the confectioners' sugar and maple syrup until smooth. 8. Dip the slightly cooled doughnuts into the maple glaze. Place them on a wire rack and dust with confectioners' sugar (if using). Let rest just until the glaze sets. Enjoy the doughnuts warm.

Full English Breakfast

Prep time: 5 minutes | Cook time: 25 minutes | Serves 2

1 cup potatoes, sliced and diced	2 eggs
2 cups beans in tomato sauce	1 tablespoon olive oil
	1 sausage
	Salt, to taste

1. Preheat the air fryer to 390°F (199°C) and allow to warm. 2. Break the eggs onto a baking dish and sprinkle with salt. 3. Lay the beans on the dish, next to the eggs. 4. In a bowl, coat the potatoes with the olive oil. Sprinkle with salt. 5. Transfer the bowl of potato slices to the air fryer and bake for 10 minutes. 6. Swap out the bowl of potatoes for the dish containing the eggs and beans. Bake for another 10 minutes. Cover the potatoes with parchment paper. 7. Slice up the sausage and throw the slices on top of the beans and eggs. Bake for another 5 minutes. 8. Serve with the potatoes.

DIY Breakfast Toaster Pastrie

Prep time: 10 minutes | Cook time: 11 minutes | Makes 6 pastries

Oil, for spraying	preserves of choice
1 (15-ounce / 425-g) package refrigerated piecrust	2 cups confectioners' sugar
	3 tablespoons milk
6 tablespoons jam or	1 to 2 tablespoons sprinkles of choice

1. Preheat the air fryer to 350°F (177°C). Line the air fryer basket with parchment and spray lightly with oil. 2. Cut the piecrust into 12 rectangles, about 3 by 4 inches each. You will need to reroll the dough scraps to get 12 rectangles. 3. Spread 1 tablespoon of jam in the center of 6 rectangles, leaving ¼ inch around the edges. 4. Pour some water into a small bowl. Use your finger to moisten the edge of each rectangle. 5. Top each rectangle with another and use your fingers to press around the edges. Using the tines of a fork, seal the edges of the dough and poke a few holes in the top of each one. Place the pastries in the prepared basket. 6. Air fry for 11 minutes. Let cool completely. 7. In a medium bowl, whisk together the confectioners' sugar and milk. Spread the icing over the tops of the pastries and add sprinkles. Serve immediately

Zesty Lemon and Blueberry Muffins

Prep time: 5 minutes | Cook time: 20 to 25 minutes | Makes 6 muffins

1¼ cups almond flour	1 tablespoon almond milk
3 tablespoons Swerve	1 tablespoon fresh lemon juice
1 teaspoon baking powder	½ cup fresh blueberries
2 large eggs	
3 tablespoons melted butter	

1. Preheat the air fryer to 350°F (177°C). Lightly coat 6 silicone muffin cups with vegetable oil. Set aside. 2. In a large mixing bowl, combine the almond flour, Swerve, and baking soda. Set aside. 3. In a separate small bowl, whisk together the eggs, butter, milk, and lemon juice. Add the egg mixture to the flour mixture and stir until just combined. Fold in the blueberries and let the batter sit for 5 minutes. 4. Spoon the muffin batter into the muffin cups, about two-thirds full. Air fry for 20 to 25 minutes, or until a toothpick inserted into the center of a muffin comes out clean. 5. Remove the basket from the air fryer and let the muffins cool for about 5 minutes before transferring them to a wire rack to cool completely.

Spring Veggie Strata

Prep time: 10 minutes | Cook time: 14 to 20 minutes | Serves 4

8 large asparagus spears, trimmed and cut into 2-inch pieces
⅓ cup shredded carrot
½ cup chopped red bell pepper
2 slices low-sodium whole-wheat bread, cut into ½-inch cubes
3 egg whites
1 egg
3 tablespoons 1% milk
½ teaspoon dried thyme

1. In a baking pan, combine the asparagus, carrot, red bell pepper, and 1 tablespoon of water. Bake in the air fryer at 330°F (166°C) for 3 to 5 minutes, or until crisp-tender. Drain well. 2. Add the bread cubes to the vegetables and gently toss. 3. In a medium bowl, whisk the egg whites, egg, milk, and thyme until frothy. 4. Pour the egg mixture into the pan. Bake for 11 to 15 minutes, or until the strata is slightly puffy and set and the top starts to brown. Serve.

Steakhouse Eggs and Strips

Prep time: 8 minutes | Cook time: 14 minutes per batch | Serves 4

Cooking oil spray
4 (4-ounce / 113-g) New York strip steaks
1 teaspoon granulated garlic, divided
1 teaspoon salt, divided
1 teaspoon freshly ground black pepper, divided
4 eggs
½ teaspoon paprika

1. Insert the crisper plate into the basket and the basket into the unit. Preheat the unit by selecting AIR FRY, setting the temperature to 360°F (182°C), and setting the time to 3 minutes. Select START/STOP to begin. 2. Once the unit is preheated, spray the crisper plate with cooking oil. Place 2 steaks into the basket; do not oil or season them at this time. 3. Select AIR FRY, set the temperature to 360°F (182°C), and set the time to 9 minutes. Select START/STOP to begin. 4. After 5 minutes, open the unit and flip the steaks. Sprinkle each with ¼ teaspoon of granulated garlic, ¼ teaspoon of salt, and ¼ teaspoon of pepper. Resume cooking until the steaks register at least 145°F (63°C) on a food thermometer. 5. When the cooking is complete, transfer the steaks to a plate and tent with aluminum foil to keep warm. Repeat steps 2, 3, and 4 with the remaining steaks. 6. Spray 4 ramekins with olive oil. Crack 1 egg into each ramekin. Sprinkle the eggs with the paprika and remaining ½ teaspoon each of salt and pepper. Working in batches, place 2 ramekins into the basket. 7. Select BAKE, set the temperature to 330°F (166°C), and set the time to 5 minutes. Select START/STOP to begin. 8. When the cooking is complete and the eggs are cooked to 160°F (71°C), remove the ramekins and repeat step 7 with the remaining 2 ramekins. 9. Serve the eggs with the steaks.

Veggie-Packed Broccoli Mushroom Frittata

Prep time: 10 minutes | Cook time: 20 minutes | Serves 2

1 tablespoon olive oil
1½ cups broccoli florets, finely chopped
½ cup sliced brown mushrooms
¼ cup finely chopped onion
½ teaspoon salt
¼ teaspoon freshly ground black pepper
6 eggs
¼ cup Parmesan cheese

1. In a nonstick cake pan, combine the olive oil, broccoli, mushrooms, onion, salt, and pepper. Stir until the vegetables are thoroughly coated with oil. Place the cake pan in the air fryer basket and set the air fryer to 400°F (204°C). Air fry for 5 minutes until the vegetables soften. 2. Meanwhile, in a medium bowl, whisk the eggs and Parmesan until thoroughly combined. Pour the egg mixture into the pan and shake gently to distribute the vegetables. Air fry for another 15 minutes until the eggs are set. 3. Remove from the air fryer and let sit for 5 minutes to cool slightly. Use a silicone spatula to gently lift the frittata onto a plate before serving.

Kale and Potato Nuggets

Prep time: 10 minutes | Cook time: 18 minutes | Serves 4

1 teaspoon extra virgin olive oil
1 clove garlic, minced
4 cups kale, rinsed and chopped
2 cups potatoes, boiled and mashed
⅛ cup milk
Salt and ground black pepper, to taste
Cooking spray

1. Preheat the air fryer to 390°F (199°C). 2. In a skillet over medium heat, sauté the garlic in the olive oil, until it turns golden brown. Sauté with the kale for an additional 3 minutes and remove from the heat. 3. Mix the mashed potatoes, kale and garlic in a bowl. Pour in the milk and sprinkle with salt and pepper. 4. Shape the mixture into nuggets and spritz with cooking spray. 5. Put in the air fryer basket and air fry for 15 minutes, flip the nuggets halfway through cooking to make sure the nuggets fry evenly. 6. Serve immediately.

Roasted Red Pepper and Feta Egg Bake

Prep time: 10 minutes | Cook time: 20 minutes | Serves 4

Olive oil cooking spray
8 large eggs
1 medium red bell pepper, diced
½ teaspoon salt
½ teaspoon black pepper
1 garlic clove, minced
½ cup feta, divided

1. Preheat the air fryer to 360°F(182°C). Lightly coat the inside of a 6-inch round cake pan with olive oil cooking spray. 2. In a large bowl, beat the eggs for 1 to 2 minutes, or until well combined. 3. Add the bell pepper, salt, black pepper, and garlic to the eggs, and mix together until the bell pepper is distributed throughout. 4. Fold in ¼ cup of the feta cheese. 5. Pour the egg mixture into the prepared cake pan, and sprinkle the remaining ¼ cup of feta over the top. 6. Place into the air fryer and bake for 18 to 20 minutes, or until the eggs are set in the center. 7. Remove from the air fryer and allow to cool for 5 minutes before serving.

Herb-Infused Turkey Sausage Patties

Prep time: 5 minutes | Cook time: 10 minutes | Serves 4

1 tablespoon chopped fresh thyme
1 tablespoon chopped fresh sage
1¼ teaspoons kosher salt
1 teaspoon chopped fennel seeds
¾ teaspoon smoked paprika
½ teaspoon onion powder
½ teaspoon garlic powder
⅛ teaspoon crushed red pepper flakes
⅛ teaspoon freshly ground black pepper
1 pound (454 g) 93% lean ground turkey
½ cup finely minced sweet apple (peeled)

1. Thoroughly combine the thyme, sage, salt, fennel seeds, paprika, onion powder, garlic powder, red pepper flakes, and black pepper in a medium bowl. 2. Add the ground turkey and apple and stir until well incorporated. Divide the mixture into 8 equal portions and shape into patties with your hands, each about ¼ inch thick and 3 inches in diameter. 3. Preheat the air fryer to 400°F (204°C). 4. Place the patties in the air fryer basket in a single layer. You may need to work in batches to avoid overcrowding. 5. Air fry for 5 minutes. Flip the patties and air fry for 5 minutes, or until the patties are nicely browned and cooked through. 6. Remove from the basket to a plate and repeat with the remaining patties. 7. Serve warm.

Roasted Cauliflower Avocado Toast

Prep time: 15 minutes | Cook time: 8 minutes | Serves 2

1 (12 ounces / 340 g) steamer bag cauliflower
1 large egg
½ cup shredded Mozzarella cheese
1 ripe medium avocado
½ teaspoon garlic powder
¼ teaspoon ground black pepper

1. Cook cauliflower according to package instructions. Remove from bag and place into cheesecloth or clean towel to remove excess moisture. 2. Place cauliflower into a large bowl and mix in egg and Mozzarella. Cut a piece of parchment to fit your air fryer basket. Separate the cauliflower mixture into two, and place it on the parchment in two mounds. Press out the cauliflower mounds into a ¼-inch-thick rectangle. Place the parchment into the air fryer basket. 3. Adjust the temperature to 400°F (204°C) and set the timer for 8 minutes. 4. Flip the cauliflower halfway through the cooking time. 5. When the timer beeps, remove the parchment and allow the cauliflower to cool 5 minutes. 6. Cut open the avocado and remove the pit. Scoop out the inside, place it in a medium bowl, and mash it with garlic powder and pepper. Spread onto the cauliflower. Serve immediately.

Cajun-Style Morning Sausage

Prep time: 10 minutes | Cook time: 15 to 20 minutes | Serves 8

1½ pounds (680 g) 85% lean ground turkey
3 cloves garlic, finely chopped
¼ onion, grated
1 teaspoon Tabasco sauce
1 teaspoon Creole seasoning
1 teaspoon dried thyme
½ teaspoon paprika
½ teaspoon cayenne

1. Preheat the air fryer to 370°F (188°C). 2. In a large bowl, combine the turkey, garlic, onion, Tabasco, Creole seasoning, thyme, paprika, and cayenne. Mix with clean hands until thoroughly combined. Shape into 16 patties, about ½ inch thick. (Wet your hands slightly if you find the sausage too sticky to handle.) 3. Working in batches if necessary, arrange the patties in a single layer in the air fryer basket. Pausing halfway through the cooking time to flip the patties, air fry for 15 to 20 minutes until a thermometer inserted into the thickest portion registers 165°F (74°C).

Spicy Bacon Breakfast Pizza

Prep time: 5 minutes | Cook time: 10 minutes | Serves 2

1 cup shredded Mozzarella cheese
1 ounce (28 g) cream cheese, broken into small pieces
4 slices cooked sugar-free bacon, chopped
¼ cup chopped pickled jalapeños
1 large egg, whisked
¼ teaspoon salt

1. Place Mozzarella in a single layer on the bottom of an ungreased round nonstick baking dish. Scatter cream cheese pieces, bacon, and jalapeños over Mozzarella, then pour egg evenly around baking dish. 2. Sprinkle with salt and place into air fryer basket. Adjust the temperature to 330°F (166°C) and bake for 10 minutes. When cheese is brown and egg is set, pizza will be done. 3. Let cool on a large plate 5 minutes before serving.

Mixed Berry Breakfast Muffin

Prep time: 15 minutes | Cook time: 12 to 17 minutes | Makes 8 muffins

1⅓ cups plus 1 tablespoon all-purpose flour, divided
¼ cup granulated sugar
2 tablespoons light brown sugar
2 teaspoons baking powder
2 eggs
⅔ cup whole milk
⅓ cup safflower oil
1 cup mixed fresh berries

1. In a medium bowl, stir together 1⅓ cups of flour, the granulated sugar, brown sugar, and baking powder until mixed well. 2. In a small bowl, whisk the eggs, milk, and oil until combined. Stir the egg mixture into the dry ingredients just until combined. 3. In another small bowl, toss the mixed berries with the remaining 1 tablespoon of flour until coated. Gently stir the berries into the batter. 4. Double up 16 foil muffin cups to make 8 cups. 5. Insert the crisper plate into the basket and the basket into the unit. Preheat the unit by selecting BAKE, setting the temperature to 315°F (157°C), and setting the time to 3 minutes. Select START/STOP to begin. 6. Once the unit is preheated, place 4 cups into the basket and fill each three-quarters full with the batter. 7. Select BAKE, set the temperature to 315°F (157°C), and set the time for 17 minutes. Select START/STOP to begin. 8. After about 12 minutes, check the muffins. If they spring back when lightly touched with your finger, they are done. If not, resume cooking. 9. When the cooking is done, transfer the muffins to a wire rack to cool. 10. Repeat steps 6, 7, and 8 with the remaining muffin cups and batter. 11. Let the muffins cool for 10 minutes before serving.

Sausage and Eggs with Tangy Mustard Sauce

Prep time: 20 minutes | Cook time: 12 minutes | Serves 8

1 pound (454 g) pork sausage
8 soft-boiled or hard-boiled eggs, peeled
1 large egg
2 tablespoons milk
1 cup crushed pork rinds

Smoky Mustard Sauce:
¼ cup mayonnaise
2 tablespoons sour cream
1 tablespoon Dijon mustard
1 teaspoon chipotle hot sauce

1. Preheat the air fryer to 390°F (199°C). 2. Divide the sausage into 8 portions. Take each portion of sausage, pat it down into a patty, and place 1 egg in the middle, gently wrapping the sausage around the egg until the egg is completely covered. (Wet your hands slightly if you find the sausage to be too sticky.) Repeat with the remaining eggs and sausage. 3. In a small shallow bowl, whisk the egg and milk until frothy. In another shallow bowl, place the crushed pork rinds. Working one at a time, dip a sausage-wrapped egg into the beaten egg and then into the pork rinds, gently rolling to coat evenly. Repeat with the remaining sausage-wrapped eggs. 4. Arrange the eggs in a single layer in the air fryer basket, and lightly spray with olive oil. Air fry for 10 to 12 minutes, pausing halfway through the baking time to turn the eggs, until the eggs are hot and the sausage is cooked through. 5. To make the sauce: In a small bowl, combine the mayonnaise, sour cream, Dijon, and hot sauce. Whisk until thoroughly combined. Serve with the Scotch eggs.

Bacon Egg Muffin Sandwiches

Prep time: 5 minutes | Cook time: 8 minutes | Serves 4

4 English muffins, split
8 slices Canadian bacon
4 slices cheese
Cooking spray

1. Preheat the air fryer to 370°F (188°C). 2. Make the sandwiches: Top each of 4 muffin halves with 2 slices of Canadian bacon, 1 slice of cheese, and finish with the remaining muffin half. 3. Put the sandwiches in the air fryer basket and spritz the tops with cooking spray. 4. Bake for 4 minutes. Flip the sandwiches and bake for another 4 minutes. 5. Divide the sandwiches among four plates and serve warm.

Spinach Bacon Egg Bites

Prep time: 7 minutes | Cook time: 12 to 14 minutes | Serves 6

6 large eggs
¼ cup heavy (whipping) cream
½ teaspoon sea salt
¼ teaspoon freshly ground black pepper
¼ teaspoon cayenne pepper (optional)
¾ cup frozen chopped spinach, thawed and drained
4 strips cooked bacon, crumbled
2 ounces (57 g) shredded Cheddar cheese

1. In a large bowl (with a spout if you have one), whisk together the eggs, heavy cream, salt, black pepper, and cayenne pepper (if using). 2. Divide the spinach and bacon among 6 silicone muffin cups. Place the muffin cups in your air fryer basket. 3. Divide the egg mixture among the muffin cups. Top with the cheese. 4. Set the air fryer to 300°F (149°C). Bake for 12 to 14 minutes, until the eggs are set and cooked through.

Broccoli Bacon Cheese Bake

Prep time: 30 minutes | Cook time: 48 minutes | Serves 2 to 4

½ pound (227 g) thick cut bacon, cut into ¼-inch pieces
3 cups brioche bread or rolls, cut into ½-inch cubes
3 eggs
1 cup milk
½ teaspoon salt
freshly ground black pepper
1 cup frozen broccoli florets, thawed and chopped
1½ cups grated Swiss cheese

1. Preheat the air fryer to 400°F (204°C). 2. Air fry the bacon for 6 to 10 minutes until crispy, shaking the basket a few times while it cooks to help it cook evenly. Remove the bacon and set it aside on a paper towel. 3. Air fry the brioche bread cubes for 2 minutes to dry and toast lightly. (If your brioche is a few days old and slightly stale, you can omit this step.) 4. Butter a cake pan. Combine all the ingredients in a large bowl and toss well. Transfer the mixture to the buttered cake pan, cover with aluminum foil and refrigerate the bread pudding overnight, or for at least 8 hours. 5. Remove the casserole from the refrigerator an hour before you plan to cook, and let it sit on the countertop to come to room temperature. 6. Preheat the air fryer to 330°F (166°C). Transfer the covered cake pan, to the basket of the air fryer, lowering the dish into the basket using a sling made of aluminum foil (fold a piece of aluminum foil into a strip about 2-inches wide by 24-inches long). Fold the ends of the aluminum foil over the top of the dish before returning the basket to the air fryer. Air fry for 20 minutes. Remove the foil and air fry for an additional 20 minutes. If the top starts to brown a little too much before the custard has set, simply return the foil to the pan. The bread pudding has cooked through when a skewer inserted into the center comes out clean.

Bell Pepper Egg Bake with Cheese

Prep time: 10 minutes | Cook time: 15 minutes | Serves 4

4 medium green bell peppers
3 ounces (85 g) cooked ham, chopped
¼ medium onion, peeled and chopped
8 large eggs
1 cup mild Cheddar cheese

1. Cut the tops off each bell pepper. Remove the seeds and the white membranes with a small knife. Place ham and onion into each pepper. 2. Crack 2 eggs into each pepper. Top with ¼ cup cheese per pepper. Place into the air fryer basket. 3. Adjust the temperature to 390°F (199°C) and air fry for 15 minutes. 4. When fully cooked, peppers will be tender and eggs will be firm. Serve immediately.

Mushroom Spinach Bite-Size Quiche

Prep time: 10 minutes | Cook time: 15 minutes | Serves 4

1 teaspoon olive oil, plus more for spraying
1 cup coarsely chopped mushrooms
1 cup fresh baby spinach, shredded
4 eggs, beaten
½ cup shredded Cheddar cheese
½ cup shredded Mozzarella cheese
¼ teaspoon salt
¼ teaspoon black pepper

1. Spray 4 silicone baking cups with olive oil and set aside. 2. In a medium sauté pan over medium heat, warm 1 teaspoon of olive oil. Add the mushrooms and sauté until soft, 3 to 4 minutes. 3. Add the spinach and cook until wilted, 1 to 2 minutes. Set aside. 4. In a medium bowl, whisk together the eggs, Cheddar cheese, Mozzarella cheese, salt, and pepper. 5. Gently fold the mushrooms and spinach into the egg mixture. 6. Pour ¼ of the mixture into each silicone baking cup. 7. Place the baking cups into the air fryer basket and air fry at 350°F (177°C) for 5 minutes. Stir the mixture in each ramekin slightly and air fry until the egg has set, an additional 3 to 5 minutes.

Sweet Squash Ricotta Frittata

Prep time: 10 minutes | Cook time: 33 minutes | Serves 2 to 3

1 cup cubed (½-inch) butternut squash (5½ ounces / 156 g)	taste
	4 fresh sage leaves, thinly sliced
2 tablespoons olive oil	6 large eggs, lightly beaten
Kosher salt and freshly ground black pepper, to	½ cup ricotta cheese
	Cayenne pepper

1. In a bowl, toss the squash with the olive oil and season with salt and black pepper until evenly coated. Sprinkle the sage on the bottom of a cake pan and place the squash on top. Place the pan in the air fryer and bake at 400°F (204°C) for 10 minutes. Stir to incorporate the sage, then cook until the squash is tender and lightly caramelized at the edges, about 3 minutes more. 2. Pour the eggs over the squash, dollop the ricotta all over, and sprinkle with cayenne. Bake at 300°F (149°C) until the eggs are set and the frittata is golden brown on top, about 20 minutes. Remove the pan from the air fryer and cut the frittata into wedges to serve.

Mediterranean Breakfast Gyro Patties

Prep time: 10 minutes | Cook time: 20 minutes per batch | Makes 16 patties

Patties:

2 pounds (907 g) ground lamb or beef	leaves
	1 teaspoon Greek seasoning
½ cup diced red onions	
¼ cup sliced black olives	2 cloves garlic, minced
2 tablespoons tomato sauce	1 teaspoon fine sea salt
1 teaspoon dried oregano	

Tzatziki:

1 cup full-fat sour cream	or 1 clove garlic, minced
1 small cucumber, chopped	¼ teaspoon dried dill weed, or 1 teaspoon finely chopped fresh dill
½ teaspoon fine sea salt	
½ teaspoon garlic powder,	

For Garnish/Serving:

½ cup crumbled feta cheese (about 2 ounces / 57 g)	Diced red onions
	Sliced black olives
	Sliced cucumbers

1. Preheat the air fryer to 350°F (177°C). 2. Place the ground lamb, onions, olives, tomato sauce, oregano, Greek seasoning, garlic, and salt in a large bowl. Mix well to combine the ingredients. 3. Using your hands, form the mixture into sixteen 3-inch patties. Place about 5 of the patties in the air fryer and air fry for 20 minutes, flipping halfway through. Remove the patties and place them on a serving platter. Repeat with the remaining patties. 4. While the patties cook, make the tzatziki: Place all the ingredients in a small bowl and stir well. Cover and store in the fridge until ready to serve. Garnish with ground black pepper before serving. 5. Serve the patties with a dollop of tzatziki, a sprinkle of crumbled feta cheese, diced red onions, sliced black olives, and sliced cucumbers. 6. Store leftovers in an airtight container in the refrigerator for up to 5 days or in the freezer for up to a month. Reheat the patties in a preheated 390°F (199°C) air fryer for a few minutes, until warmed through.

Crispy Spaghetti Squash Fritters

Prep time: 15 minutes | Cook time: 8 minutes | Serves 4

2 cups cooked spaghetti squash	¼ cup blanched finely ground almond flour
2 tablespoons unsalted butter, softened	2 stalks green onion, sliced
	½ teaspoon garlic powder
1 large egg	1 teaspoon dried parsley

1. Remove excess moisture from the squash using a cheesecloth or kitchen towel. 2. Mix all ingredients in a large bowl. Form into four patties. 3. Cut a piece of parchment to fit your air fryer basket. Place each patty on the parchment and place into the air fryer basket. 4. Adjust the temperature to 400°F (204°C) and set the timer for 8 minutes. 5. Flip the patties halfway through the cooking time. Serve warm.

Egg-in-Toast Breakfast Cup

Prep time: 5 minutes | Cook time: 6 to 7 minutes | Serves 1

1 slice bread	1 tablespoon shredded Cheddar cheese
1 teaspoon soft butter	
1 egg	2 teaspoons diced ham
Salt and pepper, to taste	

1. Place a baking dish inside air fryer basket and preheat the air fryer to 330°F (166°C). 2. Using a 2½-inch-diameter biscuit cutter, cut a hole in center of bread slice. 3. Spread softened butter on both sides of bread. 4. Lay bread slice in baking dish and crack egg into the hole. Sprinkle egg with salt and pepper to taste. 5. Cook for 5 minutes. 6. Turn toast over and top it with shredded cheese and diced ham. 7. Cook for 1 to 2 more minutes or until yolk is done to your liking.

Classic Custard Egg Tarts

Prep time: 10 minutes | Cook time: 17 to 20 minutes | Makes 2 tarts

⅓ sheet frozen puff pastry, thawed
Cooking oil spray
½ cup shredded Cheddar cheese

2 eggs
¼ teaspoon salt, divided
1 teaspoon minced fresh parsley (optional)

1. Insert the crisper plate into the basket and the basket into the unit. Preheat the unit by selecting BAKE, setting the temperature to 390°F (199°C), and setting the time to 3 minutes. Select START/STOP to begin. 2. Lay the puff pastry sheet on a piece of parchment paper and cut it in half. 3. Once the unit is preheated, spray the crisper plate with cooking oil. Transfer the 2 squares of pastry to the basket, keeping them on the parchment paper. 4. Select BAKE, set the temperature to 390°F (199°C), and set the time to 20 minutes. Select START/STOP to begin. 5. After 10 minutes, use a metal spoon to press down the center of each pastry square to make a well. Divide the cheese equally between the baked pastries. Carefully crack an egg on top of the cheese, and sprinkle each with the salt. Resume cooking for 7 to 10 minutes. 6. When the cooking is complete, the eggs will be cooked through. Sprinkle each with parsley (if using) and serve.

Chapter 2: Family Favorites

Cheesy Roasted Sweet Potatoes

Prep time: 7 minutes | Cook time: 18 to 23 minutes | Serves 4

2 large sweet potatoes, peeled and sliced
1 teaspoon olive oil
1 tablespoon white balsamic vinegar
1 teaspoon dried thyme
¼ cup grated Parmesan cheese

1. Begin by placing the sweet potato slices into a sizable mixing bowl. Drizzle them evenly with the olive oil, then toss thoroughly to ensure every piece is coated. 2. Add a sprinkling of balsamic vinegar and thyme to the bowl. Toss once more so the slices are well-seasoned. 3. Gradually sprinkle the Parmesan cheese over the sweet potatoes, continuing to toss until the slices are evenly coated. 4. Cook the sweet potato slices in batches inside the air fryer basket, setting the temperature to 400°F (204°C). Roast them for approximately 18 to 23 minutes, pausing once during the cooking time to toss the slices in the basket. Continue cooking until the slices are tender. 5. Repeat the process with any remaining sweet potato slices, and serve them promptly while still warm.

Phyllo Vegetable Triangles

Prep time: 15 minutes | Cook time: 6 to 11 minutes | Serves 6

3 tablespoons minced onion
2 garlic cloves, minced
2 tablespoons grated carrot
1 teaspoon olive oil
3 tablespoons frozen baby peas, thawed
2 tablespoons nonfat cream cheese, at room temperature
6 sheets frozen phyllo dough, thawed
Olive oil spray, for coating the dough

1. Combine the onion, garlic, carrot, and olive oil in a baking pan. Place the pan in the air fryer and cook at 390°F (199°C) for 2 to 4 minutes, until the vegetables are crisp-tender. Transfer them to a bowl. 2. Stir the peas and cream cheese into the vegetable mixture. Set it aside to cool while preparing the phyllo dough. 3. On a clean work surface, lay out one phyllo sheet. Lightly spray it with olive oil spray, then place another sheet on top. Repeat this process with the remaining 4 sheets, creating 3 stacks of 2 layers each. Cut each stack lengthwise into 4 strips, yielding a total of 12 strips. 4. Place about 2 teaspoons of filling near the bottom of each strip. Fold one corner of the strip up over the filling to form a triangle, and continue folding the triangle upward, like folding a flag, until the entire strip is wrapped. Seal the edge with a small dab of water. Repeat with the rest of the strips and filling. 5. Arrange the triangles in the air fryer in two batches. Cook each batch at 390°F (199°C) for 4 to 7 minutes, or until the triangles are golden brown. Serve immediately.

Chinese-Inspired Spareribs

Prep time: 30 minutes | Cook time: 8 minutes | Serves 4

Oil, for spraying
12 ounces (340 g) boneless pork spareribs, cut into 3-inch-long pieces
1 cup soy sauce
¾ cup sugar
½ cup beef or chicken stock
¼ cup honey
2 tablespoons minced garlic
1 teaspoon ground ginger
2 drops red food coloring (optional)

1. Begin by lining the air fryer basket with a layer of parchment paper, then give it a light coating of oil spray. 2. In a large zip-top plastic bag, mix together the ribs, soy sauce, sugar, beef stock, honey, garlic, ginger, and food coloring (if desired). Seal the bag tightly and shake it thoroughly to ensure the ribs are evenly coated. Allow the mixture to marinate in the refrigerator for a minimum of 30 minutes. 3. Once the ribs are marinated, transfer them to the prepared air fryer basket. 4. Air fry the ribs at 375°F (191°C) for approximately 8 minutes, or until their internal temperature rises to 165°F (74°C).

Berry Cheesecake

Prep time: 5 minutes | Cook time: 10 minutes | Serves 4

Oil, for spraying
8 ounces (227 g) cream cheese
6 tablespoons sugar
1 tablespoon sour cream
1 large egg
½ teaspoon vanilla extract
¼ teaspoon lemon juice
½ cup fresh mixed berries

1. Preheat the air fryer to 350°F (177°C). Line the basket with parchment paper and apply a light spray of oil. 2. Add the cream cheese, sugar, sour cream, egg, vanilla, and lemon juice to a blender. Blend until the mixture is smooth and creamy, then pour it into a 4-inch springform pan. 3. Place the pan in the lined air fryer basket. 4. Cook for 8 to 10 minutes, or until the center of the cheesecake wobbles slightly when the pan is gently shaken. 5. Once cooked, refrigerate the cheesecake in the pan for at least 2 hours. 6. After chilling, remove the springform sides, top the cheesecake with the mixed berries, and serve.

Steak Tips and Potatoes

Prep time: 10 minutes | Cook time: 20 minutes | Serves 4

Oil, for spraying
8 ounces (227 g) baby gold potatoes, cut in half
½ teaspoon salt
1 pound (454 g) steak, cut into ½-inch pieces
1 teaspoon Worcestershire sauce
1 teaspoon granulated garlic
½ teaspoon salt
½ teaspoon freshly ground black pepper

1. Line the air fryer basket with parchment paper and lightly spray it with oil. 2. Place the potatoes and salt into a microwave-safe bowl, then add enough water to reach about ½ inch deep. Microwave the potatoes for about 7 minutes, or until they are almost tender. Drain the water. 3. In a large mixing bowl, combine the steak, cooked potatoes, Worcestershire sauce, garlic, salt, and black pepper. Stir gently until everything is evenly coated, then spread the mixture in a single, even layer in the prepared air fryer basket. 4. Cook at 400°F (204°C) for 12 to 17 minutes, stirring once after 5 to 6 minutes. Adjust the cooking time based on the thickness of the steak and your preferred doneness.

Meatball Subs

Prep time: 15 minutes | Cook time: 19 minutes | Serves 6

Oil, for spraying
1 pound (454 g) 85% lean ground beef
½ cup Italian bread crumbs
1 tablespoon dried minced onion
1 tablespoon minced garlic
1 large egg
1 teaspoon salt
1 teaspoon freshly ground black pepper
6 hoagie rolls
1 (18 ounces / 510 g) jar marinara sauce
1½ cups shredded Mozzarella cheese

1. Begin by lining the air fryer basket with parchment paper and lightly spraying it with oil. 2. In a large mixing bowl, combine the ground beef, bread crumbs, onion, garlic, egg, salt, and black pepper. Use your hands to roll the mixture into 18 evenly sized meatballs. 3. Arrange the meatballs in a single layer inside the prepared basket. 4. Set the air fryer to 390°F (199°C) and cook the meatballs for 15 minutes. 5. Once cooked, place three meatballs into each hoagie roll. Spoon marinara sauce over the top and sprinkle with Mozzarella cheese. 6. Return the assembled sandwiches to the air fryer and cook for 3 to 4 minutes, until the cheese has melted. Depending on the size of your air fryer, you may need to work in batches. Serve the meatball hoagies immediately.

Fish and Vegetable Tacos

Prep time: 15 minutes | Cook time: 9 to 12 minutes | Serves 4

1 pound (454 g) white fish fillets, such as sole or cod
2 teaspoons olive oil
3 tablespoons freshly squeezed lemon juice, divided
1½ cups chopped red cabbage
1 large carrot, grated
½ cup low-sodium salsa
⅓ cup low-fat Greek yogurt
4 soft low-sodium whole-wheat tortillas

1. Brush the fish fillets with olive oil and drizzle with 1 tablespoon of lemon juice. Place the fillets in the air fryer basket and cook at 390°F (199°C) for 9 to 12 minutes, until the fish easily flakes apart when tested with a fork. 2. While the fish is cooking, mix the remaining 2 tablespoons of lemon juice with the red cabbage, carrot, salsa, and yogurt in a medium bowl. Stir until evenly combined. 3. Once the fish is done, remove it from the air fryer and break it into large chunks. 4. Serve the fish alongside tortillas and the cabbage mixture, allowing everyone to assemble their own tacos.

Puffed Egg Tarts

Prep time: 10 minutes | Cook time: 42 minutes | Makes 4 tarts

Oil, for spraying
All-purpose flour, for dusting
1 (12 ounces / 340 g) sheet frozen puff pastry, thawed
¾ cup shredded Cheddar cheese, divided
4 large eggs
2 teaspoons chopped fresh parsley
Salt and freshly ground black pepper, to taste

1. Preheat the air fryer to 390°F (199°C). Line the basket with parchment paper and lightly spray it with oil. 2. Lightly flour your work surface. Unfold the puff pastry and cut it into 4 equal squares. Place two of the squares in the prepared air fryer basket. 3. Cook the puff pastry squares for 10 minutes. 4. Carefully remove the basket and use a spoon to press down the center of each puff pastry square, creating an indentation. 5. Add 3 tablespoons of cheese into each indentation, then crack an egg into the center of each tart shell. 6. Return the basket to the air fryer and cook for another 7 to 11 minutes, adjusting the time to achieve your preferred egg doneness. 7. Repeat the process with the remaining two puff pastry squares, cheese, and eggs. 8. Garnish each tart with a sprinkle of parsley and season lightly with salt and black pepper. Serve immediately.

Meringue Cookies

Prep time: 15 minutes | Cook time: 1 hour 30 minutes | Makes 20 cookies

Oil, for spraying
4 large egg whites
1 cup sugar
Pinch cream of tartar

1. Begin by preheating the air fryer to 140°F (60°C). Prepare the basket by lining it with parchment and lightly spraying it with oil. 2. In a small heatproof bowl, whisk together the egg whites and sugar. Place a saucepan with water over medium heat and bring it to a light simmer. Set the bowl on top of the saucepan, ensuring it doesn't touch the water. Stir the mixture until the sugar fully dissolves. 3. Pour the dissolved mixture into a large mixing bowl. Add the cream of tartar and beat the mixture with an electric mixer on high speed until it turns glossy and forms stiff peaks. Scoop the mixture into a piping bag or a zip-top bag with a corner cut off. 4. Pipe the meringue rounds onto the prepared parchment in the basket. If needed, work in batches to ensure proper spacing. 5. Cook the meringues in the air fryer for 1 hour and 30 minutes. 6. Once the cooking time is complete, turn off the air fryer but leave the meringues inside until they cool entirely. The residual heat will help them dry out fully.

Fried Green Tomatoes

Prep time: 15 minutes | Cook time: 6 to 8 minutes | Serves 4

4 medium green tomatoes
⅓ cup all-purpose flour
2 egg whites
¼ cup almond milk
1 cup ground almonds
½ cup panko bread crumbs
2 teaspoons olive oil
1 teaspoon paprika
1 clove garlic, minced

1. Begin by rinsing the tomatoes under cool water, then pat them dry with a paper towel. Slice the tomatoes into ½-inch rounds, setting aside the thinner ends. 2. Arrange three separate dishes for dredging: a plate of flour, a shallow bowl containing egg whites whisked with almond milk until frothy, and another plate holding the almond mixture (a blend of almonds, bread crumbs, olive oil, paprika, and garlic). 3. Dredge each tomato slice first in the flour, then dip into the egg white mixture, and finally press into the almond mixture to fully coat. 4. Place four of the coated tomato slices into the air fryer basket, ensuring they are in a single layer. Air fry at 400°F (204°C) for 6 to 8 minutes, or until the coating is golden and crisp. Repeat the process with the remaining tomato slices, and serve the tomatoes right away.

Steak and Vegetable Kebabs

Prep time: 15 minutes | Cook time: 5 to 7 minutes | Serves 4

2 tablespoons balsamic vinegar
2 teaspoons olive oil
½ teaspoon dried marjoram
⅛ teaspoon freshly ground black pepper
¾ pound (340 g) round steak, cut into 1-inch pieces
1 red bell pepper, sliced
16 button mushrooms
1 cup cherry tomatoes

1. Combine the balsamic vinegar, olive oil, marjoram, and black pepper in a medium bowl. Stir until well mixed. 2. Add the steak into the mixture and toss until evenly coated. Allow it to rest for 10 minutes at room temperature. 3. Skewer the ingredients in an alternating pattern, placing the beef, red bell pepper, mushrooms, and tomatoes onto 8 bamboo or metal skewers that fit your air fryer. 4. Cook the skewers in the air fryer at 390°F (199°C) for 5 to 7 minutes, or until the steak is browned and reaches an internal temperature of at least 145°F (63°C) when checked with a meat thermometer. Serve the skewers immediately.

Churro Bites

Prep time: 5 minutes | Cook time: 6 minutes | Makes 36 bites

Oil, for spraying
1 (17¼ ounces / 489 g) package frozen puffed pastry, thawed
1 cup granulated sugar
1 tablespoon ground cinnamon
½ cup confectioners' sugar
1 tablespoon milk

1. Start by preheating the air fryer to 400°F (204°C). Line the basket with parchment paper and lightly coat it with oil spray. 2. Place the puff pastry on a clean surface. Use a sharp knife to divide it into 36 small squares. 3. Arrange the pastry pieces in a single layer inside the lined basket, making sure they don't touch each other or overlap. 4. Cook the pastry bites for 3 minutes, then flip them over and continue cooking for another 3 minutes, until they are puffed and golden brown. 5. In a small bowl, combine the granulated sugar and cinnamon, mixing well. 6. In a separate bowl, whisk together the confectioners' sugar and milk until smooth. 7. Toss each puff pastry piece in the cinnamon-sugar mixture, ensuring they are well-coated. 8. Serve the bites immediately, alongside the icing for dipping.

Bacon-Wrapped Hot Dogs

Prep time: 5 minutes | Cook time: 10 minutes | Serves 4

Oil, for spraying
4 bacon slices
4 all-beef hot dogs
4 hot dog buns
Toppings of choice

1. Prepare the air fryer basket by lining it with parchment and lightly spraying it with oil. 2. Tightly wrap each hot dog with a strip of bacon, making sure to cover the tips so they don't become overly crisp. Use a toothpick at each end to prevent the bacon from shrinking. 3. Arrange the bacon-wrapped hot dogs in the basket. 4. Air fry at 380°F (193°C) for about 8 to 9 minutes, or adjust the time depending on how crispy you want the bacon. For a more intense crunch, cook at 400°F (204°C) for 6 to 8 minutes. 5. Place the cooked hot dogs into buns, return them to the air fryer, and heat for 1 to 2 minutes until the buns are warm. Add any toppings you like, and serve.

Scallops with Green Vegetables

Prep time: 15 minutes | Cook time: 8 to 11 minutes | Serves 4

1 cup green beans
1 cup frozen peas
1 cup frozen chopped broccoli
2 teaspoons olive oil
½ teaspoon dried basil
½ teaspoon dried oregano
12 ounces (340 g) sea scallops

1. Start by tossing the green beans, peas, and broccoli with olive oil in a large mixing bowl. Transfer them into the air fryer basket. Air fry at 400°F (204°C) for about 4 to 6 minutes, until the vegetables reach a crisp-tender texture. 2. Take the vegetables out of the air fryer basket, sprinkle them with herbs, and set aside. 3. Place the scallops into the air fryer basket and cook them for 4 to 5 minutes, or until they become firm and reach an internal temperature of 145°F (63°C) when checked with a meat thermometer. 4. Mix the cooked scallops with the reserved vegetables and serve right away.

Mixed Berry Crumble

Prep time: 10 minutes | Cook time: 11 to 16 minutes | Serves 4

½ cup chopped fresh strawberries
½ cup fresh blueberries
⅓ cup frozen raspberries
1 tablespoon freshly squeezed lemon juice
1 tablespoon honey
⅔ cup whole-wheat pastry flour
3 tablespoons packed brown sugar
2 tablespoons unsalted butter, melted

1. Combine the strawberries, blueberries, and raspberries in a baking pan. Pour the lemon juice and honey evenly over the fruit. 2. In a separate small bowl, blend the pastry flour with the brown sugar. 3. Add the butter to the flour mixture and work it in until it forms a crumbly texture. Sprinkle this crumb topping over the fruit mixture. 4. Bake at 380°F (193°C) for 11 to 16 minutes, or until the fruit is bubbling and tender and the topping is golden brown. Serve while warm.

Avocado and Egg Burrito

Prep time: 10 minutes | Cook time: 3 to 5 minutes | Serves 4

2 hard-boiled egg whites, chopped
1 hard-boiled egg, chopped
1 avocado, peeled, pitted, and chopped
1 red bell pepper, chopped
3 tablespoons low-sodium salsa, plus additional for serving (optional)
1 (1.2 ounces / 34 g) slice low-sodium, low-fat American cheese, torn into pieces
4 low-sodium whole-wheat flour tortillas

1. Combine the egg whites, whole egg, avocado, red bell pepper, salsa, and cheese in a medium bowl. Stir until well mixed. 2. Lay the tortillas on a flat surface and divide the egg mixture evenly among them. Fold in the sides and roll each tortilla into a burrito. Use toothpicks if needed to keep them secure. 3. Place the burritos in the air fryer basket. Cook at 390°F (199°C) for 3 to 5 minutes, or until they turn golden brown and crispy. Serve with extra salsa, if desired.

Cajun Shrimp

Prep time: 15 minutes | Cook time: 9 minutes | Serves 4

Oil, for spraying
1 pound (454 g) jumbo raw shrimp, peeled and deveined
1 tablespoon Cajun seasoning
6 ounces (170 g) cooked kielbasa, cut into thick slices
½ medium zucchini, cut into ¼-inch-thick slices
½ medium yellow squash, cut into ¼-inch-thick slices
1 green bell pepper, seeded and cut into 1-inch pieces
2 tablespoons olive oil
½ teaspoon salt

1. Preheat the air fryer to 400°F (204°C). Line the air fryer basket with parchment and spray lightly with oil. 2. In a large bowl, toss together the shrimp and Cajun seasoning. Add the kielbasa, zucchini, squash, bell pepper, olive oil, and salt and mix well. 3. Transfer the mixture to the prepared basket, taking care not to overcrowd. You may need to work in batches, depending on the size of your air fryer. 4. Cook for 9 minutes, shaking and stirring every 3 minutes. Serve immediately.

Pork Stuffing Meatballs

Prep time: 10 minutes | Cook time: 12 minutes | Makes 35 meatballs

Oil, for spraying
1½ pounds (680 g) ground pork
1 cup bread crumbs
½ cup milk
¼ cup minced onion
1 large egg
1 tablespoon dried rosemary
1 tablespoon dried thyme
1 teaspoon salt
1 teaspoon freshly ground black pepper
1 teaspoon finely chopped fresh parsley

1. Line the air fryer basket with parchment paper and lightly coat it with oil spray. 2. In a large mixing bowl, combine the ground pork, bread crumbs, milk, onion, egg, rosemary, thyme, salt, black pepper, and parsley. Stir until the mixture is evenly blended. 3. Use about 2 tablespoons of the pork mixture for each meatball. Shape the mixture into balls, continuing until you have around 30 to 35 meatballs. 4. Arrange the meatballs in a single layer in the prepared basket, leaving space between them. If needed, cook them in batches based on the air fryer's capacity. 5. Cook the meatballs at 390°F (199°C) for 10 to 12 minutes, flipping them halfway through cooking, until they turn golden brown and the internal temperature reaches 160°F (71°C).

Elephant Ears

Prep time: 5 minutes | Cook time: 5 minutes | Serves 8

Oil, for spraying
1 (8 ounces / 227 g) can buttermilk biscuits
3 tablespoons sugar
1 tablespoon ground cinnamon
3 tablespoons unsalted butter, melted
8 scoops vanilla ice cream (optional)

1. Begin by lining the air fryer basket with parchment paper and lightly spraying it with oil. 2. Roll out the biscuit dough into 6- to 8-inch circles using a rolling pin. 3. Place the flattened dough rounds into the prepared air fryer basket, spraying the tops generously with oil. Work in batches if necessary, depending on the size of your air fryer. 4. Air fry at 350°F (177°C) for about 5 minutes, or until the dough is lightly browned. 5. In a small bowl, combine the sugar and cinnamon. 6. After cooking, brush the elephant ears with melted butter and sprinkle the cinnamon-sugar mixture evenly over them. 7. Optionally, serve each elephant ear with a scoop of ice cream.

Veggie Tuna Melts

Prep time: 15 minutes | Cook time: 7 to 11 minutes | Serves 4

2 low-sodium whole-wheat English muffins, split
1 (6 ounces / 170 g) can chunk light low-sodium tuna, drained
1 cup shredded carrot
⅓ cup chopped mushrooms
2 scallions, white and green parts, sliced
⅓ cup nonfat Greek yogurt
2 tablespoons low-sodium stone ground mustard
2 slices low-sodium low-fat Swiss cheese, halved

1. Place the English muffin halves in the air fryer basket. Cook them at 340°F (171°C) for 3 to 4 minutes, or until they become crisp. Once done, remove the muffins from the basket and set aside. 2. In a medium bowl, combine the tuna, carrot, mushrooms, scallions, yogurt, and mustard. Mix thoroughly until the ingredients are well blended. Spread one-fourth of the tuna mixture onto each muffin half, then top each one with a half slice of Swiss cheese. 3. Return the topped muffins to the air fryer. Cook at the same temperature for 4 to 7 minutes, or until the tuna mixture is heated through and the cheese melts and begins to brown. Serve immediately.

Chapter 3
Fast and Easy Everyday Favorites

Crispy Southern-Style Fried Okra

Prep time: 5 minutes | Cook time: 8 to 10 minutes | Serves 4

1 cup self-rising yellow cornmeal	½ teaspoon freshly ground black pepper
1 teaspoon Italian-style seasoning	2 large eggs, beaten
1 teaspoon paprika	2 cups okra slices
1 teaspoon salt	Cooking spray

1. Preheat the air fryer to 400°F (204°C). Line the air fryer basket with parchment paper. 2. In a shallow bowl, whisk the cornmeal, Italian-style seasoning, paprika, salt, and pepper until blended. Place the beaten eggs in a second shallow bowl. 3. Add the okra to the beaten egg and stir to coat. Add the egg and okra mixture to the cornmeal mixture and stir until coated. 4. Place the okra on the parchment and spritz it with oil. 5. Air fry for 4 minutes. Shake the basket, spritz the okra with oil, and air fry for 4 to 6 minutes more until lightly browned and crispy. 6. Serve immediately.

Juicy Grilled Beef Brats

Prep time: 5 minutes | Cook time: 15 minutes | Serves 4

4 (3-ounce / 85-g) beef bratwursts

1. Preheat the air fryer to 375°F (191°C). 2. Place the beef bratwursts in the air fryer basket and air fry for 15 minutes, turning once halfway through. 3. Serve hot.

Roasted Cherry Tomatoes with Garlic

Prep time: 5 minutes | Cook time: 4 to 6 minutes | Serves 2

2 cups cherry tomatoes	1 tablespoon freshly chopped basil, for topping
1 clove garlic, thinly sliced	Cooking spray
1 teaspoon olive oil	
⅛ teaspoon kosher salt	

1. Preheat the air fryer to 360°F (182°C). Spritz the air fryer baking pan with cooking spray and set aside. 2. In a large bowl, toss together the cherry tomatoes, sliced garlic, olive oil, and kosher salt. Spread the mixture in an even layer in the prepared pan. 3. Bake in the preheated air fryer for 4 to 6 minutes, or until the tomatoes become soft and wilted. 4. Transfer to a bowl and rest for 5 minutes. Top with the chopped basil and serve warm.

Spiced Brown Rice Fritters

Prep time: 10 minutes | Cook time: 8 to 10 minutes | Serves 4

1 (10 ounces / 284 g) bag frozen cooked brown rice, thawed	⅓ cup minced red bell pepper
1 egg	2 tablespoons minced fresh basil
3 tablespoons brown rice flour	3 tablespoons grated Parmesan cheese
⅓ cup finely grated carrots	2 teaspoons olive oil

1. Preheat the air fryer to 380°F (193°C). 2. In a small bowl, combine the thawed rice, egg, and flour and mix to blend. 3. Stir in the carrots, bell pepper, basil, and Parmesan cheese. 4. Form the mixture into 8 fritters and drizzle with the olive oil. 5. Put the fritters carefully into the air fryer basket. Air fry for 8 to 10 minutes, or until the fritters are golden brown and cooked through. 6. Serve immediately.

Toasted Cheese and Chile Bites

Prep time: 5 minutes | Cook time: 5 minutes | Serves 1

2 tablespoons grated Parmesan cheese	at room temperature
2 tablespoons grated Mozzarella cheese	10 to 15 thin slices serrano chile or jalapeño
2 teaspoons salted butter,	2 slices sourdough bread
	½ teaspoon black pepper

1. Preheat the air fryer to 325°F (163°C). 2. In a small bowl, stir together the Parmesan, Mozzarella, butter, and chiles. 3. Spread half the mixture onto one side of each slice of bread. Sprinkle with the pepper. Place the slices, cheese-side up, in the air fryer basket. Bake for 5 minutes, or until the cheese has melted and started to brown slightly. 4. Serve immediately.

Homemade Crunchy Croutons

Prep time: 5 minutes | Cook time: 8 minutes | Serves 4

2 slices friendly bread	Hot soup, for serving
1 tablespoon olive oil	

1. Preheat the air fryer to 390°F (199°C). 2. Cut the slices of bread into medium-size chunks. 3. Brush the air fryer basket with the oil. 4. Place the chunks inside and air fry for at least 8 minutes. 5. Serve with hot soup.

Fast and Easy Everyday Favorites

Parsley Garlic Butter Knots

Prep time: 10 minutes | Cook time: 10 minutes | Makes 8 knots

1 teaspoon dried parsley
¼ cup melted butter
2 teaspoons garlic powder
1 (11 ounces / 312 g) tube refrigerated French bread dough, cut into 8 slices

1. Preheat the air fryer to 350°F (177°C). 2. Combine the parsley, butter, and garlic powder in a bowl. Stir to mix well. 3. Place the French bread dough slices on a clean work surface, then roll each slice into a 6-inch long rope. Tie the ropes into knots and arrange them on a plate. Brush the knots with butter mixture. 4. Transfer the knots into the air fryer. You need to work in batches to avoid overcrowding. 5. Air fry for 5 minutes or until the knots are golden brown. Flip the knots halfway through the cooking time. 6. Serve immediately.

Classic Melted Queso Dip

Prep time: 10 minutes | Cook time: 25 minutes | Serves 4

4 ounces (113 g) fresh Mexican chorizo, casings removed
1 medium onion, chopped
3 cloves garlic, minced
1 cup chopped tomato
2 jalapeños, deseeded and diced
2 teaspoons ground cumin
2 cups shredded Oaxaca or Mozzarella cheese
½ cup half-and-half
Celery sticks or tortilla chips, for serving

1. Preheat the air fryer to 400°F (204°C). 2. In a baking pan, combine the chorizo, onion, garlic, tomato, jalapeños, and cumin. Stir to combine. 3. Place the pan in the air fryer basket. Air fry for 15 minutes, or until the sausage is cooked, stirring halfway through the cooking time to break up the sausage. 4. Add the cheese and half-and-half; stir to combine. Air fry for 10 minutes, or until the cheese has melted. 5. Serve with celery sticks or tortilla chips.

Quick Air Fryer Edamame Snacks

Prep time: 5 minutes | Cook time: 7 minutes | Serves 6

1½ pounds (680 g) unshelled edamame
2 tablespoons olive oil
1 teaspoon sea salt

1. Preheat the air fryer to 400°F (204°C). 2. Place the edamame in a large bowl, then drizzle with olive oil. Toss to coat well. 3. Transfer the edamame to the preheated air fryer. Cook for 7 minutes or until tender and warmed through. Shake the basket at least three times during the cooking. 4. Transfer the cooked edamame onto a plate and sprinkle with salt. Toss to combine well and set aside for 3 minutes to infuse before serving.

Garlic-Infused Zucchini Noodles

Prep time: 10 minutes | Cook time: 10 minutes | Serves 4

2 large zucchini, peeled and spiralized
2 large yellow summer squash, peeled and spiralized
1 tablespoon olive oil, divided
½ teaspoon kosher salt
1 garlic clove, whole
2 tablespoons fresh basil, chopped
Cooking spray

1. Preheat the air fryer to 360°F (182°C). Spritz the air fryer basket with cooking spray. 2. Combine the zucchini and summer squash with 1 teaspoon olive oil and salt in a large bowl. Toss to coat well. 3. Transfer the zucchini and summer squash in the preheated air fryer and add the garlic. 4. Air fry for 10 minutes or until tender and fragrant. Toss the spiralized zucchini and summer squash halfway through the cooking time. 5. Transfer the cooked zucchini and summer squash onto a plate and set aside. 6. Remove the garlic from the air fryer and allow to cool for a few minutes. Mince the garlic and combine with remaining olive oil in a small bowl. Stir to mix well. 7. Drizzle the spiralized zucchini and summer squash with garlic oil and sprinkle with basil. Toss to serve.

Creamy Butter-Glazed Sweet Potatoes

Prep time: 5 minutes | Cook time: 10 minutes | Serves 4

2 tablespoons butter, melted
1 tablespoon light brown sugar
2 sweet potatoes, peeled and cut into ½-inch cubes
Cooking spray

1. Preheat the air fryer to 400°F (204°C). Line the air fryer basket with parchment paper. 2. In a medium bowl, stir together the melted butter and brown sugar until blended. Toss the sweet potatoes in the butter mixture until coated. 3. Place the sweet potatoes on the parchment and spritz with oil. 4. Air fry for 5 minutes. Shake the basket, spritz the sweet potatoes with oil, and air fry for 5 minutes more until they're soft enough to cut with a fork. 5. Serve immediately.

Creamy Baked Cheese Grits

Prep time: 10 minutes | Cook time: 12 minutes | Serves 6

¾ cup hot water
2 (1-ounce / 28-g) packages instant grits
1 large egg, beaten
1 tablespoon butter, melted
2 cloves garlic, minced
½ to 1 teaspoon red pepper flakes
1 cup shredded Cheddar cheese or jalapeño Jack cheese

1. Preheat the air fryer to 400ºF (204ºC). 2. In a baking pan, combine the water, grits, egg, butter, garlic, and red pepper flakes. Stir until well combined. Stir in the shredded cheese. 3. Place the pan in the air fryer basket and air fry for 12 minutes, or until the grits have cooked through and a knife inserted near the center comes out clean. 4. Let stand for 5 minutes before serving.

Lemon-Garlic Roasted Asparagus

Prep time: 5 minutes | Cook time: 10 minutes | Makes 10 spears

10 spears asparagus (about ½ pound / 227 g in total), snap the ends off
1 tablespoon lemon juice
2 teaspoons minced garlic
½ teaspoon salt
¼ teaspoon ground black pepper
Cooking spray

1. Preheat the air fryer to 400ºF (204ºC). Line a parchment paper in the air fryer basket. 2. Put the asparagus spears in a large bowl. Drizzle with lemon juice and sprinkle with minced garlic, salt, and ground black pepper. Toss to coat well. 3. Transfer the asparagus in the preheated air fryer and spritz with cooking spray. Air fryer for 10 minutes or until wilted and soft. Flip the asparagus halfway through. 4. Serve immediately.

Simple Herb-Roasted Asparagus

Prep time: 5 minutes | Cook time: 6 minutes | Serves 4

1 pound (454 g) asparagus, trimmed and halved crosswise
1 teaspoon extra-virgin olive oil
Salt and pepper, to taste
Lemon wedges, for serving

1. Preheat the air fryer to 400ºF (204ºC). 2. Toss the asparagus with the oil, ⅛ teaspoon salt, and ⅛ teaspoon pepper in bowl. Transfer to air fryer basket. 3. Place the basket in air fryer and roast for 6 to 8 minutes, or until tender and bright green, tossing halfway through cooking. 4. Season with salt and pepper and serve with lemon wedges.

Spicy Cheddar Jalapeño Cornbread

Prep time: 10 minutes | Cook time: 20 minutes | Serves 8

⅔ cup cornmeal
⅓ cup all-purpose flour
¾ teaspoon baking powder
2 tablespoons buttery spread, melted
½ teaspoon kosher salt
1 tablespoon granulated sugar
¾ cup whole milk
1 large egg, beaten
1 jalapeño pepper, thinly sliced
⅓ cup shredded sharp Cheddar cheese
Cooking spray

1. Preheat the air fryer to 300ºF (149ºC). Spritz the air fryer basket with cooking spray. 2. Combine all the ingredients in a large bowl. Stir to mix well. Pour the mixture in a baking pan. 3. Arrange the pan in the preheated air fryer. Bake for 20 minutes or until a toothpick inserted in the center of the bread comes out clean. 4. When the cooking is complete, remove the baking pan from the air fryer and allow the bread to cool for a few minutes before slicing to serve.

Fresh Beet Salad with Lemon Dressing

Prep time: 10 minutes | Cook time: 12 to 15 minutes | Serves 4

6 medium red and golden beets, peeled and sliced
1 teaspoon olive oil
¼ teaspoon kosher salt
Vinaigrette:
2 teaspoons olive oil
2 tablespoons chopped
½ cup crumbled feta cheese
8 cups mixed greens
Cooking spray
fresh chives
Juice of 1 lemon

1. Preheat the air fryer to 360ºF (182ºC). 2. In a large bowl, toss the beets, olive oil, and kosher salt. 3. Spray the air fryer basket with cooking spray, then place the beets in the basket and air fry for 12 to 15 minutes or until tender. 4. While the beets cook, make the vinaigrette in a large bowl by whisking together the olive oil, lemon juice, and chives. 5. Remove the beets from the air fryer, toss in the vinaigrette, and allow to cool for 5 minutes. Add the feta and serve on top of the mixed greens.

Crispy Roasted Green Beans

Prep time: 5 minutes | Cook time: 10 minutes | Makes 2 cups

½ teaspoon lemon pepper
2 teaspoons granulated garlic
½ teaspoon salt
1 tablespoon olive oil
2 cups fresh green beans, trimmed and snapped in half

1. Preheat the air fryer to 370°F (188°C). 2. Combine the lemon pepper, garlic, salt, and olive oil in a bowl. Stir to mix well. 3. Add the green beans to the bowl of mixture and toss to coat well. 4. Arrange the green beans in the preheated air fryer. Bake for 10 minutes or until tender and crispy. Shake the basket halfway through to make sure the green beans are cooked evenly. 5. Serve immediately.

Traditional Canadian Poutine

Prep time: 15 minutes | Cook time: 25 minutes | Serves 2

2 russet potatoes, scrubbed and cut into ½-inch sticks
2 teaspoons vegetable oil
2 tablespoons butter
¼ onion, minced
¼ teaspoon dried thyme
1 clove garlic, smashed
3 tablespoons all-purpose flour
1 teaspoon tomato paste
1½ cups beef stock
2 teaspoons Worcestershire sauce
Salt and freshly ground black pepper, to taste
⅔ cup chopped string cheese

1. Bring a pot of water to a boil, then put in the potato sticks and blanch for 4 minutes. 2. Preheat the air fryer to 400°F (204°C). 3. Drain the potato sticks and rinse under running cold water, then pat dry with paper towels. 4. Transfer the sticks in a large bowl and drizzle with vegetable oil. Toss to coat well. 5. Place the potato sticks in the preheated air fryer. Air fry for 25 minutes or until the sticks are golden brown. Shake the basket at least three times during the frying. 6. Meanwhile, make the gravy: Heat the butter in a saucepan over medium heat until melted. 7. Add the onion, thyme, and garlic and sauté for 5 minutes or until the onion is translucent. 8. Add the flour and sauté for an additional 2 minutes. Pour in the tomato paste and beef stock and cook for 1 more minute or until lightly thickened. 9. Drizzle the gravy with Worcestershire sauce and sprinkle with salt and ground black pepper. Reduce the heat to low to keep the gravy warm until ready to serve. 10. Transfer the fried potato sticks onto a plate, then sprinkle with salt and ground black pepper. Scatter with string cheese and pour the gravy over. Serve warm.

Veggie Spinach and Carrot Bites

Prep time: 10 minutes | Cook time: 10 minutes | Serves 4

2 slices toasted bread
1 carrot, peeled and grated
1 package fresh spinach, blanched and chopped
½ onion, chopped
1 egg, beaten
½ teaspoon garlic powder
1 teaspoon minced garlic
1 teaspoon salt
½ teaspoon black pepper
1 tablespoon nutritional yeast
1 tablespoon flour

1. Preheat the air fryer to 390°F (199°C). 2. In a food processor, pulse the toasted bread to form bread crumbs. Transfer into a shallow dish or bowl. 3. In a bowl, mix together all the other ingredients. 4. Use your hands to shape the mixture into small-sized balls. Roll the balls in the bread crumbs, ensuring to cover them well. 5. Put in the air fryer basket and air fry for 10 minutes. 6. Serve immediately.

Zesty Old Bay Air Fried Shrimp

Prep time: 7 minutes | Cook time: 10 minutes | Makes 2 cups

½ teaspoon Old Bay Seasoning
1 teaspoon ground cayenne pepper
½ teaspoon paprika
1 tablespoon olive oil
⅛ teaspoon salt
½ pound (227 g) shrimps, peeled and deveined
Juice of half a lemon

1. Preheat the air fryer to 390°F (199°C). 2. Combine the Old Bay Seasoning, cayenne pepper, paprika, olive oil, and salt in a large bowl, then add the shrimps and toss to coat well. 3. Put the shrimps in the preheated air fryer. Air fry for 10 minutes or until opaque. Flip the shrimps halfway through. 4. Serve the shrimps with lemon juice on top.

Chapter 4
Snacks and Appetizers

Buffalo Bites

Prep time: 15 minutes | Cook time: 11 to 12 minutes per batch | Makes 16 meatballs

1½ cups cooked jasmine or sushi rice	8 tablespoons buffalo wing sauce
¼ teaspoon salt	2 ounces (57 g) Gruyère cheese, cut into 16 cubes
1 pound (454 g) ground chicken	1 tablespoon maple syrup

1. Mix 4 tablespoons of buffalo wing sauce into the ground chicken until well combined. 2. Form the chicken into a log and divide it into 16 equal portions. 3. With dampened hands, wrap each portion of chicken around a cube of cheese, shaping it into a firm meatball. Once you've shaped 8 meatballs, place them in the air fryer basket. 4. Cook the meatballs at 390°F (199°C) for 5 minutes. Shake the basket, lower the temperature to 360°F (182°C), and cook for an additional 5 to 6 minutes. 5. While the first batch cooks, shape the remaining chicken portions into 8 more meatballs. 6. Cook the second batch of meatballs using the same method as before. 7. In a medium bowl, combine the remaining 4 tablespoons of buffalo wing sauce with the maple syrup. Toss the cooked meatballs in this mixture until they are evenly coated. 8. Return all the meatballs to the air fryer basket and cook at 390°F (199°C) for 2 to 3 minutes, allowing the glaze to set. Skewer each meatball with a toothpick and serve.

Eggplant Fries

Prep time: 10 minutes | Cook time: 7 to 8 minutes per batch | Serves 4

1 medium eggplant	1 cup crushed panko bread crumbs
1 teaspoon ground coriander	1 large egg
1 teaspoon cumin	2 tablespoons water
1 teaspoon garlic powder	Oil for misting or cooking spray
½ teaspoon salt	

1. Peel the eggplant and cut it into fries about ⅜ to ½ inch thick. 2. Preheat your air fryer to 390°F (199°C). 3. In a small cup, mix together the coriander, cumin, garlic, and salt. 4. Combine 1 teaspoon of the seasoning blend with the panko crumbs in a shallow dish. 5. Put the eggplant fries in a large bowl, sprinkle with the remaining seasoning, and toss to coat evenly. 6. Beat the eggs with the water, pour this mixture over the eggplant fries, and stir until well-coated. 7. Take the eggplant fries out of the egg wash, letting the excess drip off, and coat them in the seasoned panko crumbs. 8. Lightly spray the coated eggplant fries with oil. 9. Place half the fries in the air fryer basket, arranging them in a single layer, though a slight overlap is fine. 10. Air fry for 5 minutes. Shake the basket, mist with oil, and cook for another 2 to 3 minutes, until golden and crispy. 11. Repeat the cooking process with the remaining eggplant fries.

Cream Cheese Wontons

Prep time: 15 minutes | Cook time: 6 minutes | Makes 20 wontons

Oil, for spraying	4 ounces (113 g) cream cheese
20 wonton wrappers	

1. Begin by lining the air fryer basket with parchment paper and giving it a light spray of oil. 2. Fill a small bowl with a bit of water. 3. Take a wonton wrapper and place it flat, then add 1 teaspoon of cream cheese right in the middle. 4. Use your finger to dip into the water and lightly wet the edges of the wrapper. Bring the opposite corners together to form a triangle, pressing the edges firmly to seal. 5. Gently pinch the corners of the triangle to create the traditional wonton shape. Carefully place the wonton into the prepared basket. Continue this process with the remaining wrappers and cream cheese, working in batches if your air fryer is on the smaller side. 6. Set the air fryer to 400°F (204°C) and cook for 6 minutes, or until the edges turn a beautiful golden brown.

Black Bean Corn Dip

Prep time: 10 minutes | Cook time: 10 minutes | Serves 4

½ (15 ounces / 425 g) can black beans, drained and rinsed	cream cheese, softened
½ (15 ounces / 425 g) can corn, drained and rinsed	¼ cup shredded reduced-fat Cheddar cheese
¼ cup chunky salsa	½ teaspoon ground cumin
2 ounces (57 g) reduced-fat	½ teaspoon paprika
	Salt and freshly ground black pepper, to taste

1. Begin by preheating the air fryer to 325°F (163°C). 2. In a medium-sized bowl, combine the black beans, corn, salsa, cream cheese, Cheddar cheese, cumin, and paprika. Season the mixture with salt and pepper, then stir until all ingredients are thoroughly blended. 3. Transfer the mixture into a baking dish, spreading it evenly. 4. Place the baking dish in the air fryer basket and bake for approximately 10 minutes, or until the dip is heated through and bubbly. 5. Serve the dip hot, accompanied by your favorite chips or vegetables for dipping.

Greek Potato Skins with Olives and Feta

Prep time: 5 minutes | Cook time: 45 minutes | Serves 4

2 russet potatoes	cilantro, chopped, plus more for serving
3 tablespoons olive oil, divided, plus more for drizzling (optional)	¼ cup Kalamata olives, diced
1 teaspoon kosher salt, divided	¼ cup crumbled feta
¼ teaspoon black pepper	Chopped fresh parsley, for garnish (optional)
2 tablespoons fresh	

1. Preheat the air fryer to 380°F (193°C). 2. Poke 2 to 3 holes into each potato using a fork. Rub each potato with about ½ tablespoon of olive oil and ½ teaspoon of salt until fully coated. 3. Arrange the potatoes in the air fryer basket and bake for 30 minutes. 4. Once done, carefully remove the potatoes from the air fryer. Cut each potato in half and scoop out the flesh, leaving about a ½-inch layer inside the skins. Set the potato skins aside. 5. In a medium bowl, combine the scooped-out potato flesh with the remaining 2 tablespoons of olive oil, ½ teaspoon of salt, black pepper, and cilantro. Mash everything together until well mixed. 6. Spoon the seasoned potato mixture back into the potato skins, dividing it evenly. Sprinkle each filled skin with 1 tablespoon of olives and 1 tablespoon of feta. 7. Return the stuffed potato skins to the air fryer and cook for another 15 minutes. 8. Serve hot, garnished with extra chopped cilantro or parsley and a drizzle of olive oil, if desired.

Spicy Tortilla Chips

Prep time: 5 minutes | Cook time: 8 to 12 minutes | Serves 4

½ teaspoon ground cumin	Pinch cayenne pepper
½ teaspoon paprika	8 (6-inch) corn tortillas, each cut into 6 wedges
½ teaspoon chili powder	Cooking spray
½ teaspoon salt	

1. Preheat the air fryer to 375°F (191°C). Lightly spray the air fryer basket with cooking spray. 2. In a small bowl, mix together the cumin, paprika, chili powder, salt, and pepper. 3. Arrange the tortilla wedges in a single layer in the prepared basket. Work in batches if needed. Lightly mist the wedges with cooking spray and sprinkle them with the seasoning mixture. 4. Air fry for 4 to 6 minutes, shaking the basket halfway through cooking, until the chips are golden and crispy. 5. Repeat the process with any remaining tortilla wedges and seasoning. 6. Allow the tortilla chips to cool for about 5 minutes before serving.

Bacon-Wrapped Pickle Spears

Prep time: 10 minutes | Cook time: 8 minutes | Serves 4

8 to 12 slices bacon	cheese
¼ cup (2 ounces / 57 g) cream cheese, softened	8 dill pickle spears
¼ cup shredded Mozzarella	½ cup ranch dressing

1. Arrange the bacon slices flat on a clean surface. In a medium-sized bowl, mix the cream cheese and Mozzarella until thoroughly combined. Spread this cheese mixture evenly over the bacon slices. 2. Take a pickle spear and place it on one end of a bacon slice. Roll the bacon around the pickle in a tight spiral, making sure the pickle is completely enclosed. (If necessary, use additional bacon slices to fully cover the pickle.) Secure the ends by tucking them in to prevent unraveling. Repeat this process to wrap all the pickles. 3. Carefully place the bacon-wrapped pickles in the air fryer basket, ensuring they are arranged in a single layer. Set the air fryer to 400°F (204°C) and cook for 8 minutes, or until the bacon is fully cooked and the edges are crispy. 4. Serve the bacon-wrapped pickles warm, accompanied by ranch dressing for dipping.

Kale Chips with Tex-Mex Dip

Prep time: 10 minutes | Cook time: 5 to 6 minutes | Serves 8

1 cup Greek yogurt	1 bunch curly kale
1 tablespoon chili powder	1 teaspoon olive oil
⅓ cup low-sodium salsa, well drained	¼ teaspoon coarse sea salt

1. In a small bowl, mix together the yogurt, chili powder, and drained salsa, then place it in the refrigerator to chill. 2. Thoroughly rinse the kale and pat it dry. Using a sharp knife, remove the stems and ribs from the kale leaves. Cut or tear the leaves into 3-inch pieces. 3. In a large bowl, toss the kale pieces with olive oil until evenly coated. 4. Air fry the kale in small batches at 390°F (199°C) for 5 to 6 minutes, or until the leaves become crisp. Shake the basket once halfway through the cooking process. 5. As you take the kale chips out of the air fryer, lightly sprinkle them with sea salt. 6. Once all the kale chips are prepared, serve them alongside the chilled dip for a delicious combination.

Ranch Oyster Snack Crackers

Prep time: 3 minutes | Cook time: 12 minutes | Serves 6

Oil, for spraying
¼ cup olive oil
2 teaspoons dry ranch seasoning
1 teaspoon chili powder
½ teaspoon dried dill
½ teaspoon granulated garlic
½ teaspoon salt
1 (9 ounces / 255 g) bag oyster crackers

1. Begin by preheating the air fryer to 325°F (163°C). Line the air fryer basket with parchment paper and lightly spray it with oil. 2. In a large mixing bowl, combine the olive oil, ranch seasoning, chili powder, dill, garlic, and salt, stirring until well blended. Add the crackers to the mixture and toss them gently until they are evenly coated. 3. Transfer the coated crackers to the prepared air fryer basket, spreading them out in an even layer. 4. Cook for 10 to 12 minutes, shaking or stirring the crackers every 3 to 4 minutes to ensure even cooking, until they are crisp and turn a golden brown color.

Corn Dog Muffins

Prep time: 10 minutes | Cook time: 8 to 10 minutes per batch | Makes 8 muffins

1¼ cups sliced kosher hotdogs (3 or 4, depending on size)
½ cup flour
½ cup yellow cornmeal
2 teaspoons baking powder
½ cup skim milk
1 egg
2 tablespoons canola oil
8 foil muffin cups, paper liners removed
Cooking spray
Mustard or your favorite dipping sauce

1. Start by slicing each hotdog in half lengthwise, then cutting them into ¼-inch half-moon pieces. Set these aside for later use. 2. Preheat your air fryer to 390°F (199°C) to ensure it's ready for baking. 3. In a large mixing bowl, combine the flour, cornmeal, and baking powder, stirring them together thoroughly. 4. In a separate small bowl, whisk together the milk, egg, and oil until the mixture is just combined. 5. Pour the wet ingredients into the dry ingredients and mix well using a spoon until fully incorporated. 6. Gently fold the sliced hot dogs into the batter, ensuring they are evenly distributed. 7. Lightly coat the foil cups with cooking spray to prevent sticking. 8. Evenly distribute the batter among the muffin cups, filling them appropriately. 9. Place 4 muffin cups into the air fryer basket and cook for 5 minutes at the initial temperature. 10. Lower the temperature to 360°F (182°C) and continue cooking for an additional 3 to 5 minutes, or until a toothpick inserted into the center of a muffin comes out clean. 11. Repeat the process of cooking 4 muffin cups at a time until all the batter is used. 12. Serve the corn dog muffins warm, accompanied by mustard or your preferred dipping sauces.

Roasted Grape Dip

Prep time: 10 minutes | Cook time: 8 to 12 minutes | Serves 6

2 cups seedless red grapes, rinsed and patted dry
1 tablespoon apple cider vinegar
1 tablespoon honey
1 cup low-fat Greek yogurt
2 tablespoons 2% milk
2 tablespoons minced fresh basil

1. Place the grapes in the air fryer basket and sprinkle them with cider vinegar, followed by a drizzle of honey. Toss the grapes gently to ensure they are evenly coated. Roast them at 380°F (193°C) for 8 to 12 minutes, or until they become slightly shriveled but remain tender. Once done, remove the grapes from the air fryer. 2. In a medium bowl, combine the yogurt and milk, stirring until smooth. 3. Carefully fold in the roasted grapes and basil, mixing gently to incorporate. Serve the mixture right away, or cover and refrigerate for 1 to 2 hours to allow the flavors to meld before serving.

Poutine with Waffle Fries

Prep time: 10 minutes | Cook time: 15 to 17 minutes | Serves 4

2 cups frozen waffle cut fries
2 teaspoons olive oil
1 red bell pepper, chopped
2 green onions, sliced
1 cup shredded Swiss cheese
½ cup bottled chicken gravy

1. Start by preheating the air fryer to 380°F (193°C). 2. Toss the waffle fries with olive oil until evenly coated, then place them in the air fryer basket. Air fry for 10 to 12 minutes, shaking the basket halfway through, until the fries are crispy and lightly golden brown. 3. Transfer the fries to a baking pan and evenly top them with the pepper, green onions, and cheese. Return the pan to the air fryer and cook for an additional 3 minutes, or until the vegetables are tender and slightly crisp. 4. Take the pan out of the air fryer and drizzle the gravy over the fries. Place the pan back in the air fryer for 2 minutes, or until the gravy is heated through. 5. Serve the dish immediately while hot for the best flavor and texture.

Snacks and Appetizers

Parmesan French Fries

Prep time: 10 minutes | Cook time: 25 minutes | Serves 2 to 3

- 2 to 3 large russet potatoes, peeled and cut into ½-inch sticks
- 2 teaspoons vegetable or canola oil
- ¾ cup grated Parmesan cheese
- ½ teaspoon salt
- Freshly ground black pepper, to taste
- 1 teaspoon fresh chopped parsley

1. Start by filling a large saucepan with salted water and bringing it to a boil on the stovetop. As the water heats, peel and cut the potatoes into sticks. Blanch the potato sticks in the boiling water for 4 minutes. Meanwhile, preheat the air fryer to 400°F (204°C). Once the potatoes are blanched, strain them and rinse under cold water to stop the cooking process. Pat them dry thoroughly using a clean kitchen towel. 2. Gently toss the dried potato sticks with oil to coat them evenly, then place them in the air fryer basket. Air fry for 25 minutes, shaking the basket several times during cooking to ensure the fries brown evenly on all sides. 3. In a small bowl, mix together the Parmesan cheese, salt, and pepper. When there are 2 minutes remaining in the cooking time, sprinkle the Parmesan mixture over the fries. Toss the fries gently to coat them with the cheese mixture, then continue air frying for the final 2 minutes, or until the cheese has melted and begins to turn golden. Finish by sprinkling the fries with chopped parsley and an extra dusting of grated Parmesan cheese if desired, then serve immediately.

Crispy Breaded Beef Cubes

Prep time: 10 minutes | Cook time: 12 to 16 minutes | Serves 4

- 1 pound (454 g) sirloin tip, cut into 1-inch cubes
- 1 cup cheese pasta sauce
- 1½ cups soft bread crumbs
- 2 tablespoons olive oil
- ½ teaspoon dried marjoram

1. Begin by preheating the air fryer to 360°F (182°C). 2. In a medium-sized bowl, toss the beef cubes with the pasta sauce, ensuring they are evenly coated. 3. In a separate shallow bowl, mix together the bread crumbs, oil, and marjoram until well combined. Take the beef cubes one at a time and roll them in the bread crumb mixture, making sure they are fully coated. 4. Air fry the beef in two batches for 6 to 8 minutes, shaking the basket once during the cooking process to ensure even browning. Cook until the beef reaches an internal temperature of at least 145°F (63°C) and the exterior is crispy and golden brown. 5. Serve the beef immediately while hot for the best flavor and texture.

Stuffed Fried Mushrooms

Prep time: 20 minutes | Cook time: 10 to 11 minutes | Serves 10

- ½ cup panko bread crumbs
- ½ teaspoon freshly ground black pepper
- ½ teaspoon onion powder
- ½ teaspoon cayenne pepper
- 1 (8-ounce / 227-g) package cream cheese, at room temperature
- 20 cremini or button mushrooms, stemmed
- 1 to 2 tablespoons oil

1. In a medium-sized bowl, whisk together the bread crumbs, black pepper, onion powder, and cayenne until thoroughly combined. 2. Add the cream cheese to the mixture and stir until fully blended. Scoop 1 teaspoon of the cream cheese mixture and fill each mushroom cap evenly. 3. Preheat the air fryer to 360°F (182°C). Line the air fryer basket with a piece of parchment paper for easy cleanup. 4. Arrange the stuffed mushrooms on the parchment paper in a single layer and lightly spray them with oil. 5. Cook the mushrooms for 5 minutes, then shake the basket to ensure even cooking. Continue air frying for an additional 5 to 6 minutes, or until the filling is firm and the mushrooms are tender. Serve warm.

Old Bay Chicken Wings

Prep time: 10 minutes | Cook time: 12 to 15 minutes | Serves 4

- 2 tablespoons Old Bay seasoning
- 2 teaspoons baking powder
- 2 teaspoons salt
- 2 pounds (907 g) chicken wings, patted dry
- Cooking spray

1. Preheat the air fryer to 400°F (204°C) and lightly spray the air fryer basket with cooking spray. 2. In a large zip-top plastic bag, mix together the Old Bay seasoning, baking powder, and salt. Add the chicken wings to the bag, seal it, and shake vigorously until the wings are evenly coated with the seasoning mixture. 3. Arrange the seasoned chicken wings in the air fryer basket in a single layer, ensuring they are not overcrowded. Lightly mist the wings with cooking spray. If necessary, cook in batches to maintain proper air circulation. 4. Air fry the wings for 12 to 15 minutes, flipping them halfway through the cooking time, until they are lightly browned and the internal temperature reaches at least 165°F (74°C) when checked with a meat thermometer. 5. Transfer the cooked wings to a plate and repeat the process with any remaining wings. 6. Serve the wings hot for the best flavor and texture.

Italian Rice Balls

Prep time: 20 minutes | Cook time: 10 minutes | Makes 8 rice balls

1½ cups cooked sticky rice	(small enough to stuff into olives)
½ teaspoon Italian seasoning blend	2 eggs
¾ teaspoon salt, divided	⅓ cup Italian bread crumbs
8 black olives, pitted	¾ cup panko bread crumbs
1 ounce (28 g) Mozzarella cheese, cut into tiny pieces	Cooking spray

1. Preheat the air fryer to 390ºF (199ºC). 2. Take each black olive and stuff it with a small piece of Mozzarella cheese, then set them aside. 3. In a mixing bowl, combine the cooked sticky rice, Italian seasoning blend, and ½ teaspoon of salt, stirring until well mixed. Shape the rice mixture into a log using your hands, then divide it into 8 equal portions. Mold each portion around a stuffed olive, rolling it into a smooth ball. 4. Place the rice balls in the freezer for 10 to 15 minutes to firm up. 5. In a shallow dish, spread out the Italian bread crumbs. In another shallow dish, whisk the eggs. In a third dish, mix the panko bread crumbs with the remaining salt. 6. Working one at a time, roll each rice ball in the Italian bread crumbs, dip it into the whisked eggs, and then coat it thoroughly with the panko bread crumbs. 7. Arrange the coated rice balls in the air fryer basket and lightly spray both sides with cooking spray. 8. Air fry for 10 minutes, flipping the balls halfway through, until they are golden brown and crispy. 9. Serve the rice balls warm for the best taste and texture.

Mozzarella Arancini

Prep time: 5 minutes | Cook time: 8 to 11 minutes | Makes 16 arancini

2 cups cooked rice, cooled	2 tablespoons minced fresh basil
2 eggs, beaten	
1½ cups panko bread crumbs, divided	16 ¾-inch cubes Mozzarella cheese
½ cup grated Parmesan cheese	2 tablespoons olive oil

1. Begin by preheating the air fryer to 400ºF (204ºC). 2. In a medium bowl, mix together the rice, eggs, ½ cup of bread crumbs, Parmesan cheese, and basil until well combined. Shape the mixture into 16 balls, each about 1½ inches in diameter. 3. Use your finger to create a small hole in each ball, then insert a cube of Mozzarella cheese. Reshape the rice mixture firmly around the cheese to ensure it is fully enclosed. 4. On a shallow plate, combine the remaining 1 cup of bread crumbs with the olive oil, mixing until evenly distributed. Roll each rice ball in the bread crumb mixture to coat it thoroughly. 5. Air fry the arancini in batches for 8 to 11 minutes, or until they turn a golden brown color and become crispy. 6. Serve the arancini hot for the best flavor and texture.

Garlic-Parmesan Croutons

Prep time: 3 minutes | Cook time: 12 minutes | Serves 4

Oil, for spraying	3 tablespoons olive oil
4 cups cubed French bread	1 tablespoon granulated garlic
1 tablespoon grated Parmesan cheese	½ teaspoon unsalted salt

1. Start by lining the air fryer basket with parchment paper and lightly spraying it with oil. 2. In a large bowl, combine the bread cubes, Parmesan cheese, olive oil, garlic, and salt. Use your hands to toss the mixture thoroughly, ensuring the bread is evenly coated with the seasonings. Transfer the seasoned bread cubes to the prepared air fryer basket. 3. Air fry at 350ºF (177ºC) for 10 to 12 minutes, stirring the cubes once after 5 minutes, until they are crispy and golden brown. Serve warm as a delicious snack or accompaniment.

Rosemary-Garlic Shoestring Fries

Prep time: 5 minutes | Cook time: 18 minutes | Serves 2

1 large russet potato (about 12 ounces / 340 g), scrubbed clean, and julienned	rosemary
	Kosher salt and freshly ground black pepper, to taste
1 tablespoon vegetable oil	1 garlic clove, thinly sliced
Leaves from 1 sprig fresh	Flaky sea salt, for serving

1. Start by preheating the air fryer to 400ºF (204ºC). 2. Take the julienned potatoes and place them in a large colander, rinsing them under cold running water until the water runs clear. Spread the rinsed potatoes on a double layer of paper towels and pat them dry thoroughly. 3. In a large mixing bowl, toss the potatoes with oil and rosemary, seasoning generously with kosher salt and pepper to ensure even coating. Transfer the potatoes to the air fryer and cook for 18 minutes, shaking the basket every 5 minutes to promote even cooking. Add the garlic during the last 5 minutes of cooking, continuing until the fries are golden brown and crispy. 4. Once done, transfer the fries to a plate and sprinkle them with flaky sea salt while they're still hot. Serve immediately for the best texture and flavor.

Authentic Scotch Eggs

Prep time: 15 minutes | Cook time: 11 to 13 minutes | Serves 6

1½ pounds (680 g) bulk lean chicken or turkey sausage
3 raw eggs, divided
1½ cups dried bread crumbs, divided
½ cup all-purpose flour
6 hardboiled eggs, peeled
Cooking oil spray

1. In a large bowl, mix together the chicken sausage, 1 raw egg, and ½ cup of bread crumbs until well combined. Divide the mixture into 6 equal portions and shape each into a long oval. 2. In a shallow bowl, beat the remaining 2 raw eggs. 3. Place the flour in a small bowl. 4. Place the remaining 1 cup of bread crumbs in another small bowl. 5. Roll each hardboiled egg in the flour, then wrap one of the chicken sausage ovals around each egg, ensuring it is completely covered. 6. One at a time, roll the sausage-wrapped eggs in the flour, dip them into the beaten eggs, and finally coat them with the bread crumbs. 7. Insert the crisper plate into the air fryer basket and place the basket into the unit. Preheat the air fryer by selecting AIR FRY, setting the temperature to 375°F (191°C), and setting the time to 3 minutes. Press START/STOP to begin preheating. 8. Once preheated, lightly spray the crisper plate with cooking oil. Arrange the coated eggs in a single layer in the basket and spray them with oil. 9. Select AIR FRY, set the temperature to 375°F (191°C), and set the time to 13 minutes. Press START/STOP to begin cooking. 10. After about 6 minutes, use tongs to carefully turn the eggs and spray them with additional oil. Continue cooking for another 5 to 7 minutes, or until the chicken sausage is fully cooked and the Scotch eggs are golden brown. 11. Once cooking is complete, serve the Scotch eggs warm for the best flavor and texture.

Spicy Chicken Bites

Prep time: 10 minutes | Cook time: 10 to 12 minutes | Makes 30 bites

8 ounces boneless and skinless chicken thighs, cut into 30 pieces
¼ teaspoon kosher salt
2 tablespoons hot sauce
Cooking spray

1. Begin by preheating the air fryer to 390°F (199°C). 2. Lightly spray the air fryer basket with cooking spray. Season the chicken bites with kosher salt, then place them in the basket in a single layer. Air fry for 10 to 12 minutes, or until the chicken is crispy and cooked through. 3. While the chicken bites are cooking, pour the hot sauce into a large mixing bowl. 4. Once the chicken bites are done, remove them from the air fryer and immediately add them to the bowl of hot sauce. Toss the bites gently until they are evenly coated. Serve warm for the best flavor and texture.

Fried Artichoke Hearts

Prep time: 10 minutes | Cook time: 12 minutes | Serves 10

Oil, for spraying
3 (14 ounces / 397 g) cans quartered artichokes, drained and patted dry
½ cup mayonnaise
1 cup panko bread crumbs
⅓ cup grated Parmesan cheese
Salt and freshly ground black pepper, to taste

1. Begin by lining the air fryer basket with parchment paper and giving it a light spray of oil. 2. Arrange the artichokes on a plate and prepare two separate bowls, one with mayonnaise and the other with bread crumbs. 3. Take one artichoke piece at a time, coating it first in the mayonnaise and then rolling it in the bread crumbs until fully covered. 4. Transfer the coated artichokes to the prepared basket, working in batches if necessary to avoid overcrowding, depending on the size of your air fryer. 5. Air fry at 370°F (188°C) for 10 to 12 minutes, or until the artichokes turn crispy and achieve a golden brown color. 6. Once done, sprinkle the artichokes with Parmesan cheese and season with salt and black pepper to taste. Serve immediately for the best flavor and texture.

Red Pepper Tapenade

Prep time: 5 minutes | Cook time: 5 minutes | Serves 4

1 large red bell pepper
2 tablespoons plus 1 teaspoon olive oil, divided
½ cup Kalamata olives, pitted and roughly chopped
1 garlic clove, minced
½ teaspoon dried oregano
1 tablespoon lemon juice

1. Start by preheating the air fryer to 380°F (193°C). 2. Lightly brush the outside of a whole red pepper with 1 teaspoon of olive oil and place it in the air fryer basket. Roast for 5 minutes to soften the pepper. 3. While the pepper is roasting, prepare the olive mixture by combining the remaining 2 tablespoons of olive oil, olives, garlic, oregano, and lemon juice in a medium bowl. 4. Carefully remove the roasted red pepper from the air fryer. Slice off the stem, remove the seeds, and roughly chop the pepper into small pieces. 5. Add the chopped roasted pepper to the olive mixture and stir everything together until well combined. 6. Serve the flavorful mixture with pita chips, crackers, or crusty bread for a delicious appetizer or snack.

Carrot Chips

Prep time: 15 minutes | Cook time: 8 to 10 minutes | Serves 4

1 tablespoon olive oil, plus more for greasing the basket	4 to 5 medium carrots, trimmed and thinly sliced
	1 teaspoon seasoned salt

1. Start by preheating the air fryer to 390°F (199°C). Lightly grease the air fryer basket with olive oil to prevent sticking. 2. In a medium bowl, toss the carrot slices with 1 tablespoon of olive oil and salt, ensuring they are evenly coated. 3. Arrange the carrot slices in a single layer in the greased basket, working in batches if necessary to avoid overcrowding. 4. Air fry the carrots for 8 to 10 minutes, shaking the basket once during cooking, until they are crisp-tender and slightly caramelized. 5. Transfer the cooked carrot slices to a bowl and repeat the process with any remaining carrots. 6. Let the carrots cool for about 5 minutes before serving to allow them to firm up slightly. Enjoy warm as a tasty side dish or snack.

Lemon Shrimp with Garlic Olive Oil

Prep time: 5 minutes | Cook time: 6 minutes | Serves 4

1 pound (454 g) medium shrimp, cleaned and deveined	½ teaspoon salt
¼ cup plus 2 tablespoons olive oil, divided	¼ teaspoon red pepper flakes
Juice of ½ lemon	Lemon wedges, for serving (optional)
3 garlic cloves, minced and divided	Marinara sauce, for dipping (optional)

1. Begin by preheating the air fryer to 380°F (193°C). 2. In a large bowl, toss the shrimp with 2 tablespoons of olive oil, lemon juice, ⅓ of the minced garlic, salt, and red pepper flakes, ensuring the shrimp are evenly coated. 3. In a small ramekin, mix together the remaining ¼ cup of olive oil and the rest of the minced garlic. 4. Tear off a 12-by-12-inch sheet of aluminum foil and place the shrimp in the center. Fold the sides of the foil up and crimp the edges to create an open-top foil bowl. Carefully place this packet into the air fryer basket. 5. Roast the shrimp for 4 minutes, then open the air fryer and add the ramekin of garlic olive oil to the basket beside the shrimp packet. Continue cooking for an additional 2 minutes. 6. Transfer the shrimp to a serving plate or platter, placing the ramekin of garlic olive oil alongside for dipping. If desired, serve with lemon wedges and marinara sauce for added flavor.

Lemony Pear Chips

Prep time: 15 minutes | Cook time: 9 to 13 minutes | Serves 4

2 firm Bosc pears, cut crosswise into ⅛-inch-thick slices	½ teaspoon ground cinnamon
1 tablespoon freshly squeezed lemon juice	⅛ teaspoon ground cardamom

1. Start by preheating the air fryer to 380°F (193°C). 2. Separate the pear slices into smaller stem-end rounds and larger rounds with seeds. Remove the core and seeds from the larger slices. Lightly sprinkle all slices with lemon juice, cinnamon, and cardamom for added flavor. 3. Place the smaller pear chips into the air fryer basket. Air fry for 3 to 5 minutes, shaking the basket once during cooking, until the chips turn a light golden brown. Remove the smaller chips from the air fryer. 4. Repeat the process with the larger pear slices, air frying them for 6 to 8 minutes, shaking the basket once, until they achieve a light golden brown color. 5. Once done, remove the chips from the air fryer and let them cool. Serve immediately, or store in an airtight container at room temperature for up to 2 days to maintain their crispness.

Cinnamon-Apple Chips

Prep time: 10 minutes | Cook time: 32 minutes | Serves 4

Oil, for spraying	¼ teaspoon ground cinnamon, divided
2 Red Delicious or Honeycrisp apples	

1. Start by lining the air fryer basket with parchment paper and lightly spraying it with oil. 2. Trim any uneven ends from the apples. Using a mandoline set to the thinnest setting or a sharp knife, slice the apples into very thin pieces, discarding the cores. 3. Arrange half of the apple slices in a single layer in the prepared basket and sprinkle them evenly with half of the cinnamon. 4. Place a metal air fryer trivet on top of the apple slices to prevent them from moving around during cooking. 5. Air fry at 300°F (149°C) for 16 minutes, flipping the slices every 5 minutes to ensure they cook evenly. Repeat the process with the remaining apple slices and cinnamon. 6. Allow the apple chips to cool to room temperature before serving. As they cool, the chips will become firmer and crispier.

Pepperoni Pizza Dip

Prep time: 10 minutes | Cook time: 10 minutes | Serves 6

6 ounces (170 g) cream cheese, softened
¾ cup shredded Italian cheese blend
¼ cup sour cream
1½ teaspoons dried Italian seasoning
¼ teaspoon garlic salt
¼ teaspoon onion powder
¾ cup pizza sauce
½ cup sliced miniature pepperoni
¼ cup sliced black olives
1 tablespoon thinly sliced green onion
Cut-up raw vegetables, toasted baguette slices, pita chips, or tortilla chips, for serving

1. In a small bowl, mix together the cream cheese, ¼ cup of shredded cheese, sour cream, Italian seasoning, garlic salt, and onion powder until the mixture is smooth and all ingredients are thoroughly combined. 2. Spread the mixture evenly in a baking pan. Layer the pizza sauce on top, spreading it to the edges of the pan. Sprinkle the remaining ½ cup of shredded cheese over the sauce, then arrange the pepperoni slices on top. Finish by adding the black olives and green onion as the final layer. 3. Place the pan in the air fryer basket. Set the air fryer to 350°F (177°C) and cook for 10 minutes, or until the pepperoni edges begin to brown and the cheese becomes bubbly and lightly golden. 4. Allow the dish to stand for 5 minutes before serving. Pair it with vegetables, toasted baguette slices, pita chips, or tortilla chips for a delicious and versatile appetizer.

Rumaki

Prep time: 30 minutes | Cook time: 10 to 12 minutes per batch | Makes about 24 rumaki

10 ounces (283 g) raw chicken livers
1 can sliced water chestnuts, drained
¼ cup low-sodium teriyaki sauce
12 slices turkey bacon

1. Begin by cutting the livers into 1½-inch pieces, carefully removing any tough veins as you slice. 2. Place the liver pieces, water chestnuts, and teriyaki sauce in a small container with a lid. If necessary, add an extra tablespoon of teriyaki sauce to ensure the livers are fully submerged. Refrigerate the mixture for 1 hour to allow the flavors to meld. 3. When ready to cook, cut the bacon slices in half crosswise to create shorter strips. 4. Take one piece of liver and one slice of water chestnut, then wrap them together in a bacon strip. Secure the bundle with a toothpick to hold it in place. 5. After wrapping half of the livers, arrange them in a single layer in the air fryer basket. 6. Air fry at 390°F (199°C) for 10 to 12 minutes, or until the liver is fully cooked and the bacon turns crispy. 7. While the first batch is cooking, continue wrapping the remaining livers. Once the first batch is done, repeat the cooking process for the second batch. Serve warm and enjoy!

Crispy Cajun Dill Pickle Chips

Prep time: 5 minutes | Cook time: 10 minutes | Makes 16 slices

¼ cup all-purpose flour
½ cup panko bread crumbs
1 large egg, beaten
2 teaspoons Cajun seasoning
2 large dill pickles, sliced into 8 rounds each
Cooking spray

1. Begin by preheating the air fryer to 390°F (199°C). 2. Prepare three shallow bowls: one with all-purpose flour mixed with Cajun seasoning, one with panko bread crumbs, and one with beaten egg. 3. Coat each pickle chip by first dredging it in the seasoned flour, then dipping it into the egg, and finally rolling it in the panko bread crumbs. Shake off any excess coating and place the coated pickle chips on a plate. 4. Lightly spray the air fryer basket with cooking spray. Arrange 8 pickle chips in a single layer in the basket and air fry for 5 minutes, or until they are crispy and golden brown. Repeat the process with the remaining pickle chips. 5. Once cooked, transfer the pickle chips to a wire rack to cool slightly before serving. Enjoy them warm for the best texture and flavor.

Garlic-Roasted Tomatoes and Olives

Prep time: 5 minutes | Cook time: 20 minutes | Serves 6

2 cups cherry tomatoes
4 garlic cloves, roughly chopped
½ red onion, roughly chopped
1 cup black olives
1 cup green olives
1 tablespoon fresh basil, minced
1 tablespoon fresh oregano, minced
2 tablespoons olive oil
¼ to ½ teaspoon salt

1. Begin by preheating the air fryer to 380°F (193°C). 2. In a large bowl, combine all the ingredients and toss them together, ensuring the tomatoes and olives are evenly coated with the olive oil and herbs. 3. Transfer the mixture to the air fryer basket and roast for 10 minutes. Stir the mixture thoroughly, then continue roasting for another 10 minutes. 4. Remove the mixture from the air fryer, transfer it to a serving bowl, and enjoy immediately.

Spinach and Crab Meat Cups

Prep time: 10 minutes | Cook time: 10 minutes | Makes 30 cups

1 (6 ounces / 170 g) can crab meat, drained to yield ⅓ cup meat
¼ cup frozen spinach, thawed, drained, and chopped
1 clove garlic, minced
½ cup grated Parmesan cheese
3 tablespoons plain yogurt
¼ teaspoon lemon juice
½ teaspoon Worcestershire sauce
30 mini frozen phyllo shells, thawed
Cooking spray

1. Begin by preheating the air fryer to 390°F (199°C). 2. Carefully inspect the crab meat and remove any remaining bits of shell. 3. In a mixing bowl, combine the crab meat, spinach, garlic, and cheese, ensuring they are well blended. 4. Add the yogurt, lemon juice, and Worcestershire sauce to the mixture, stirring thoroughly until everything is evenly incorporated. 5. Spoon approximately a teaspoon of the filling into each phyllo shell, ensuring they are evenly filled. 6. Lightly spray the air fryer basket with cooking spray and arrange half of the filled shells in a single layer. Air fry for 5 minutes, then repeat the process with the remaining shells. 7. Serve the crab-filled phyllo shells immediately while warm for the best flavor and texture.

Shrimp Egg Rolls

Prep time: 15 minutes | Cook time: 10 minutes per batch | Serves 4

1 tablespoon vegetable oil
½ head green or savoy cabbage, finely shredded
1 cup shredded carrots
1 cup canned bean sprouts, drained
1 tablespoon soy sauce
½ teaspoon sugar
1 teaspoon sesame oil
¼ cup hoisin sauce
Freshly ground black pepper, to taste
1 pound (454 g) cooked shrimp, diced
¼ cup scallions
8 egg roll wrappers
Vegetable oil
Duck sauce

1. Heat a large sauté pan over medium-high heat. Add the oil and sauté the cabbage, carrots, and bean sprouts until they begin to wilt, approximately 3 minutes. Incorporate the soy sauce, sugar, sesame oil, hoisin sauce, and black pepper, stirring well. Continue cooking for a few more minutes. Add the shrimp and scallions, cooking until the vegetables are just tender. Transfer the mixture to a colander placed over a bowl to cool. Press or squeeze out any excess liquid from the filling to prevent soggy egg rolls. 2. Prepare the egg rolls: Lay the egg roll wrappers on a flat surface with one corner pointing toward you, resembling diamonds. Evenly divide the filling among the eight wrappers, spooning it onto the center of each. Spread the filling horizontally across the center, leaving about 2 inches of space at each corner. Lightly brush the empty edges of the wrapper with water. Fold the bottom corner tightly over the filling, ensuring no air pockets remain. Fold the left and right corners inward toward the center, creating an envelope shape. Roll the wrapper tightly from the bottom to the top corner, sealing the edge with a bit of water if necessary. Repeat this process for all eight egg rolls. 3. Preheat the air fryer to 370°F (188°C). 4. Lightly spray or brush all sides of the egg rolls with vegetable oil. Air fry four egg rolls at a time for 10 minutes, flipping them halfway through the cooking time to ensure even crispiness. 5. Serve the egg rolls hot, accompanied by duck sauce or your preferred dipping sauce.

Baked Spanakopita Dip

Prep time: 10 minutes | Cook time: 15 minutes | Serves 2

Olive oil cooking spray
3 tablespoons olive oil, divided
2 tablespoons minced white onion
2 garlic cloves, minced
4 cups fresh spinach
4 ounces (113 g) cream cheese, softened
4 ounces (113 g) feta cheese, divided
Zest of 1 lemon
¼ teaspoon ground nutmeg
1 teaspoon dried dill
½ teaspoon salt
Pita chips, carrot sticks, or sliced bread for serving (optional)

1. Preheat the air fryer to 360°F (182°C). Lightly coat the inside of a 6-inch ramekin or baking dish with olive oil cooking spray. 2. In a large skillet over medium heat, warm 1 tablespoon of olive oil. Add the onion and cook for 1 minute. 3. Stir in the garlic and cook for an additional minute, stirring frequently. 4. Reduce the heat to low and mix in the spinach and water. Cook for 2 to 3 minutes, or until the spinach has fully wilted. Remove the skillet from the heat. 5. In a medium bowl, combine the cream cheese, 2 ounces (57 g) of feta, the remaining 2 tablespoons of olive oil, lemon zest, nutmeg, dill, and salt. Mix until just combined. 6. Add the cooked vegetables to the cheese mixture and stir until evenly incorporated. 7. Transfer the dip mixture into the prepared ramekin and sprinkle the remaining 2 ounces (57 g) of feta cheese on top. 8. Place the ramekin in the air fryer basket and cook for 10 minutes, or until the dip is heated through and bubbling. 9. Serve the dip warm with pita chips, carrot sticks, or sliced bread for dipping.

Snacks and Appetizers

Veggie Shrimp Toast

Prep time: 15 minutes | Cook time: 3 to 6 minutes | Serves 4

8 large raw shrimp, peeled and finely chopped
1 egg white
2 garlic cloves, minced
3 tablespoons minced red bell pepper
1 medium celery stalk, minced
2 tablespoons cornstarch
¼ teaspoon Chinese five-spice powder
3 slices firm thin-sliced no-sodium whole-wheat bread

1. Begin by preheating the air fryer to 350°F (177°C). 2. In a small bowl, combine the shrimp, egg white, garlic, red bell pepper, celery, cornstarch, and five-spice powder, stirring until well mixed. Spread one-third of the shrimp mixture evenly over each slice of bread, ensuring it reaches the edges. Using a sharp knife, cut each slice of bread into 4 equal strips. 3. Arrange the shrimp toasts in the air fryer basket in a single layer, cooking in batches if necessary. Air fry for 3 to 6 minutes, or until the toasts are crisp and golden brown. 4. Serve the shrimp toasts immediately while hot for the best flavor and texture.

Feta and Quinoa Stuffed Mushrooms

Prep time: 5 minutes | Cook time: 8 minutes | Serves 6

2 tablespoons finely diced red bell pepper
1 garlic clove, minced
¼ cup cooked quinoa
⅛ teaspoon salt
¼ teaspoon dried oregano
24 button mushrooms, stemmed
2 ounces (57 g) crumbled feta
3 tablespoons whole wheat bread crumbs
Olive oil cooking spray

1. Start by preheating the air fryer to 360°F (182°C). 2. In a small bowl, mix together the bell pepper, garlic, quinoa, salt, and oregano until well combined. 3. Spoon the quinoa stuffing into the mushroom caps, filling them just to the top. 4. Place a small piece of feta cheese on top of each stuffed mushroom. 5. Sprinkle a pinch of bread crumbs over the feta on each mushroom for added texture. 6. Lightly spray the air fryer basket with olive oil cooking spray. Gently place the mushrooms in the basket, ensuring they do not touch each other. (Depending on the size of your air fryer, you may need to cook them in two batches.) 7. Insert the basket into the air fryer and bake for 8 minutes. 8. Once done, remove the mushrooms from the air fryer and serve warm.

Peppery Chicken Meatballs

Prep time: 5 minutes | Cook time: 13 to 20 minutes | Makes 16 meatballs

2 teaspoons olive oil
¼ cup minced onion
¼ cup minced red bell pepper
2 vanilla wafers, crushed
1 egg white
½ teaspoon dried thyme
½ pound (227 g) ground chicken breast

1. Begin by preheating the air fryer to 370°F (188°C). 2. In a baking pan, combine the olive oil, onion, and red bell pepper. Place the pan in the air fryer and cook for 3 to 5 minutes, or until the vegetables become tender. 3. In a medium bowl, mix the cooked vegetables, crushed wafers, egg white, and thyme until the ingredients are well blended. 4. Gently fold in the chicken, ensuring everything is thoroughly combined without overmixing. 5. Shape the mixture into 16 meatballs and place them in the air fryer basket. Air fry for 10 to 15 minutes, or until the meatballs reach an internal temperature of 165°F (74°C) when checked with a meat thermometer. 6. Serve the meatballs immediately while hot for the best flavor and texture.

Cheese Drops

Prep time: 15 minutes | Cook time: 10 minutes per batch | Serves 8

¾ cup all-purpose flour
½ teaspoon kosher salt
¼ teaspoon cayenne pepper
¼ teaspoon smoked paprika
¼ teaspoon black pepper
Dash garlic powder (optional)
¼ cup butter, softened
1 cup shredded sharp Cheddar cheese, at room temperature
Olive oil spray

1. In a small bowl, mix together the flour, salt, cayenne, paprika, pepper, and garlic powder (if using). 2. Using a food processor, blend the butter and cheese until smooth. Gradually add the seasoned flour and process until the dough is well combined, smooth, and no longer sticky. (Alternatively, use a stand mixer fitted with the paddle attachment: Cream the butter and cheese on medium speed until smooth, then add the seasoned flour and beat at low speed until the dough is smooth.) 3. Divide the dough into 32 equal-sized pieces. On a lightly floured surface, roll each piece into a small ball. 4. Lightly spray the air fryer basket with oil spray. Arrange 16 cheese drops in the basket. Set the air fryer to 325°F (163°C) and cook for 10 minutes, or until the drops begin to brown slightly. Transfer them to a wire rack. Repeat with the remaining dough, checking for doneness at 8 minutes. 5. Allow the cheese drops to cool completely on the wire rack. Store them in an airtight container until ready to serve, or for up to 1 or 2 days.

Lebanese Muhammara

Prep time: 15 minutes | Cook time: 15 minutes | Serves 6

2 large red bell peppers
¼ cup plus 2 tablespoons extra-virgin olive oil
1 cup walnut halves
1 tablespoon agave nectar or honey
1 teaspoon fresh lemon juice
1 teaspoon ground cumin
1 teaspoon kosher salt
1 teaspoon red pepper flakes
Raw vegetables (such as cucumber, carrots, zucchini slices, or cauliflower) or toasted pita chips, for serving

1. Start by drizzling the peppers with 2 tablespoons of olive oil and placing them in the air fryer basket. Set the air fryer to 400°F (204°C) and cook for 10 minutes. 2. Add the walnuts to the basket, arranging them around the peppers. Set the air fryer to 400°F (204°C) and cook for an additional 5 minutes. 3. Remove the peppers and seal them in a resealable plastic bag, allowing them to rest for 5 to 10 minutes to soften. Transfer the walnuts to a plate and let them cool. 4. In a food processor, combine the softened peppers, walnuts, agave, lemon juice, cumin, salt, and ½ teaspoon of the pepper flakes. Purée the mixture until smooth and well combined. 5. Transfer the dip to a serving bowl and create a small indentation in the center. Pour the remaining ¼ cup of olive oil into the indentation. Sprinkle the remaining ½ teaspoon of pepper flakes over the top as a garnish. 6. Serve the dip with fresh vegetables or toasted pita chips for a delicious and flavorful snack or appetizer.

Chapter 5
Poultry

Spicy Jalapeño Chicken Bites

Prep time: 10 minutes | Cook time: 25 minutes | Serves 4

1 medium red onion, minced
2 garlic cloves, minced
1 jalapeño pepper, minced
2 teaspoons extra-virgin olive oil
3 tablespoons ground almonds
1 egg
1 teaspoon dried thyme
1 pound (454 g) ground chicken breast
Cooking oil spray

1. Insert the crisper plate into the basket and the basket into the unit. Preheat the unit by selecting BAKE, setting the temperature to 400°F (204°C), and setting the time to 3 minutes. Select START/STOP to begin. 2. In a 6-by-2-inch round pan, combine the red onion, garlic, jalapeño, and olive oil. 3. Once the unit is preheated, place the pan into the basket. 4. Select BAKE, set the temperature to 400°F (204°C), and set the time to 4 minutes. Select START/STOP to begin. 5. When the cooking is complete, the vegetables should be crisp-tender. Transfer to a medium bowl. 6. Mix the almonds, egg, and thyme into the vegetable mixture. Add the chicken and mix until just combined. Form the chicken mixture into about 24 (1-inch) balls. 7. Insert the crisper plate into the basket and the basket into the unit. Preheat the unit by selecting BAKE, setting the temperature to 400°F (204°C), and setting the time to 3 minutes. Select START/STOP to begin. 8. Once the unit is preheated, spray the crisper plate with cooking oil. Working in batches, place half the meatballs in a single layer, not touching, into the basket. 9. Select BAKE, set the temperature to 400°F (204°C), and set the time to 10 minutes. Select START/STOP to begin. 10. When the cooking is complete, a food thermometer inserted into the meatballs should register at least 165°F (74°C). 11. Repeat steps 8 and 9 with the remaining meatballs. Serve warm.

Sweet and Spicy Korean Wings

Prep time: 10 minutes | Cook time: 25 minutes per batch | Serves 4

¼ cup gochujang, or red pepper paste
¼ cup mayonnaise
2 tablespoons honey
1 tablespoon sesame oil
2 teaspoons minced garlic
1 tablespoon sugar
2 teaspoons ground ginger
3 pounds (1.4 kg) whole chicken wings
Olive oil spray
1 teaspoon salt
½ teaspoon freshly ground black pepper

1. In a large bowl, whisk the gochujang, mayonnaise, honey, sesame oil, garlic, sugar, and ginger. Set aside. 2. Insert the crisper plate into the basket and the basket into the unit. Preheat the unit by selecting AIR FRY, setting the temperature to 400°F (204°C), and setting the time to 3 minutes. Select START/STOP to begin. 3. To prepare the chicken wings, cut the wings in half. The meatier part is the drumette. Cut off and discard the wing tip from the flat part (or save the wing tips in the freezer to make chicken stock). 4. Once the unit is preheated, spray the crisper plate with olive oil. Working in batches, place half the chicken wings into the basket, spray them with olive oil, and sprinkle with the salt and pepper. 5. Select AIR FRY, set the temperature to 400°F (204°C), and set the time to 20 minutes. Select START/STOP to begin. 6. After 10 minutes, remove the basket, flip the wings, and spray them with more olive oil. Reinsert the basket to resume cooking. 7. Cook the wings to an internal temperature of 165°F (74°C), then transfer them to the bowl with the prepared sauce and toss to coat. 8. Repeat steps 4, 5, 6, and 7 for the remaining chicken wings. 9. Return the coated wings to the basket and air fry for 4 to 6 minutes more until the sauce has glazed the wings and the chicken is crisp. After 3 minutes, check the wings to make sure they aren't burning. Serve hot.

Sweet and Tangy Pineapple Peach Chicken

Prep time: 10 minutes | Cook time: 14 to 15 minutes | Serves 4

1 pound (454 g) low-sodium boneless, skinless chicken breasts, cut into 1-inch pieces
1 medium red onion, chopped
1 (8-ounce / 227-g) can pineapple chunks, drained, ¼ cup juice reserved
1 tablespoon peanut oil or safflower oil
1 peach, peeled, pitted, and cubed
1 tablespoon cornstarch
½ teaspoon ground ginger
¼ teaspoon ground allspice
Brown rice, cooked (optional)

1. Preheat the air fryer to 380°F (193°C). 2. In a medium metal bowl, mix the chicken, red onion, pineapple, and peanut oil. Bake in the air fryer for 9 minutes. Remove and stir. 3. Add the peach and return the bowl to the air fryer. Bake for 3 minutes more. Remove and stir again. 4. In a small bowl, whisk the reserved pineapple juice, the cornstarch, ginger, and allspice well. Add to the chicken mixture and stir to combine. 5. Bake for 2 to 3 minutes more, or until the chicken reaches an internal temperature of 165°F (74°C) on a meat thermometer and the sauce is slightly thickened. 6. Serve immediately over hot cooked brown rice, if desired.

Fajita-Style Stuffed Chicken

Prep time: 15 minutes | Cook time: 25 minutes | Serves 4

2 (6-ounce / 170-g) boneless, skinless chicken breasts
¼ medium white onion, peeled and sliced
1 medium green bell pepper, seeded and sliced
1 tablespoon coconut oil
2 teaspoons chili powder
1 teaspoon ground cumin
½ teaspoon garlic powder

1. Slice each chicken breast completely in half lengthwise into two even pieces. Using a meat tenderizer, pound out the chicken until it's about ¼-inch thickness. 2. Lay each slice of chicken out and place three slices of onion and four slices of green pepper on the end closest to you. Begin rolling the peppers and onions tightly into the chicken. Secure the roll with either toothpicks or a couple pieces of butcher's twine. 3. Drizzle coconut oil over chicken. Sprinkle each side with chili powder, cumin, and garlic powder. Place each roll into the air fryer basket. 4. Adjust the temperature to 350°F (177°C) and air fry for 25 minutes. 5. Serve warm.

Crispy Chicken Chimichangas

Prep time: 20 minutes | Cook time: 8 to 10 minutes | Serves 4

2 cups cooked chicken, shredded
2 tablespoons chopped green chiles
½ teaspoon oregano
½ teaspoon cumin
½ teaspoon onion powder
Chimichanga Sauce:
2 tablespoons butter
2 tablespoons flour
1 cup chicken broth
¼ cup light sour cream
¼ teaspoon garlic powder
Salt and pepper, to taste
8 flour tortillas (6- or 7-inch diameter)
Oil for misting or cooking spray
¼ teaspoon salt
2 ounces (57 g) Pepper Jack or Monterey Jack cheese, shredded

1. Make the sauce by melting butter in a saucepan over medium-low heat. Stir in flour until smooth and slightly bubbly. Gradually add broth, stirring constantly until smooth. Cook and stir 1 minute, until the mixture slightly thickens. Remove from heat and stir in sour cream and salt. Set aside. 2. In a medium bowl, mix together the chicken, chiles, oregano, cumin, onion powder, garlic, salt, and pepper. Stir in 3 to 4 tablespoons of the sauce, using just enough to make the filling moist but not soupy. 3. Divide filling among the 8 tortillas. Place filling down the center of tortilla, stopping about 1 inch from edges. Fold one side of tortilla over filling, fold the two sides in, and then roll up. Mist all sides with oil or cooking spray. 4. Place chimichangas in air fryer basket seam side down. To fit more into the basket, you can stand them on their sides with the seams against the sides of the basket. 5. Air fry at 360°F (182°C) for 8 to 10 minutes or until heated through and crispy brown outside. 6. Add the shredded cheese to the remaining sauce. Stir over low heat, warming just until the cheese melts. Don't boil or sour cream may curdle. 7. Drizzle the sauce over the chimichangas.

Lettuce-Wrapped Savory Turkey Meatballs

Prep time: 10 minutes | Cook time: 15 minutes | Serves 6

Sauce:
2 tablespoons tamari
2 tablespoons tomato sauce
1 tablespoon lime juice
¼ teaspoon peeled and grated fresh ginger
1 clove garlic, smashed to a paste
½ cup chicken broth
⅓ cup sugar
2 tablespoons toasted sesame oil
Cooking spray
Meatballs:
2 pounds (907 g) ground turkey
¾ cup finely chopped button mushrooms
2 large eggs, beaten
1½ teaspoons tamari
¼ cup finely chopped green onions, plus more for garnish
2 teaspoons peeled and grated fresh ginger
1 clove garlic, smashed
2 teaspoons toasted sesame oil
2 tablespoons sugar
For Serving:
Lettuce leaves, for serving
Sliced red chiles, for garnish (optional)
Toasted sesame seeds, for garnish (optional)

1. Preheat the air fryer to 350°F (177°C). Spritz a baking pan with cooking spray. 2. Combine the ingredients for the sauce in a small bowl. Stir to mix well. Set aside. 3. Combine the ingredients for the meatballs in a large bowl. Stir to mix well, then shape the mixture in twelve 1½-inch meatballs. 4. Arrange the meatballs in a single layer on the baking pan, then baste with the sauce. You may need to work in batches to avoid overcrowding. 5. Arrange the pan in the air fryer. Air fry for 15 minutes or until the meatballs are golden brown. Flip the balls halfway through the cooking time. 6. Unfold the lettuce leaves on a large serving plate, then transfer the cooked meatballs on the leaves. Spread the red chiles and sesame seeds over the balls, then serve.

Dijon Chicken and Ham Meatballs

Prep time: 10 minutes | Cook time: 15 minutes | Serves 4

Meatballs:
½ pound (227 g) ham, diced
½ pound (227 g) ground chicken
½ cup grated Swiss cheese
1 large egg, beaten
Dijon Sauce:
3 tablespoons Dijon mustard
2 tablespoons lemon juice
¼ cup chicken broth, warmed
3 cloves garlic, minced
¼ cup chopped onions
1½ teaspoons sea salt
1 teaspoon ground black pepper
Cooking spray
¾ teaspoon sea salt
¼ teaspoon ground black pepper
Chopped fresh thyme leaves, for garnish

1. Preheat the air fryer to 390°F (199°C). Spritz the air fryer basket with cooking spray. 2. Combine the ingredients for the meatballs in a large bowl. Stir to mix well, then shape the mixture in twelve 1½-inch meatballs. 3. Arrange the meatballs in a single layer in the air fryer basket. Air fry for 15 minutes or until lightly browned. Flip the balls halfway through. You may need to work in batches to avoid overcrowding. 4. Meanwhile, combine the ingredients, except for the thyme leaves, for the sauce in a small bowl. Stir to mix well. 5. Transfer the cooked meatballs on a large plate, then baste the sauce over. Garnish with thyme leaves and serve.

Spiced Turkish Chicken Skewers

Prep time: 30 minutes | Cook time: 15 minutes | Serves 4

¼ cup plain Greek yogurt
1 tablespoon minced garlic
1 tablespoon tomato paste
1 tablespoon fresh lemon juice
1 tablespoon vegetable oil
1 teaspoon kosher salt
1 teaspoon ground cumin
1 teaspoon sweet Hungarian paprika
½ teaspoon ground cinnamon
½ teaspoon black pepper
½ teaspoon cayenne pepper
1 pound (454 g) boneless, skinless chicken thighs, quartered crosswise

1. In a large bowl, combine the yogurt, garlic, tomato paste, lemon juice, vegetable oil, salt, cumin, paprika, cinnamon, black pepper, and cayenne. Stir until the spices are blended into the yogurt. 2. Add the chicken to the bowl and toss until well coated. Marinate at room temperature for 30 minutes, or cover and refrigerate for up to 24 hours. 3. Arrange the chicken in a single layer in the air fryer basket. Set the air fryer to 375°F (191°C) for 10 minutes. Turn the chicken and cook for 5 minutes more. Use a meat thermometer to ensure the chicken has reached an internal temperature of 165°F (74°C).

Individual Cauliflower Crust Pizzas

Prep time: 10 minutes | Cook time: 25 minutes | Serves 2

1 (12-ounce / 340-g) bag frozen riced cauliflower
⅓ cup shredded Mozzarella cheese
¼ cup almond flour
¼ grated Parmesan cheese
1 large egg
½ teaspoon salt
1 teaspoon garlic powder
1 teaspoon dried oregano
4 tablespoons no-sugar-added marinara sauce, divided
4 ounces (113 g) fresh Mozzarella, chopped, divided
1 cup cooked chicken breast, chopped, divided
½ cup chopped cherry tomatoes, divided
¼ cup fresh baby arugula, divided

1. Preheat the air fryer to 400°F (204°C). Cut 4 sheets of parchment paper to fit the basket of the air fryer. Brush with olive oil and set aside. 2. In a large glass bowl, microwave the cauliflower according to package directions. Place the cauliflower on a clean towel, draw up the sides, and squeeze tightly over a sink to remove the excess moisture. Return the cauliflower to the bowl and add the shredded Mozzarella along with the almond flour, Parmesan, egg, salt, garlic powder, and oregano. Stir until thoroughly combined. 3. Divide the dough into two equal portions. Place one piece of dough on the prepared parchment paper and pat gently into a thin, flat disk 7 to 8 inches in diameter. Air fry for 15 minutes until the crust begins to brown. Let cool for 5 minutes. 4. Transfer the parchment paper with the crust on top to a baking sheet. Place a second sheet of parchment paper over the crust. While holding the edges of both sheets together, carefully lift the crust off the baking sheet, flip it, and place it back in the air fryer basket. The new sheet of parchment paper is now on the bottom. Remove the top piece of paper and air fry the crust for another 15 minutes until the top begins to brown. Remove the basket from the air fryer. 5. Spread 2 tablespoons of the marinara sauce on top of the crust, followed by half the fresh Mozzarella, chicken, cherry tomatoes, and arugula. Air fry for 5 to 10 minutes longer, until the cheese is melted and beginning to brown. Remove the pizza from the oven and let it sit for 10 minutes before serving. Repeat with the remaining ingredients to make a second pizza.

Classic Cobb Salad with Bacon and Avocado

Prep time: 15 minutes | Cook time: 8 minutes | Serves 4

8 slices reduced-sodium bacon
8 chicken breast tenders (about 1½ pounds / 680 g)
8 cups chopped romaine lettuce

Avocado-Lime Dressing:
½ cup plain Greek yogurt
¼ cup almond milk
½ avocado
Juice of ½ lime
3 scallions, coarsely chopped
1 cup cherry tomatoes, halved
¼ red onion, thinly sliced
2 hard-boiled eggs, peeled and sliced
1 clove garlic
2 tablespoons fresh cilantro
⅛ teaspoon ground cumin
Salt and freshly ground black pepper, to taste

1. Preheat the air fryer to 400ºF (204ºC). 2. Wrap a piece of bacon around each piece of chicken and secure with a toothpick. Working in batches if necessary, arrange the bacon-wrapped chicken in a single layer in the air fryer basket. Air fry for 8 minutes until the bacon is browned and a thermometer inserted into the thickest piece of chicken register 165ºF (74ºC). Let cool for a few minutes, then slice into bite-size pieces. 3. To make the dressing: In a blender or food processor, combine the yogurt, milk, avocado, lime juice, scallions, garlic, cilantro, and cumin. Purée until smooth. Season to taste with salt and freshly ground pepper. 4. To assemble the salad, in a large bowl, combine the lettuce, tomatoes, and onion. Drizzle the dressing over the vegetables and toss gently until thoroughly combined. Arrange the chicken and eggs on top just before serving.

Smoky Chipotle Aioli Wings

Prep time: 5 minutes | Cook time: 25 minutes | Serves 6

2 pounds (907 g) bone-in chicken wings
½ teaspoon salt
¼ teaspoon ground black pepper
2 tablespoons mayonnaise
2 teaspoons chipotle powder
2 tablespoons lemon juice

1. In a large bowl, toss wings in salt and pepper, then place into ungreased air fryer basket. Adjust the temperature to 400ºF (204ºC) and air fry for 25 minutes, shaking the basket twice while cooking. Wings will be done when golden and have an internal temperature of at least 165ºF (74ºC). 2. In a small bowl, whisk together mayonnaise, chipotle powder, and lemon juice. Place cooked wings into a large serving bowl and drizzle with aioli. Toss to coat. Serve warm.

Middle Eastern Chicken Shawarma

Prep time: 30 minutes | Cook time: 15 minutes | Serves 4

Shawarma Spice:
2 teaspoons dried oregano
1 teaspoon ground cinnamon
1 teaspoon ground cumin
1 teaspoon ground coriander
1 teaspoon kosher salt
½ teaspoon ground allspice
½ teaspoon cayenne pepper

Chicken:
1 pound (454 g) boneless, skinless chicken thighs, cut into large bite-size chunks
2 tablespoons vegetable oil

For Serving:
Tzatziki
Pita bread

1. For the shawarma spice: In a small bowl, combine the oregano, cayenne, cumin, coriander, salt, cinnamon, and allspice. 2. For the chicken: In a large bowl, toss together the chicken, vegetable oil, and shawarma spice to coat. Marinate at room temperature for 30 minutes or cover and refrigerate for up to 24 hours. 3. Place the chicken in the air fryer basket. Set the air fryer to 350ºF (177ºC) for 15 minutes, or until the chicken reaches an internal temperature of 165ºF (74ºC). 4. Transfer the chicken to a serving platter. Serve with tzatziki and pita bread.

Lemon and Herb Roasted Chicken

Prep time: 10 minutes | Cook time: 60 minutes | Serves 6

1 (4-pound / 1.8-kg) chicken
2 teaspoons dried thyme
1 teaspoon garlic powder
½ teaspoon onion powder
2 teaspoons dried parsley
1 teaspoon baking powder
1 medium lemon
2 tablespoons salted butter, melted

1. Rub chicken with thyme, garlic powder, onion powder, parsley, and baking powder. 2. Slice lemon and place four slices on top of chicken, breast side up, and secure with toothpicks. Place remaining slices inside of the chicken. 3. Place entire chicken into the air fryer basket, breast side down. 4. Adjust the temperature to 350ºF (177ºC) and air fry for 60 minutes. 5. After 30 minutes, flip chicken so breast side is up. 6. When done, internal temperature should be 165ºF (74ºC) and the skin golden and crispy. To serve, pour melted butter over entire chicken.

Crispy Garlic Dill Wings

Prep time: 5 minutes | Cook time: 25 minutes | Serves 4

2 pounds (907 g) bone-in chicken wings, separated at joints
½ teaspoon salt
½ teaspoon ground black pepper
½ teaspoon onion powder
½ teaspoon garlic powder
1 teaspoon dried dill

1. In a large bowl, toss wings with salt, pepper, onion powder, garlic powder, and dill until evenly coated. Place wings into ungreased air fryer basket in a single layer, working in batches if needed. 2. Adjust the temperature to 400ºF (204ºC) and air fry for 25 minutes, shaking the basket every 7 minutes during cooking. Wings should have an internal temperature of at least 165ºF (74ºC) and be golden brown when done. Serve warm.

Thai Peanut Chicken Tacos

Prep time: 10 minutes | Cook time: 6 minutes | Serves 4

1 pound (454 g) ground chicken
¼ cup diced onions (about 1 small onion)
2 cloves garlic, minced
¼ teaspoon fine sea salt

Sauce:
¼ cup creamy peanut butter, room temperature
2 tablespoons chicken broth, plus more if needed
2 tablespoons lime juice
2 tablespoons grated fresh ginger
2 tablespoons wheat-free tamari or coconut aminos
1½ teaspoons hot sauce
5 drops liquid stevia (optional)

For Serving:
2 small heads butter lettuce, leaves separated
Lime slices (optional)

For Garnish (Optional):
Cilantro leaves
Shredded purple cabbage
Sliced green onions

1. Preheat the air fryer to 350ºF (177ºC). 2. Place the ground chicken, onions, garlic, and salt in a pie pan or a dish that will fit in your air fryer. Break up the chicken with a spatula. Place in the air fryer and bake for 5 minutes, or until the chicken is browned and cooked through. Break up the chicken again into small crumbles. 3. Make the sauce: In a medium-sized bowl, stir together the peanut butter, broth, lime juice, ginger, tamari, hot sauce, and stevia (if using) until well combined. If the sauce is too thick, add another tablespoon or two of broth. Taste and add more hot sauce if desired. 4. Add half of the sauce to the pan with the chicken. Cook for another minute, until heated through, and stir well to combine. 5. Assemble the tacos: Place several lettuce leaves on a serving plate. Place a few tablespoons of the chicken mixture in each lettuce leaf and garnish with cilantro leaves, purple cabbage, and sliced green onions, if desired. Serve the remaining sauce on the side. Serve with lime slices, if desired. 6. Store leftover meat mixture in an airtight container in the refrigerator for up to 4 days; store leftover sauce, lettuce leaves, and garnishes separately. Reheat the meat mixture in a lightly greased pie pan in a preheated 350ºF (177ºC) air fryer for 3 minutes, or until heated through.

Satay-Style Chicken Strips

Prep time: 15 minutes | Cook time: 10 minutes | Serves 4

4 (6-ounce / 170-g) boneless, skinless chicken breasts, sliced into 16 (1-inch) strips
1 teaspoon fine sea salt
1 teaspoon paprika

Sauce:
¼ cup creamy almond butter (or sunflower seed butter for nut-free)
2 tablespoons chicken broth
1½ tablespoons coconut vinegar or unseasoned rice vinegar
1 clove garlic, minced
1 teaspoon peeled and minced fresh ginger
½ teaspoon hot sauce
⅛ teaspoon stevia glycerite, or 2 to 3 drops liquid stevia

For Garnish/Serving (Optional):
¼ cup chopped cilantro leaves
Red pepper flakes
Sea salt flakes
Thinly sliced red, orange, and yellow bell peppers

Special Equipment:
16 wooden or bamboo skewers, soaked in water for 15 minutes

1. Spray the air fryer basket with avocado oil. Preheat the air fryer to 400ºF (204ºC). 2. Thread the chicken strips onto the skewers. Season on all sides with the salt and paprika. Place the chicken skewers in the air fryer basket and air fry for 5 minutes, flip, and cook for another 5 minutes, until the chicken is cooked through and the internal temperature reaches 165ºF (74ºC). 3. While the chicken skewers cook, make the sauce: In a medium-sized bowl, stir together all the sauce ingredients until well combined. Taste and adjust the sweetness and heat to your liking. 4. Garnish the chicken with cilantro, red pepper flakes, and salt flakes, if desired, and serve with sliced bell peppers, if desired. Serve the sauce on the side. 5. Store leftovers in an airtight container in the fridge for up to 4 days or in the freezer for up to a month. Reheat in a preheated 350ºF (177ºC) air fryer for 3 minutes per side, or until heated through.

Southwestern Turkey Burgers

Prep time: 10 minutes | Cook time: 14 to 16 minutes | Serves 4

⅓ cup finely crushed corn tortilla chips
1 egg, beaten
¼ cup salsa
⅓ cup shredded pepper Jack cheese
Pinch salt
Freshly ground black pepper, to taste
1 pound (454 g) ground turkey
1 tablespoon olive oil
1 teaspoon paprika

1. Preheat the air fryer to 330°F (166°C). 2. In a medium bowl, combine the tortilla chips, egg, salsa, cheese, salt, and pepper, and mix well. 3. Add the turkey and mix gently but thoroughly with clean hands. 4. Form the meat mixture into patties about ½ inch thick. Make an indentation in the center of each patty with your thumb so the burgers don't puff up while cooking. 5. Brush the patties on both sides with the olive oil and sprinkle with paprika. 6. Put in the air fryer basket and air fry for 14 to 16 minutes or until the meat registers at least 165°F (74°C). 7. Let sit for 5 minutes before serving.

Spinach and Cheese-Stuffed Chicken

Prep time: 10 minutes | Cook time: 27 minutes | Serves 4

1 (10 ounces / 283 g) package frozen spinach, thawed and drained well
1 cup feta cheese, crumbled
½ teaspoon freshly ground black pepper
4 boneless chicken breasts
Salt and freshly ground black pepper, to taste
1 tablespoon olive oil

1. Prepare the filling. Squeeze out as much liquid as possible from the thawed spinach. Rough chop the spinach and transfer it to a mixing bowl with the feta cheese and the freshly ground black pepper. 2. Prepare the chicken breast. Place the chicken breast on a cutting board and press down on the chicken breast with one hand to keep it stabilized. Make an incision about 1-inch long in the fattest side of the breast. Move the knife up and down inside the chicken breast, without poking through either the top or the bottom, or the other side of the breast. The inside pocket should be about 3-inches long, but the opening should only be about 1-inch wide. If this is too difficult, you can make the incision longer, but you will have to be more careful when cooking the chicken breast since this will expose more of the stuffing. 3. Once you have prepared the chicken breasts, use your fingers to stuff the filling into each pocket, spreading the mixture down as far as you can. 4. Preheat the air fryer to 380°F (193°C). 5. Lightly brush or spray the air fryer basket and the chicken breasts with olive oil. Transfer two of the stuffed chicken breasts to the air fryer. Air fry for 12 minutes, turning the chicken breasts over halfway through the cooking time. Remove the chicken to a resting plate and air fry the second two breasts for 12 minutes. Return the first batch of chicken to the air fryer with the second batch and air fry for 3 more minutes. When the chicken is cooked, an instant read thermometer should register 165°F (74°C) in the thickest part of the chicken, as well as in the stuffing. 6. Remove the chicken breasts and let them rest on a cutting board for 2 to 3 minutes. Slice the chicken on the bias and serve with the slices fanned out.

Garlic-Butter French Chicken

Prep time: 30 minutes | Cook time: 27 minutes | Serves 4

2 tablespoon extra-virgin olive oil
1 tablespoon Dijon mustard
1 tablespoon apple cider vinegar
3 cloves garlic, minced
2 teaspoons herbes de Provence
½ teaspoon kosher salt
1 teaspoon black pepper
1 pound (454 g) boneless, skinless chicken thighs, halved crosswise
2 tablespoons butter
8 cloves garlic, chopped
¼ cup heavy whipping cream

1. In a small bowl, combine the olive oil, mustard, vinegar, minced garlic, herbes de Provence, salt, and pepper. Use a wire whisk to emulsify the mixture. 2. Pierce the chicken all over with a fork to allow the marinade to penetrate better. Place the chicken in a resealable plastic bag, pour the marinade over, and seal. Massage until the chicken is well coated. Marinate at room temperature for 30 minutes or in the refrigerator for up to 24 hours. 3. When you are ready to cook, place the butter and chopped garlic in a baking pan and place it in the air fryer basket. Set the air fryer to 400°F (204°C) for 5 minutes, or until the butter has melted and the garlic is sizzling. 4. Add the chicken and the marinade to the seasoned butter. Set the air fryer to 350°F (177°C) for 15 minutes. Use a meat thermometer to ensure the chicken has reached an internal temperature of 165°F (74°C). Transfer the chicken to a plate and cover lightly with foil to keep warm. 5. Add the cream to the pan, stirring to combine with the garlic, butter, and cooking juices. Place the pan in the air fryer basket. Set the air fryer to 350°F (177°C) for 7 minutes. 6. Pour the thickened sauce over the chicken and serve.

Traditional Hungarian Goulash

Prep time: 5 minutes | Cook time: 17 minutes | Serves 2

2 red bell peppers, chopped
1 pound (454 g) ground chicken
2 medium tomatoes, diced
½ cup chicken broth
Salt and ground black pepper, to taste
Cooking spray

1. Preheat the air fryer to 365°F (185°C). Spritz a baking pan with cooking spray. 2. Set the bell pepper in the baking pan and put in the air fry to broil for 5 minutes or until the bell pepper is tender. Shake the basket halfway through. 3. Add the ground chicken and diced tomatoes in the baking pan and stir to mix well. Broil for 6 more minutes or until the chicken is lightly browned. 4. Pour the chicken broth over and sprinkle with salt and ground black pepper. Stir to mix well. Broil for an additional 6 minutes. 5. Serve immediately.

Creamy Chicken Broccoli Bake

Prep time: 5 minutes | Cook time: 20 to 25 minutes | Serves 4

½ pound (227 g) broccoli, chopped into florets
2 cups shredded cooked chicken
4 ounces (113 g) cream cheese
⅓ cup heavy cream
1½ teaspoons Dijon mustard
½ teaspoon garlic powder
Salt and freshly ground black pepper, to taste
2 tablespoons chopped fresh basil
1 cup shredded Cheddar cheese

1. Preheat the air fryer to 390°F (199°C). Lightly coat a casserole dish that will fit in air fryer, with olive oil and set aside. 2. Place the broccoli in a large glass bowl with 1 tablespoon of water and cover with a microwavable plate. Microwave on high for 2 to 3 minutes until the broccoli is bright green but not mushy. Drain if necessary and add to another large bowl along with the shredded chicken. 3. In the same glass bowl used to microwave the broccoli, combine the cream cheese and cream. Microwave for 30 seconds to 1 minute on high and stir until smooth. Add the mustard and garlic powder and season to taste with salt and freshly ground black pepper. Whisk until the sauce is smooth. 4. Pour the warm sauce over the broccoli and chicken mixture and then add the basil. Using a silicone spatula, gently fold the mixture until thoroughly combined. 5. Transfer the chicken mixture to the prepared casserole dish and top with the cheese. Air fry for 20 to 25 minutes until warmed through and the cheese has browned.

Golden Crispy Fried Chicken Breasts

Prep time: 30 minutes | Cook time: 12 to 14 minutes | Serves 4

1 pound (454 g) boneless, skinless chicken breasts
¾ cup dill pickle juice
¾ cup finely ground blanched almond flour
¾ cup finely grated Parmesan cheese
½ teaspoon sea salt
½ teaspoon freshly ground black pepper
2 large eggs
Avocado oil spray

1. Place the chicken breasts in a zip-top bag or between two pieces of plastic wrap. Using a meat mallet or heavy skillet, pound the chicken to a uniform ½-inch thickness. 2. Place the chicken in a large bowl with the pickle juice. Cover and allow to brine in the refrigerator for up to 2 hours. 3. In a shallow dish, combine the almond flour, Parmesan cheese, salt, and pepper. In a separate, shallow bowl, beat the eggs. 4. Drain the chicken and pat it dry with paper towels. Dip in the eggs and then in the flour mixture, making sure to press the coating into the chicken. Spray both sides of the coated breasts with oil. 5. Spray the air fryer basket with oil and put the chicken inside. Set the temperature to 400°F (204°C) and air fry for 6 to 7 minutes. 6. Carefully flip the breasts with a spatula. Spray the breasts again with oil and continue cooking for 6 to 7 minutes more, until golden and crispy.

Smoky BBQ Chicken Nuggets

Prep time: 5 minutes | Cook time: 19 minutes | Serves 4

Oil, for spraying
2 (6-ounce / 170-g) boneless, skinless chicken breasts, cut into bite-size pieces
½ cup all-purpose flour
1 tablespoon granulated garlic
2 teaspoons seasoned salt
1 cup barbecue sauce

1. Line the air fryer basket with parchment and spray lightly with oil. 2. Place the chicken, flour, garlic, and seasoned salt in a zip-top plastic bag, seal, and shake well until evenly coated. 3. Place the chicken in an even layer in the prepared basket and spray liberally with oil. You may need to work in batches, depending on the size of your air fryer. 4. Roast at 390°F (199°C) for 8 minutes, flip, spray with more oil, and cook for another 8 minutes, or until the internal temperature reaches 165°F (74°C) and the juices run clear. 5. Transfer the chicken to a large bowl and toss with the barbecue sauce. 6. Line the air fryer basket with fresh parchment, return the chicken to the basket, and cook for another 3 minutes.

Crispy Air-Fried Buffalo Wings

Prep time: 10 minutes | Cook time: 20 minutes | Serves 6

16 chicken drumettes (party wings)
Chicken seasoning or rub, to taste
1 teaspoon garlic powder
Ground black pepper, to taste
¼ cup buffalo wings sauce
Cooking spray

1. Preheat the air fryer to 400°F (204°C). Spritz the air fryer basket with cooking spray. 2. Rub the chicken wings with chicken seasoning, garlic powder, and ground black pepper on a clean work surface. 3. Arrange the chicken wings in the preheated air fryer. Spritz with cooking spray. Air fry for 10 minutes or until lightly browned. Shake the basket halfway through. 4. Transfer the chicken wings in a large bowl, then pour in the buffalo wings sauce and toss to coat well. 5. Put the wings back to the air fryer and cook for an additional 7 minutes. 6. Serve immediately.

Crispy General Tso's Chicken

Prep time: 10 minutes | Cook time: 14 minutes | Serves 4

1 tablespoon sesame oil
1 teaspoon minced garlic
½ teaspoon ground ginger
1 cup chicken broth
4 tablespoons soy sauce, divided
½ teaspoon sriracha, plus more for serving
2 tablespoons hoisin sauce
4 tablespoons cornstarch, divided
4 boneless, skinless chicken breasts, cut into 1-inch pieces
Olive oil spray
2 medium scallions, sliced, green parts only
Sesame seeds, for garnish

1. In a small saucepan over low heat, combine the sesame oil, garlic, and ginger and cook for 1 minute. 2. Add the chicken broth, 2 tablespoons of soy sauce, the sriracha, and hoisin. Whisk to combine. 3. Whisk in 2 tablespoons of cornstarch and continue cooking over low heat until the sauce starts to thicken, about 5 minutes. Remove the pan from the heat, cover it, and set aside. 4. Insert the crisper plate into the basket and the basket into the unit. Preheat the unit by selecting BAKE, setting the temperature to 400°F (204°C), and setting the time to 3 minutes. Select START/STOP to begin. 5. In a medium bowl, toss together the chicken, remaining 2 tablespoons of soy sauce, and remaining 2 tablespoons of cornstarch. 6. Once the unit is preheated, spray the crisper plate with olive oil. Place the chicken into the basket and spray it with olive oil. 7. Select BAKE, set the temperature to 400°F (204°C), and set the time to 9 minutes. Select START/STOP to begin. 8. After 5 minutes, remove the basket, shake, and spray the chicken with more olive oil. Reinsert the basket to resume cooking. 9. When the cooking is complete, a food thermometer inserted into the chicken should register at least 165°F (74°C). Transfer the chicken to a large bowl and toss it with the sauce. Garnish with the scallions and sesame seeds and serve.

Zesty Lemon Herb Chicken

Prep time: 5 minutes | Cook time: 20 to 25 minutes | Serves 4

8 bone-in chicken thighs, skin on
1 tablespoon olive oil
1½ teaspoons lemon-pepper seasoning
½ teaspoon paprika
½ teaspoon garlic powder
¼ teaspoon freshly ground black pepper
Juice of ½ lemon

1. Preheat the air fryer to 360°F (182°C). 2. Place the chicken in a large bowl and drizzle with the olive oil. Top with the lemon-pepper seasoning, paprika, garlic powder, and freshly ground black pepper. Toss until thoroughly coated. 3. Working in batches if necessary, arrange the chicken in a single layer in the basket of the air fryer. Pausing halfway through the cooking time to turn the chicken, air fry for 20 to 25 minutes, until a thermometer inserted into the thickest piece registers 165°F (74°C). 4. Transfer the chicken to a serving platter and squeeze the lemon juice over the top.

Cranberry Turkey Quesadilla Melts

Prep time: 7 minutes | Cook time: 4 to 8 minutes | Serves 4

6 low-sodium whole-wheat tortillas
⅓ cup shredded low-sodium low-fat Swiss cheese
¾ cup shredded cooked low-sodium turkey breast
2 tablespoons cranberry sauce
2 tablespoons dried cranberries
½ teaspoon dried basil
Olive oil spray, for spraying the tortillas

1. Preheat the air fryer to 400°F (204°C). 2. Put 3 tortillas on a work surface. 3. Evenly divide the Swiss cheese, turkey, cranberry sauce, and dried cranberries among the tortillas. Sprinkle with the basil and top with the remaining tortillas. 4. Spray the outsides of the tortillas with olive oil spray. 5. One at a time, air fry the quesadillas in the air fryer for 4 to 8 minutes, or until crisp and the cheese is melted. Cut into quarters and serve.

Easy Turkey Meatballs

Prep time: 10 minutes | Cook time: 7 to 10 minutes | Serves 4

1 red bell pepper, seeded and coarsely chopped	lean ground turkey
2 cloves garlic, coarsely chopped	1 egg, lightly beaten
	½ cup grated Parmesan cheese
¼ cup chopped fresh parsley	1 teaspoon salt
1½ pounds (680 g) 85%	½ teaspoon freshly ground black pepper

1. Preheat the air fryer to 400°F (204°C). 2. In a food processor fitted with a metal blade, combine the bell pepper, garlic, and parsley. Pulse until finely chopped. Transfer the vegetables to a large mixing bowl. 3. Add the turkey, egg, Parmesan, salt, and black pepper. Mix gently until thoroughly combined. Shape the mixture into 1¼-inch meatballs. 4. Working in batches if necessary, arrange the meatballs in a single layer in the air fryer basket; coat lightly with olive oil spray. Pausing halfway through the cooking time to shake the basket, air fry for 7 to 10 minutes, until lightly browned and a thermometer inserted into the center of a meatball registers 165°F (74°C).

Grilled Mediterranean Chicken Skewers

Prep time: 35 minutes | Cook time: 25 minutes | Serves 4

¼ cup olive oil	1 pound (454 g) boneless skinless chicken thighs, cut into 1-inch pieces
1 teaspoon garlic powder	
1 teaspoon onion powder	
1 teaspoon ground cumin	1 red bell pepper, cut into 1-inch pieces
½ teaspoon dried oregano	
½ teaspoon dried basil	1 red onion, cut into 1-inch pieces
¼ cup lemon juice	
1 tablespoon apple cider vinegar	1 zucchini, cut into 1-inch pieces
Olive oil cooking spray	12 cherry tomatoes

1. In a large bowl, mix together the olive oil, garlic powder, onion powder, cumin, oregano, basil, lemon juice, and apple cider vinegar. 2. Spray six skewers with olive oil cooking spray. 3. On each skewer, slide on a piece of chicken, then a piece of bell pepper, onion, zucchini, and finally a tomato and then repeat. Each skewer should have at least two pieces of each item. 4. Once all of the skewers are prepared, place them in a 9-by-13-inch baking dish and pour the olive oil marinade over the top of the skewers. Turn each skewer so that all sides of the chicken and vegetables are coated. 5. Cover the dish with plastic wrap and place it in the refrigerator for 30 minutes. 6. After 30 minutes, preheat the air fryer to 380°F(193°C). (If using a grill attachment, make sure it is inside the air fryer during preheating.) 7. Remove the skewers from the marinade and lay them in a single layer in the air fryer basket. If the air fryer has a grill attachment, you can also lay them on this instead. 8. Cook for 10 minutes. Rotate the kebabs, then cook them for 15 minutes more. 9. Remove the skewers from the air fryer and let them rest for 5 minutes before serving.

Buffalo-Style Crunchy Chicken Strips

Prep time: 15 minutes | Cook time: 13 to 17 minutes per batch | Serves 4

¾ cup all-purpose flour	black pepper
2 eggs	16 chicken breast strips, or 3 large boneless, skinless chicken breasts, cut into 1-inch strips
2 tablespoons water	
1 cup seasoned panko bread crumbs	
2 teaspoons granulated garlic	Olive oil spray
	¼ cup Buffalo sauce, plus more as needed
1 teaspoon salt	
1 teaspoon freshly ground	

1. Put the flour in a small bowl. 2. In another small bowl, whisk the eggs and the water. 3. In a third bowl, stir together the panko, granulated garlic, salt, and pepper. 4. Dip each chicken strip in the flour, in the egg, and in the panko mixture to coat. Press the crumbs onto the chicken with your fingers. 5. Insert the crisper plate into the basket and the basket into the unit. Preheat the unit by selecting AIR FRY, setting the temperature to 375°F (191°C), and setting the time to 3 minutes. Select START/STOP to begin. 6. Once the unit is preheated, place a parchment paper liner into the basket. Working in batches if needed, place the chicken strips into the basket. Do not stack unless using a wire rack for the second layer. Spray the top of the chicken with olive oil. 7. Select AIR FRY, set the temperature to 375°F (191°C), and set the time to 17 minutes. Select START/STOP to begin. 8. After 10 or 12 minutes, remove the basket, flip the chicken, and spray again with olive oil. Reinsert the basket to resume cooking. 9. When the cooking is complete, the chicken should be golden brown and crispy and a food thermometer inserted into the chicken should register 165°F (74°C). 10. Repeat steps 6, 7, and 8 with any remaining chicken. 11. Transfer the chicken to a large bowl. Drizzle the Buffalo sauce over the top of the cooked chicken, toss to coat, and serve.

Herb-Roasted Thanksgiving Turkey Breast

Prep time: 5 minutes | Cook time: 30 minutes | Serves 4

1½ teaspoons fine sea salt	tarragon
1 teaspoon ground black pepper	1 teaspoon chopped fresh thyme leaves
1 teaspoon chopped fresh rosemary leaves	1 (2 pounds / 907 g) turkey breast
1 teaspoon chopped fresh sage	3 tablespoons ghee or unsalted butter, melted
1 teaspoon chopped fresh	3 tablespoons Dijon mustard

1. Spray the air fryer with avocado oil. Preheat the air fryer to 390°F (199°C). 2. In a small bowl, stir together the salt, pepper, and herbs until well combined. Season the turkey breast generously on all sides with the seasoning. 3. In another small bowl, stir together the ghee and Dijon. Brush the ghee mixture on all sides of the turkey breast. 4. Place the turkey breast in the air fryer basket and air fry for 30 minutes, or until the internal temperature reaches 165°F (74°C). Transfer the breast to a cutting board and allow it to rest for 10 minutes before cutting it into ½-inch-thick slices. 5. Store leftovers in an airtight container in the refrigerator for up to 4 days or in the freezer for up to a month. Reheat in a preheated 350°F (177°C) air fryer for 4 minutes, or until warmed through.

Golden Duck with Sweet Cherry Glaze

Prep time: 10 minutes | Cook time: 33 minutes | Serves 2 to 4

1 whole duck (up to 5 pounds / 2.3 kg), split in half, back and rib bones removed	1 teaspoon olive oil
	Salt and freshly ground black pepper, to taste
Cherry Sauce:	
1 tablespoon butter	vinegar
1 shallot, minced	1 teaspoon fresh thyme leaves
½ cup sherry	
¾ cup cherry preserves	Salt and freshly ground black pepper, to taste
1 cup chicken stock	
1 teaspoon white wine	

1. Preheat the air fryer to 400°F (204°C). 2. Trim some of the fat from the duck. Rub olive oil on the duck and season with salt and pepper. Place the duck halves in the air fryer basket, breast side up and facing the center of the basket. 3. Air fry the duck for 20 minutes. Turn the duck over and air fry for another 6 minutes. 4. While duck is air frying, make the cherry sauce. Melt the butter in a large sauté pan. Add the shallot and sauté until it is just starting to brown, about 2 to 3 minutes. Add the sherry and deglaze the pan by scraping up any brown bits from the bottom of the pan. Simmer the liquid for a few minutes, until it has reduced by half. Add the cherry preserves, chicken stock and white wine vinegar. Whisk well to combine all the ingredients. Simmer the sauce until it thickens and coats the back of a spoon, about 5 to 7 minutes. Season with salt and pepper and stir in the fresh thyme leaves. 5. When the air fryer timer goes off, spoon some cherry sauce over the duck and continue to air fry at 400°F (204°C) for 4 more minutes. Then, turn the duck halves back over so that the breast side is facing up. Spoon more cherry sauce over the top of the duck, covering the skin completely. Air fry for 3 more minutes and then remove the duck to a plate to rest for a few minutes. 6. Serve the duck in halves, or cut each piece in half again for a smaller serving. Spoon any additional sauce over the duck or serve it on the side.

Italian Herb Chicken with Roma Tomatoes

Prep time: 10 minutes | Cook time: 60 minutes | Serves 8

3 pounds (1.4 kg) chicken breasts, bone-in	1 teaspoon cayenne pepper
	½ teaspoon salt
1 teaspoon minced fresh basil	½ teaspoon freshly ground black pepper
1 teaspoon minced fresh rosemary	4 medium Roma tomatoes, halved
2 tablespoons minced fresh parsley	Cooking spray

1. Preheat the air fryer to 370°F (188°C). Spritz the air fryer basket with cooking spray. 2. Combine all the ingredients, except for the chicken breasts and tomatoes, in a large bowl. Stir to mix well. 3. Dunk the chicken breasts in the mixture and press to coat well. 4. Transfer the chicken breasts in the preheated air fryer. You may need to work in batches to avoid overcrowding. 5. Air fry for 25 minutes or until the internal temperature of the thickest part of the breasts reaches at least 165°F (74°C). Flip the breasts halfway through the cooking time. 6. Remove the cooked chicken breasts from the basket and adjust the temperature to 350°F (177°C). 7. Place the tomatoes in the air fryer and spritz with cooking spray. Sprinkle with a touch of salt and cook for 10 minutes or until tender. Shake the basket halfway through the cooking time. 8. Serve the tomatoes with chicken breasts on a large serving plate.

Crispy Israeli Chicken Schnitzel

Prep time: 5 minutes | Cook time: 10 minutes | Serves 4

2 large boneless, skinless chicken breasts, each weighing about 1 pound (454 g)	1 teaspoon black pepper
	1 teaspoon paprika
	2 eggs beaten with 2 tablespoons water
1 cup all-purpose flour	2 cups panko bread crumbs
2 teaspoons garlic powder	Vegetable oil spray
2 teaspoons kosher salt	Lemon juice, for serving

1. Preheat the air fryer to 375°F (191°C). 2. Place 1 chicken breast between 2 pieces of plastic wrap. Use a mallet or a rolling pin to pound the chicken until it is ¼ inch thick. Set aside. Repeat with the second breast. Whisk together the flour, garlic powder, salt, pepper, and paprika on a large plate. Place the panko in a separate shallow bowl or pie plate. 3. Dredge 1 chicken breast in the flour, shaking off any excess, then dip it in the egg mixture. Dredge the chicken breast in the panko, making sure to coat it completely. Shake off any excess panko. Place the battered chicken breast on a plate. Repeat with the second chicken breast. 4. Spray the air fryer basket with oil spray. Place 1 of the battered chicken breasts in the basket and spray the top with oil spray. Air fry until the top is browned, about 5 minutes. Flip the chicken and spray the second side with oil spray. Air fry until the second side is browned and crispy and the internal temperature reaches 165°F (74°C). Remove the first chicken breast from the air fryer and repeat with the second chicken breast. 5. Serve hot with lemon juice.

Spiced Fennel Chicken Curry

Prep time: 30 minutes | Cook time: 15 minutes | Serves 4

1 pound (454 g) boneless, skinless chicken thighs, cut crosswise into thirds	1 teaspoon ground fennel
	1 teaspoon garam masala
	1 teaspoon ground turmeric
1 yellow onion, cut into 1½-inch-thick slices	1 teaspoon kosher salt
	½ to 1 teaspoon cayenne pepper
1 tablespoon coconut oil, melted	Vegetable oil spray
2 teaspoons minced fresh ginger	2 teaspoons fresh lemon juice
2 teaspoons minced garlic	¼ cup chopped fresh cilantro or parsley
1 teaspoon smoked paprika	

1. Use a fork to pierce the chicken all over to allow the marinade to penetrate better. 2. In a large bowl, combine the onion, coconut oil, ginger, garlic, paprika, fennel, garam masala, turmeric, salt, and cayenne. Add the chicken, toss to combine, and marinate at room temperature for 30 minutes, or cover and refrigerate for up to 24 hours. 3. Place the chicken and onion in the air fryer basket. (Discard remaining marinade.) Spray with some vegetable oil spray. Set the air fryer to 350°F (177°C) for 15 minutes. Halfway through the cooking time, remove the basket, spray the chicken and onion with more vegetable oil spray, and toss gently to coat. At the end of the cooking time, use a meat thermometer to ensure the chicken has reached an internal temperature of 165°F (74°C). 4. Transfer the chicken and onion to a serving platter. Sprinkle with the lemon juice and cilantro and serve.

Herb-Roasted Peruvian Chicken

Prep time: 30 minutes | Cook time: 15 minutes | Serves 4

Chicken:

4 boneless, skinless chicken thighs (about 1½ pounds / 680 g)	olive oil
	1 serrano chile, seeded and minced
2 teaspoons grated lemon zest	1 teaspoon ground cumin
2 tablespoons fresh lemon juice	½ teaspoon dried oregano, crushed
1 tablespoon extra-virgin	½ teaspoon kosher salt

Sauce:

1 cup fresh cilantro leaves	olive oil
1 jalapeño, seeded and coarsely chopped	2½ teaspoons fresh lime juice
1 garlic clove, minced	¼ teaspoon kosher salt
1 tablespoon extra-virgin	⅓ cup mayonnaise

1. For the chicken: Use a fork to pierce the chicken all over to allow the marinade to penetrate better. In a small bowl, combine the lemon zest, lemon juice, olive oil, serrano, cumin, oregano, and salt. Place the chicken in a large bowl or large resealable plastic bag. Pour the marinade over the chicken. Toss to coat. Marinate at room temperature for 30 minutes, or cover and refrigerate for up to 24 hours. 2. Place the chicken in the air fryer basket. (Discard remaining marinade.) Set the air fryer to 350°F (177°C) for 15 minutes, turning halfway through the cooking time. 3. Meanwhile, for the sauce: Combine the cilantro, jalapeño, garlic, olive oil, lime juice, and salt in a blender. Blend until combined. Add the mayonnaise and blend until puréed. Transfer to a small bowl. Cover and chill until ready to serve. 4. At the end of the cooking time, use a meat thermometer to ensure the chicken has reached an internal temperature of 165°F (74°C). Serve the chicken with the sauce.

Paprika-Seasoned Crispy Drumsticks

Prep time: 5 minutes | Cook time: 22 minutes | Serves 2

2 teaspoons paprika
1 teaspoon packed brown sugar
1 teaspoon garlic powder
½ teaspoon dry mustard
½ teaspoon salt
Pinch pepper
4 (5 ounces / 142 g) chicken drumsticks, trimmed
1 teaspoon vegetable oil
1 scallion, green part only, sliced thin on bias

1. Preheat the air fryer to 400°F (204°C). 2. Combine paprika, sugar, garlic powder, mustard, salt, and pepper in a bowl. Pat drumsticks dry with paper towels. Using metal skewer, poke 10 to 15 holes in skin of each drumstick. Rub with oil and sprinkle evenly with spice mixture. 3. Arrange drumsticks in air fryer basket, spaced evenly apart, alternating ends. Air fry until chicken is crisp and registers 195°F (91°C), 22 to 25 minutes, flipping chicken halfway through cooking. 4. Transfer chicken to serving platter, tent loosely with aluminum foil, and let rest for 5 minutes. Sprinkle with scallion and serve.

Spicy Merguez-Style Meatballs

Prep time: 30 minutes | Cook time: 10 minutes | Serves 4

1 pound (454 g) ground chicken
2 garlic cloves, finely minced
1 tablespoon sweet Hungarian paprika
1 teaspoon kosher salt
1 teaspoon sugar
1 teaspoon ground cumin
½ teaspoon black pepper
½ teaspoon ground fennel
½ teaspoon ground coriander
½ teaspoon cayenne pepper
¼ teaspoon ground allspice

1. In a large bowl, gently mix the chicken, garlic, paprika, salt, sugar, cumin, black pepper, fennel, coriander, cayenne, and allspice until all the ingredients are incorporated. Let stand for 30 minutes at room temperature, or cover and refrigerate for up to 24 hours. 2. Form the mixture into 16 meatballs. Arrange them in a single layer in the air fryer basket. Set the air fryer to 400°F (204°C) for 10 minutes, turning the meatballs halfway through the cooking time. Use a meat thermometer to ensure the meatballs have reached an internal temperature of 165°F (74°C).

Bacon-Wrapped Stuffed Chicken Rolls

Prep time: 10 minutes | Cook time: 15 minutes | Serves 4

¼ cup chopped fresh chives
2 tablespoons lemon juice
1 teaspoon dried sage
1 teaspoon fresh rosemary leaves
½ cup fresh parsley leaves
4 cloves garlic, peeled
1 teaspoon ground fennel
3 teaspoons sea salt
½ teaspoon red pepper flakes
4 (4-ounce / 113-g) boneless, skinless chicken breasts, pounded to ¼ inch thick
8 slices bacon
Sprigs of fresh rosemary, for garnish
Cooking spray

1. Preheat the air fryer to 340°F (171°C). Spritz the air fryer basket with cooking spray. 2. Put the chives, lemon juice, sage, rosemary, parsley, garlic, fennel, salt, and red pepper flakes in a food processor, then pulse to purée until smooth. 3. Unfold the chicken breasts on a clean work surface, then brush the top side of the chicken breasts with the sauce. 4. Roll the chicken breasts up from the shorter side, then wrap each chicken rolls with 2 bacon slices to cover. Secure with toothpicks. 5. Arrange the rolls in the preheated air fryer, then cook for 10 minutes. Flip the rolls halfway through. 6. Increase the heat to 390°F (199°C) and air fry for 5 more minutes or until the bacon is browned and crispy. 7. Transfer the rolls to a large plate. Discard the toothpicks and spread with rosemary sprigs before serving.

Pepperoni Chicken Cheese Pizza

Prep time: 15 minutes | Cook time: 15 minutes | Serves 6

2 cups cooked chicken, cubed
1 cup pizza sauce
20 slices pepperoni
¼ cup grated Parmesan cheese
1 cup shredded Mozzarella cheese
Cooking spray

1. Preheat the air fryer to 375°F (191°C). Spritz a baking pan with cooking spray. 2. Arrange the chicken cubes in the prepared baking pan, then top the cubes with pizza sauce and pepperoni. Stir to coat the cubes and pepperoni with sauce. 3. Scatter the cheeses on top, then place the baking pan in the preheated air fryer. Air fryer for 15 minutes or until frothy and the cheeses melt. 4. Serve immediately.

Chapter 6
Beef, Pork, and Lamb

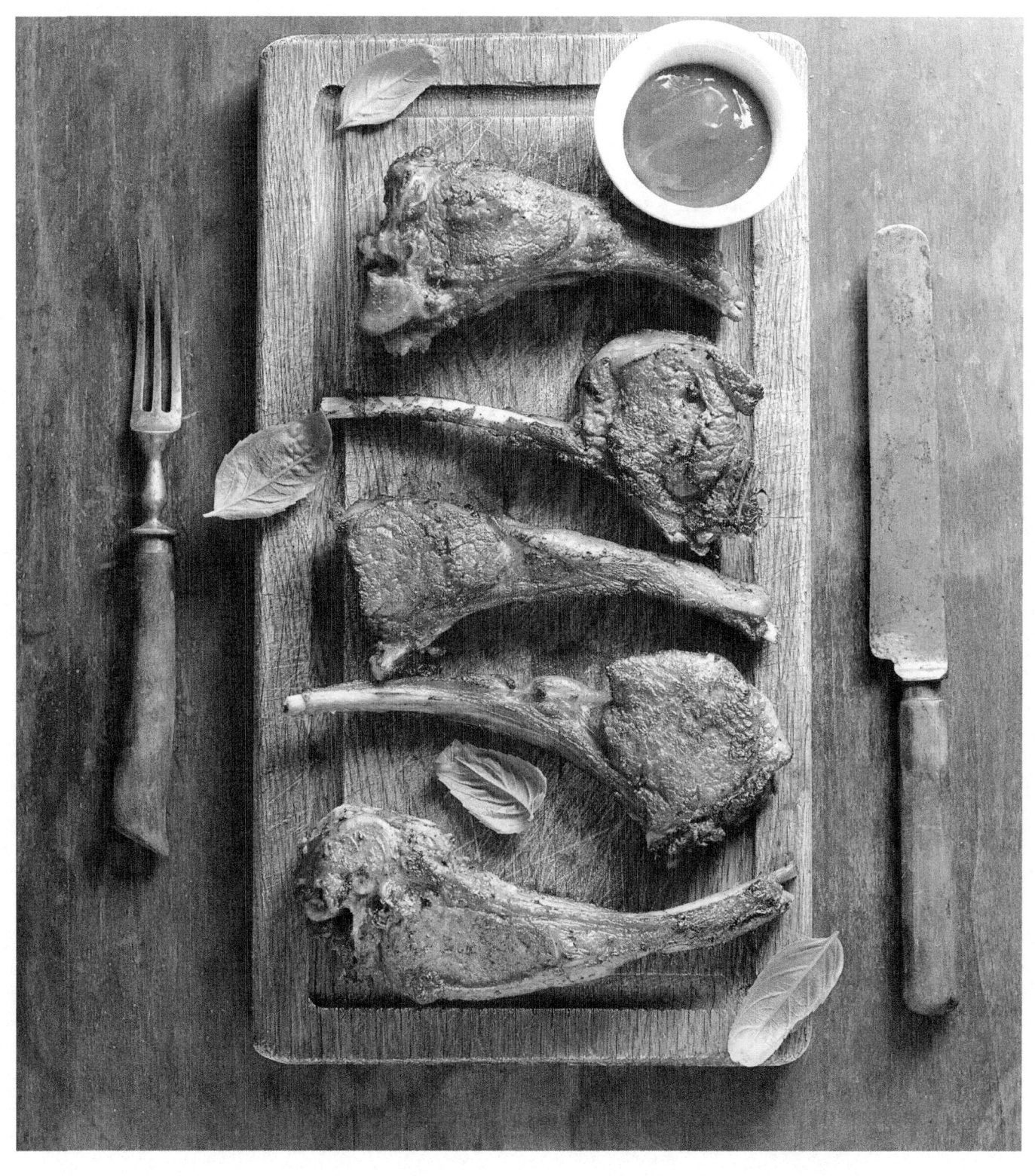

Chinese-Style Baby Back Ribs

Prep time: 30 minutes | Cook time: 30 minutes | Serves 4

1 tablespoon toasted sesame oil
1 tablespoon fermented black bean paste
1 tablespoon Shaoxing wine (rice cooking wine)
1 tablespoon dark soy sauce
1 tablespoon agave nectar or honey
1 teaspoon minced garlic
1 teaspoon minced fresh ginger
1 (1½-pound / 680-g) slab baby back ribs, cut into individual ribs

1. In a large bowl, combine the sesame oil, black bean paste, wine, soy sauce, agave, garlic, and ginger, stirring until well mixed. Add the ribs to the bowl and toss thoroughly to ensure they are evenly coated with the marinade. Let the ribs marinate at room temperature for 30 minutes, or cover the bowl and refrigerate for up to 24 hours for deeper flavor. 2. Transfer the ribs to the air fryer basket, discarding any remaining marinade. Set the air fryer to 350°F (177°C) and cook for 30 minutes, or until the ribs are tender and cooked through. Serve warm.

Swedish Meatloaf

Prep time: 10 minutes | Cook time: 35 minutes | Serves 8

1½ pounds (680 g) ground beef (85% lean)
¼ pound (113 g) ground pork
1 large egg (omit for egg-free)
½ cup minced onions
Sauce:
½ cup (1 stick) unsalted butter
½ cup shredded Swiss or mild Cheddar cheese (about 2 ounces / 57 g)
2 ounces (57 g) cream
¼ cup tomato sauce
2 tablespoons dry mustard
2 cloves garlic, minced
2 teaspoons fine sea salt
1 teaspoon ground black pepper, plus more for garnish

cheese (¼ cup), softened
⅓ cup beef broth
⅛ teaspoon ground nutmeg
Halved cherry tomatoes, for serving (optional)

1. Start by preheating the air fryer to 390°F (199°C). 2. In a large bowl, combine the ground beef, ground pork, egg, onions, tomato sauce, dry mustard, garlic, salt, and pepper. Use your hands to mix the ingredients thoroughly until well combined. 3. Transfer the meatloaf mixture into a loaf pan and place it in the air fryer. Bake for 35 minutes, or until the meatloaf is fully cooked and reaches an internal temperature of 145°F (63°C). Check the meatloaf after 25 minutes; if the top is browning too quickly, loosely cover it with foil to prevent burning. 4. While the meatloaf is cooking, prepare the sauce: Heat the butter in a saucepan over medium-high heat until it sizzles and develops brown flecks, stirring constantly to avoid burning. Reduce the heat to low and whisk in the Swiss cheese, cream cheese, broth, and nutmeg. Let the sauce simmer for at least 10 minutes, allowing the flavors to meld and deepen. 5. Once the meatloaf is done, transfer it to a serving tray and pour the sauce over the top. Garnish with ground black pepper and serve with cherry tomatoes if desired. Let the meatloaf rest for 10 minutes before slicing to ensure it holds together. 6. Store any leftovers in an airtight container in the refrigerator for up to 3 days or freeze for up to a month. To reheat, place the meatloaf in a preheated 350°F (177°C) air fryer for 4 minutes, or until warmed through.

Barbecue Ribs

Prep time: 5 minutes | Cook time: 30 minutes | Serves 4

1 (2 pounds / 907 g) rack baby back ribs
1 teaspoon onion powder
1 teaspoon garlic powder
1 teaspoon light brown sugar
1 teaspoon dried oregano
Salt and freshly ground black pepper, to taste
Cooking oil spray
½ cup barbecue sauce

1. Using a sharp knife, remove the thin membrane from the back of the ribs. Cut the rack into halves or smaller sections, such as 4- or 5-rib pieces, to ensure they fit comfortably in the air fryer basket. 2. In a small bowl, mix together the onion powder, garlic powder, brown sugar, and oregano, then season with salt and pepper. Generously rub the spice mixture onto both the front and back of the ribs. 3. Cover the ribs with plastic wrap or foil and let them sit at room temperature for 30 minutes to allow the flavors to penetrate. 4. Insert the crisper plate into the basket and place the basket into the air fryer unit. Preheat the unit by selecting AIR ROAST, setting the temperature to 360°F (182°C), and setting the time to 3 minutes. Press START/STOP to begin preheating. 5. Once preheated, lightly spray the crisper plate with cooking oil. Arrange the ribs in the basket, stacking them if necessary. 6. Select AIR ROAST, set the temperature to 360°F (182°C), and set the time to 30 minutes. Press START/STOP to begin cooking. 7. After 15 minutes, flip the ribs to ensure even cooking. Continue cooking for another 15 minutes, or until a food thermometer inserted into the ribs registers 190°F (88°C). 8. Once cooking is complete, transfer the ribs to a serving dish. Drizzle them with barbecue sauce and serve immediately.

Buttery Pork Chops

Prep time: 5 minutes | Cook time: 12 minutes | Serves 4

4 (4-ounce / 113-g) boneless pork chops
½ teaspoon salt
¼ teaspoon ground black pepper
2 tablespoons salted butter, softened

1. Season the pork chops on all sides with salt and pepper. Arrange the chops in a single layer in the ungreased air fryer basket. Set the air fryer to 400°F (204°C) and cook for 12 minutes, or until the pork chops are golden and reach an internal temperature of at least 145°F (63°C). 2. Using tongs, carefully remove the cooked pork chops from the air fryer and place them on a large plate. Top each chop with ½ tablespoon of butter and let them sit for 2 minutes to allow the butter to melt. Serve the pork chops warm and enjoy!

Pork and Tricolor Vegetables Kebabs

Prep time: 1 hour 20 minutes | Cook time: 8 minutes per batch | Serves 4

For the Pork:
1 pound (454 g) pork steak, cut in cubes
1 tablespoon white wine vinegar
3 tablespoons steak sauce
¼ cup soy sauce
1 teaspoon powdered chili
1 teaspoon red chili flakes
2 teaspoons smoked paprika
1 teaspoon garlic salt

For the Vegetable:
1 green squash, deseeded and cut in cubes
1 yellow squash, deseeded and cut in cubes
1 red pepper, cut in cubes
1 green pepper, cut in cubes
Salt and ground black pepper, to taste
Cooking spray

Special Equipment:
4 bamboo skewers, soaked in water for at least 30 minutes

1. In a large bowl, combine the ingredients for the pork marinade. Press the pork into the marinade to ensure it is fully submerged. Cover the bowl with plastic wrap and refrigerate for at least 1 hour to allow the flavors to infuse. 2. Preheat the air fryer to 370°F (188°C) and lightly spray the basket with cooking spray. 3. Remove the pork from the marinade and thread it onto skewers, alternating with vegetables. Season the skewers with salt and pepper to taste. 4. Arrange the skewers in the preheated air fryer basket, ensuring they are not overcrowded. Lightly spray the skewers with cooking spray. Air fry for 8 minutes, flipping them halfway through, until the pork is browned and the vegetables are lightly charred and tender. Cook in batches if necessary. 5. Serve the skewers immediately while hot for the best flavor and texture.

Garlic Balsamic London Broil

Prep time: 30 minutes | Cook time: 8 to 10 minutes | Serves 8

2 pounds (907 g) London broil
3 large garlic cloves, minced
3 tablespoons balsamic vinegar
3 tablespoons whole-grain mustard
2 tablespoons olive oil
Sea salt and ground black pepper, to taste
½ teaspoon dried hot red pepper flakes

1. Use a sharp knife to score both sides of the cleaned London broil, creating shallow cuts to help the marinade penetrate. 2. In a bowl, thoroughly mix the remaining ingredients, then massage the mixture into the meat, ensuring it is evenly coated on all sides. Allow the meat to marinate for at least 3 hours to enhance the flavor. 3. Preheat the air fryer to 400°F (204°C). Place the marinated London broil in the air fryer and cook for 15 minutes. Flip the meat over and continue cooking for an additional 10 to 12 minutes, or until it reaches your desired level of doneness. Enjoy your meal!

Italian Lamb Chops with Avocado Mayo

Prep time: 5 minutes | Cook time: 12 minutes | Serves 2

2 lamp chops
2 teaspoons Italian herbs
2 avocados
½ cup mayonnaise
1 tablespoon lemon juice

1. Season the lamb chops generously with Italian herbs and let them sit for 5 minutes to allow the flavors to infuse. 2. Preheat the air fryer to 400°F (204°C) and insert the rack into the basket. 3. Place the seasoned lamb chops on the rack and air fry for 12 minutes, or until cooked to your desired level of doneness. 4. While the chops are cooking, cut the avocados in half and remove the pits. Scoop the avocado flesh into a blender. 5. Add the mayonnaise and lemon juice to the blender and pulse until the mixture reaches a smooth, creamy consistency. 6. Carefully remove the lamb chops from the air fryer and plate them. Serve immediately with the avocado mayo on the side. Enjoy!

Mexican-Style Shredded Beef

Prep time: 5 minutes | Cook time: 35 minutes | Serves 6

1 (2-pound / 907-g) beef chuck roast, cut into 2-inch cubes
1 teaspoon salt
½ teaspoon ground black pepper
½ cup no-sugar-added chipotle sauce

1. In a large bowl, season the beef cubes with salt and pepper, tossing to ensure they are evenly coated. Place the beef cubes in the ungreased air fryer basket. Set the air fryer to 400°F (204°C) and cook for 30 minutes, shaking the basket halfway through to promote even cooking. The beef is done when it reaches an internal temperature of at least 160°F (71°C). 2. Transfer the cooked beef to a large bowl and use two forks to shred it into smaller pieces. Pour the chipotle sauce over the shredded beef and toss until it is well coated. 3. Return the sauced beef to the air fryer basket and cook for an additional 5 minutes at 400°F (204°C) to allow the sauce to crisp and adhere to the beef. Serve the beef warm for the best flavor and texture.

Provolone Stuffed Beef and Pork Meatballs

Prep time: 15 minutes | Cook time: 12 minutes | Serves 4 to 6

1 tablespoon olive oil
1 small onion, finely chopped
1 to 2 cloves garlic, minced
¾ pound (340 g) ground beef
¾ pound (340 g) ground pork
¾ cup bread crumbs
¼ cup grated Parmesan cheese
¼ cup finely chopped fresh parsley
½ teaspoon dried oregano
1½ teaspoons salt
Freshly ground black pepper, to taste
2 eggs, lightly beaten
5 ounces (142 g) sharp or aged provolone cheese, cut into 1-inch cubes

1. Heat a skillet over medium-high heat and add the oil. Cook the onion and garlic until they are tender but not browned. 2. Transfer the cooked onion and garlic to a large bowl. Add the beef, pork, bread crumbs, Parmesan cheese, parsley, oregano, salt, pepper, and eggs. Mix thoroughly until all ingredients are well combined. Divide the mixture into 12 equal portions. To form each meatball, press a hole into the mixture with your finger, insert a piece of provolone cheese, and mold the meat back into a ball to fully enclose the cheese. 3. Preheat the air fryer to 380°F (193°C). 4. Cook the meatballs in two batches. Place six meatballs in the air fryer basket and air fry for 12 minutes, shaking the basket and turning the meatballs twice during cooking to ensure even browning. Repeat with the remaining six meatballs. Serve the meatballs warm for the best flavor and texture.

Italian Sausage and Cheese Meatballs

Prep time: 10 minutes | Cook time: 20 minutes | Serves 4

½ pound (227 g) bulk Italian sausage
½ pound (227 g) 85% lean ground beef
½ cup shredded sharp Cheddar cheese
½ teaspoon onion powder
½ teaspoon garlic powder
½ teaspoon black pepper

1. In a large bowl, gently mix the sausage, ground beef, cheese, onion powder, garlic powder, and pepper until well combined. 2. Form the mixture into 16 meatballs. Place the meatballs in a single layer in the air fryer basket. Set the air fryer to 350°F (177°C) for 20 minutes, turning the meatballs halfway through the cooking time. Use a meat thermometer to ensure the meatballs have reached an internal temperature of 160°F / 71°C (medium).

Peppercorn-Crusted Beef Tenderloin

Prep time: 10 minutes | Cook time: 25 minutes | Serves 6

2 tablespoons salted butter, melted
2 teaspoons minced roasted garlic
3 tablespoons ground 4-peppercorn blend
1 (2 pounds / 907 g) beef tenderloin, trimmed of visible fat

1. Combine the butter and roasted garlic in a small bowl, stirring until well blended. Generously brush this mixture over the entire surface of the beef tenderloin. 2. Spread the ground peppercorns evenly on a plate and roll the tenderloin through them, ensuring a thorough coating to form a flavorful crust. Carefully place the coated tenderloin into the air fryer basket. 3. Set the air fryer temperature to 400°F (204°C) and roast the tenderloin for 25 minutes. 4. Midway through the cooking process, turn the tenderloin to ensure even browning and cooking on all sides. 5. Once the roasting is complete, let the meat rest for 10 minutes to allow the juices to redistribute before slicing and serving.

Cinnamon-Beef Kofta

Prep time: 10 minutes | Cook time: 13 minutes per batch | Makes 12 koftas

1½ pounds (680 g) lean ground beef	1 teaspoon ground cumin
1 teaspoon onion powder	¾ teaspoon salt
¾ teaspoon ground cinnamon	¼ teaspoon cayenne
¾ teaspoon ground dried turmeric	12 (3½- to 4-inch-long) cinnamon sticks
	Cooking spray

1. Preheat the air fryer to 375°F (191°C) and lightly spray the air fryer basket with cooking spray. 2. In a large bowl, combine all the ingredients except for the cinnamon sticks, tossing until well mixed. 3. Divide the mixture into 12 equal portions and shape each into a ball. Wrap each ball around a cinnamon stick, leaving about a quarter of the stick uncovered. 4. Arrange the beef-wrapped cinnamon sticks in the preheated air fryer, ensuring they are not overcrowded. Lightly spray them with cooking spray. Cook in batches if necessary. 5. Air fry for 13 minutes, flipping the sticks halfway through, until the beef is browned and cooked through. 6. Serve the beef-cinnamon sticks immediately while hot for the best flavor and texture.

Sausage and Cauliflower Arancini

Prep time: 30 minutes | Cook time: 28 to 32 minutes | Serves 6

Avocado oil spray	cheese
6 ounces (170 g) Italian sausage, casings removed	4 ounces (113 g) Cheddar cheese, shredded
¼ cup diced onion	1 large egg
1 teaspoon minced garlic	½ cup finely ground blanched almond flour
1 teaspoon dried thyme	
Sea salt and freshly ground black pepper, to taste	¼ cup finely grated Parmesan cheese
2½ cups cauliflower rice	Keto-friendly marinara sauce, for serving
3 ounces (85 g) cream	

1. Lightly coat a large skillet with oil and heat it over medium-high heat. Once the skillet is hot, add the sausage and cook for 7 minutes, using the back of a spoon to break the meat into smaller pieces. 2. Lower the heat to medium and incorporate the onion, cooking for 5 minutes until softened. Add the garlic, thyme, salt, and pepper, and cook for an additional minute to release the aromas. 3. Stir in the cauliflower rice and cream cheese, cooking for 7 minutes while stirring frequently until the cream cheese melts and the cauliflower becomes tender. 4. Remove the skillet from the heat and mix in the Cheddar cheese until fully combined. Using a cookie scoop, shape the mixture into 1½-inch balls and place them on a parchment paper-lined baking sheet. Freeze the balls for 30 minutes to firm them up. 5. In a shallow bowl, beat the egg with a fork. In another bowl, combine the almond flour and Parmesan cheese, stirring until evenly mixed. 6. Dip each cauliflower ball into the beaten egg, then roll it in the almond flour mixture, gently pressing to ensure the coating adheres well. 7. Preheat the air fryer to 400°F (204°C). Lightly spray the cauliflower balls with oil and arrange them in a single layer in the air fryer basket, working in batches if needed. Air fry for 5 minutes, then flip the balls, spray them with more oil, and cook for an additional 3 to 7 minutes, or until they turn golden brown and crispy. 8. Serve the cauliflower rice balls warm, accompanied by marinara sauce for dipping.

Steaks with Walnut-Blue Cheese Butter

Prep time: 30 minutes | Cook time: 10 minutes | Serves 6

½ cup unsalted butter, at room temperature	1 teaspoon minced garlic
½ cup crumbled blue cheese	¼ teaspoon cayenne pepper
	Sea salt and freshly ground black pepper, to taste
2 tablespoons finely chopped walnuts	1½ pounds (680 g) New York strip steaks, at room temperature
1 tablespoon minced fresh rosemary	

1. In a medium bowl, mix together the butter, blue cheese, walnuts, rosemary, garlic, cayenne pepper, and salt and black pepper to taste. Use your hands to ensure the mixture is thoroughly combined. Transfer the mixture onto a sheet of parchment paper and shape it into a log. Wrap it tightly in plastic wrap and refrigerate for at least 2 hours, or freeze for 30 minutes to firm up. 2. Generously season the steaks with salt and pepper on both sides. 3. Insert the air fryer basket or grill pan into the air fryer. Preheat the air fryer to 400°F (204°C) for 5 minutes. 4. Place the steaks in the basket in a single layer and air fry for 5 minutes. Flip the steaks and cook for an additional 5 minutes, or until an instant-read thermometer reads 120°F (49°C) for medium-rare (adjust time for your preferred doneness). 5. Transfer the steaks to a plate. Slice the chilled butter into pieces and place the desired amount on top of the steaks. Cover the steaks loosely with aluminum foil and let them rest for 10 minutes before serving. 6. Store any leftover butter in a sealed container in the refrigerator for up to 2 weeks.

Mustard Lamb Chops

Prep time: 5 minutes | Cook time: 14 minutes | Serves 4

Oil, for spraying
1 tablespoon Dijon mustard
2 teaspoons lemon juice
½ teaspoon dried tarragon
¼ teaspoon salt
¼ teaspoon freshly ground black pepper
4 (1¼-inch-thick) loin lamb chops

1. Begin by preheating the air fryer to 390ºF (199ºC). Line the air fryer basket with parchment paper and lightly spray it with oil. 2. In a small bowl, combine the mustard, lemon juice, tarragon, salt, and black pepper, mixing until well blended. 3. Use a paper towel to pat the lamb chops dry. Brush both sides of the chops generously with the mustard mixture. 4. Arrange the lamb chops in the prepared basket, working in batches if necessary to avoid overcrowding. 5. Cook the chops for 8 minutes, then flip them and cook for an additional 6 minutes, or until they reach your desired level of doneness: 125ºF (52ºC) for rare, 145ºF (63ºC) for medium-rare, or 155ºF (68ºC) for medium. Serve immediately.

Beef and Goat Cheese Stuffed Peppers

Prep time: 10 minutes | Cook time: 30 minutes | Serves 4

1 pound (454 g) lean ground beef
½ cup cooked brown rice
2 Roma tomatoes, diced
3 garlic cloves, minced
½ yellow onion, diced
2 tablespoons fresh oregano, chopped
1 teaspoon salt
½ teaspoon black pepper
¼ teaspoon ground allspice
2 bell peppers, halved and seeded
4 ounces (113 g) goat cheese
¼ cup fresh parsley, chopped

1. Begin by preheating the air fryer to 360ºF (182ºC). 2. In a large bowl, combine the ground beef, rice, tomatoes, garlic, onion, oregano, salt, pepper, and allspice, mixing thoroughly until all ingredients are well incorporated. 3. Evenly divide the beef mixture among the halved bell peppers, filling each one. Top each pepper with approximately 1 ounce (28 g, or a quarter of the total) of goat cheese. 4. Arrange the stuffed peppers in the air fryer basket in a single layer, ensuring they do not touch each other. Bake for 30 minutes. 5. Once cooked, remove the peppers from the air fryer and garnish with fresh parsley before serving. Enjoy warm!

Beef and Tomato Sauce Meatloaf

Prep time: 15 minutes | Cook time: 25 minutes | Serves 4

1½ pounds (680 g) ground beef
1 cup tomato sauce
½ cup breadcrumbs
2 egg whites
½ cup grated Parmesan cheese
1 diced onion
2 tablespoons chopped parsley
2 tablespoons minced ginger
2 garlic cloves, minced
½ teaspoon dried basil
1 teaspoon cayenne pepper
Salt and ground black pepper, to taste
Cooking spray

1. Start by preheating the air fryer to 360ºF (182ºC) and lightly spraying a meatloaf pan with cooking spray. 2. In a large bowl, combine all the ingredients and mix thoroughly until well blended. 3. Transfer the meat mixture into the prepared meatloaf pan, using a spatula to press it down firmly and evenly. 4. Place the pan in the preheated air fryer and bake for 25 minutes, or until the meatloaf is well browned and cooked through. 5. Serve the meatloaf immediately while hot for the best flavor and texture.

Cajun Bacon Pork Loin Fillet

Prep time: 30 minutes | Cook time: 20 minutes | Serves 6

1½ pounds (680 g) pork loin fillet or pork tenderloin
3 tablespoons olive oil
2 tablespoons Cajun spice mix
Salt, to taste
6 slices bacon
Olive oil spray

1. Cut the pork into two equal pieces to ensure they fit comfortably in the air fryer basket. 2. Place both pieces of pork in a resealable plastic bag. Add the oil, Cajun seasoning, and salt (if using). Seal the bag and massage it to evenly coat the meat with the oil and seasonings. Allow the pork to marinate in the refrigerator for at least 1 hour or up to 24 hours. 3. Remove the pork from the bag and wrap 3 slices of bacon around each piece. Lightly spray the air fryer basket with olive oil spray. Place the bacon-wrapped pork in the air fryer. Set the air fryer to 350ºF (177ºC) and cook for 15 minutes. Then, increase the temperature to 400ºF (204ºC) and cook for an additional 5 minutes. Use a meat thermometer to ensure the pork reaches an internal temperature of 145ºF (63ºC). 4. Let the pork rest for 10 minutes before slicing it into 6 medallions. Serve warm and enjoy!

Meat and Rice Stuffed Bell Peppers

Prep time: 20 minutes | Cook time: 18 minutes | Serves 4

¾ pound (340 g) lean ground beef
4 ounces (113 g) lean ground pork
¼ cup onion, minced
1 (15-ounce / 425-g) can crushed tomatoes
1 teaspoon Worcestershire sauce
1 teaspoon barbecue seasoning
1 teaspoon honey
½ teaspoon dried basil
½ cup cooked brown rice
½ teaspoon garlic powder
½ teaspoon oregano
½ teaspoon salt
2 small bell peppers, cut in half, stems removed, deseeded
Cooking spray

1. Preheat the air fryer to 360°F (182°C) and lightly spray a baking pan with cooking spray. 2. Arrange the beef, pork, and onion in the prepared baking pan and bake in the preheated air fryer for 8 minutes. Break the ground meat into smaller chunks halfway through the cooking time. 3. Meanwhile, in a saucepan, combine the tomatoes, Worcestershire sauce, barbecue seasoning, honey, and basil, stirring until well mixed. 4. Transfer the cooked meat mixture to a large bowl and add the cooked rice, garlic powder, oregano, salt, and ¼ cup of the tomato mixture. Stir thoroughly to combine. 5. Stuff the pepper halves with the meat and rice mixture, then place them in the air fryer. Air fry for 10 minutes, or until the peppers are lightly charred and tender. 6. Serve the stuffed peppers warm, topped with the remaining tomato sauce for added flavor.

Rack of Lamb with Pistachio Crust

Prep time: 10 minutes | Cook time: 19 minutes | Serves 2

½ cup finely chopped pistachios
3 tablespoons panko bread crumbs
1 teaspoon chopped fresh rosemary
2 teaspoons chopped fresh oregano
Salt and freshly ground black pepper, to taste
1 tablespoon olive oil
1 rack of lamb, bones trimmed of fat and frenched
1 tablespoon Dijon mustard

1. Begin by preheating the air fryer to 380°F (193°C). 2. In a small bowl (or using a food processor for convenience), combine the pistachios, bread crumbs, rosemary, oregano, salt, and pepper. Drizzle in the olive oil and mix until the ingredients are well combined. 3. Season the rack of lamb generously with salt and pepper on all sides. Place it in the air fryer basket with the fat side facing up. Air fry the lamb for 12 minutes. Remove the lamb and brush the fat side with Dijon mustard. Press the pistachio mixture onto the mustard-coated side, using your hands to ensure it adheres well. Roll the bottom of the rack in any crumbs that fall off. 4. Return the lamb to the air fryer and cook for an additional 3 to 7 minutes, or until an instant-read thermometer registers 140°F (60°C) for medium doneness. Adjust the cooking time slightly for more or less well-done lamb, depending on the size of the rack. 5. Allow the lamb to rest for at least 5 minutes before slicing it into individual chops. Serve immediately and enjoy!

Blue Cheese Steak Salad

Prep time: 30 minutes | Cook time: 22 minutes | Serves 4

2 tablespoons balsamic vinegar
2 tablespoons red wine vinegar
1 tablespoon Dijon mustard
1 tablespoon Swerve
1 teaspoon minced garlic
Sea salt and freshly ground black pepper, to taste
¾ cup extra-virgin olive oil
1 pound (454 g) boneless sirloin steak
Avocado oil spray
1 small red onion, cut into ¼-inch-thick rounds
6 ounces (170 g) baby spinach
½ cup cherry tomatoes, halved
3 ounces (85 g) blue cheese, crumbled

1. In a blender, combine the balsamic vinegar, red wine vinegar, Dijon mustard, Swerve, and garlic. Season with salt and pepper, then blend until smooth. While the blender is running, slowly drizzle in the olive oil and continue blending until the dressing is well combined. Transfer the dressing to a jar with a tight-fitting lid and refrigerate until ready to use. It can be stored for up to 2 weeks. 2. Season the steak generously with salt and pepper, then let it sit at room temperature for at least 45 minutes, if time allows. 3. Preheat the air fryer to 400°F (204°C). Lightly spray the steak with oil and place it in the air fryer basket. Cook for 6 minutes, then flip the steak, spray it with more oil, and cook for an additional 6 minutes for medium-rare, or until it reaches your desired level of doneness. 4. Transfer the steak to a plate, tent it with aluminum foil, and let it rest for a few minutes. 5. Lightly spray the onion slices with oil and place them in the air fryer basket. Cook at 400°F (204°C) for 5 minutes, then flip the slices, spray them with more oil, and cook for another 5 minutes. 6. Slice the steak diagonally into thin strips. In a large bowl, combine the spinach, cherry tomatoes, onion slices, and steak. Toss with the desired amount of dressing, then sprinkle with crumbled blue cheese. Serve immediately and enjoy!

Zesty London Broil

Prep time: 30 minutes | Cook time: 20 to 28 minutes | Serves 4 to 6

⅔ cup ketchup
¼ cup honey
¼ cup olive oil
2 tablespoons apple cider vinegar
2 tablespoons Worcestershire sauce
2 tablespoons minced onion
½ teaspoon paprika
1 teaspoon salt
1 teaspoon freshly ground black pepper
2 pounds (907 g) London broil, top round or flank steak (about 1-inch thick)

1. In a small bowl, whisk together the ketchup, honey, olive oil, apple cider vinegar, Worcestershire sauce, minced onion, paprika, salt, and pepper until well combined. 2. Use a fork or meat tenderizer to generously pierce both sides of the steak. Place the steak in a shallow dish and pour the marinade over it, ensuring all sides are thoroughly coated. Cover the dish and refrigerate overnight to allow the flavors to penetrate the meat. 3. Preheat the air fryer to 400°F (204°C). 4. Transfer the marinated London broil to the air fryer basket. Air fry for 20 to 28 minutes, depending on your preferred level of doneness, flipping the steak halfway through the cooking time. 5. Remove the steak from the air fryer and let it rest on a cutting board for 5 minutes. Thinly slice the meat against the grain and transfer it to a serving platter. Serve immediately.

Pork Milanese

Prep time: 10 minutes | Cook time: 12 minutes | Serves 4

4 (1-inch) boneless pork chops
Fine sea salt and ground black pepper, to taste
2 large eggs
¾ cup powdered Parmesan cheese
Chopped fresh parsley, for garnish
Lemon slices, for serving

1. Lightly spray the air fryer basket with avocado oil and preheat the air fryer to 400°F (204°C). 2. Place the pork chops between two sheets of plastic wrap and use the flat side of a meat tenderizer to pound them until they are ¼ inch thick. Season both sides of the chops lightly with salt and pepper. 3. In a shallow bowl, lightly beat the eggs. Divide the Parmesan cheese evenly between two bowls and set them up in this order: Parmesan, eggs, Parmesan. Dredge each chop in the first bowl of Parmesan, dip it into the eggs, and then coat it again in the second bowl of Parmesan, ensuring all sides and edges are well covered. Repeat with the remaining chops. 4. Arrange the coated chops in the air fryer basket and air fry for 12 minutes, flipping halfway through, or until the internal temperature reaches 145°F (63°C). 5. Garnish the chops with fresh parsley and serve immediately with lemon slices. Store any leftovers in an airtight container in the refrigerator for up to 3 days. To reheat, place the chops in a preheated 390°F (199°C) air fryer for 5 minutes, or until warmed through.

Pork Tenderloin with Avocado Lime Sauce

Prep time: 30 minutes | Cook time: 15 minutes | Serves 4

Marinade:
½ cup lime juice
Grated zest of 1 lime
2 teaspoons stevia glycerite, or ¼ teaspoon liquid stevia
3 cloves garlic, minced
1½ teaspoons fine sea salt
1 teaspoon chili powder, or more for more heat
1 teaspoon smoked paprika
1 pound (454 g) pork tenderloin

Avocado Lime Sauce:
1 medium-sized ripe avocado, roughly chopped
½ cup full-fat sour cream (or coconut cream for dairy-free)
Grated zest of 1 lime
Juice of 1 lime
2 cloves garlic, roughly chopped
½ teaspoon fine sea salt
¼ teaspoon ground black pepper
Chopped fresh cilantro leaves, for garnish
Lime slices, for serving
Pico de gallo, for serving

1. In a medium-sized casserole dish, combine all the marinade ingredients and stir until well mixed. Add the pork tenderloin, ensuring it is fully coated in the marinade. Cover the dish and refrigerate for at least 2 hours, or preferably overnight, to allow the flavors to infuse. 2. Lightly spray the air fryer basket with avocado oil and preheat the air fryer to 400°F (204°C). 3. Remove the pork from the marinade and place it in the air fryer basket. Air fry for 13 to 15 minutes, flipping the tenderloin after 7 minutes, until the internal temperature reaches 145°F (63°C). Transfer the pork to a cutting board and let it rest for 8 to 10 minutes before slicing it into ½-inch-thick pieces. 4. While the pork cooks, prepare the avocado lime sauce: Place all the sauce ingredients in a food processor and blend until smooth. Taste and adjust the seasoning as needed. 5. Arrange the pork slices on a serving platter and drizzle the avocado lime sauce over the top. Garnish with fresh cilantro leaves and serve with lime slices and pico de gallo on the side. 6. Store any leftovers in an airtight container in the refrigerator for up to 4 days. To reheat, place the pork in a preheated 400°F (204°C) air fryer for 5 minutes, or until thoroughly warmed.

Fajita Meatball Lettuce Wraps

Prep time: 10 minutes | Cook time: 10 minutes | Serves 4

1 pound (454 g) ground beef (85% lean)
½ cup salsa, plus more for serving if desired
¼ cup chopped onions
¼ cup diced green or red bell peppers
1 large egg, beaten
1 teaspoon fine sea salt
½ teaspoon chili powder
½ teaspoon ground cumin
1 clove garlic, minced

For Serving (Optional):
8 leaves Boston lettuce
Pico de gallo or salsa
Lime slices

1. Lightly spray the air fryer basket with avocado oil and preheat the air fryer to 350°F (177°C). 2. In a large mixing bowl, combine all the ingredients thoroughly until they are well blended. 3. Shape the mixture into eight 1-inch balls, ensuring they are evenly sized. Arrange the meatballs in the air fryer basket, leaving a small gap between each one to allow for even cooking. Air fry for 10 minutes, or until the meatballs are fully cooked, no longer pink inside, and reach an internal temperature of 145°F (63°C). 4. Serve each meatball on a crisp lettuce leaf, optionally topped with pico de gallo or salsa for added flavor. Accompany with lime slices if desired. 5. Store any leftovers in an airtight container in the refrigerator for up to 3 days or freeze for up to a month. To reheat, place the meatballs in a preheated 350°F (177°C) air fryer for 4 minutes, or until thoroughly warmed.

Greek Stuffed Tenderloin

Prep time: 10 minutes | Cook time: 10 minutes | Serves 4

1½ pounds (680 g) venison or beef tenderloin, pounded to ¼ inch thick
3 teaspoons fine sea salt
1 teaspoon ground black pepper
2 ounces (57 g) creamy goat cheese
½ cup crumbled feta cheese (about 2 ounces / 57 g)
¼ cup finely chopped onions
2 cloves garlic, minced

For Garnish/Serving (Optional):
Prepared yellow mustard
Halved cherry tomatoes
Extra-virgin olive oil
Sprigs of fresh rosemary
Lavender flowers

1. Lightly spray the air fryer basket with avocado oil and preheat the air fryer to 400°F (204°C). 2. Season the pork tenderloin generously on all sides with salt and pepper. 3. In a medium-sized mixing bowl, combine the goat cheese, feta, onions, and garlic. Spread this mixture evenly over the center of the tenderloin. Starting at the end closest to you, tightly roll the tenderloin like a jelly roll. Secure the roll by tying it tightly with kitchen twine. 4. Place the rolled tenderloin in the air fryer basket and cook for 5 minutes. Flip the meat over and cook for an additional 5 minutes, or until the internal temperature reaches 135°F (57°C) for medium-rare. 5. To serve, spread a line of prepared yellow mustard on a platter. Place the cooked tenderloin next to the mustard and arrange halved cherry tomatoes on the side if desired. Drizzle with olive oil and garnish with rosemary sprigs and lavender flowers for an elegant touch. 6. This dish is best served fresh. Store any leftovers in an airtight container in the refrigerator for up to 3 days. To reheat, place the tenderloin in a preheated 350°F (177°C) air fryer for 4 minutes, or until warmed through.

Bacon Wrapped Pork with Apple Gravy

Prep time: 10 minutes | Cook time: 25 minutes | Serves 4

Pork:
1 tablespoons Dijon mustard
1 pork tenderloin
3 strips bacon

Apple Gravy:
3 tablespoons ghee, divided
1 small shallot, chopped
2 apples
1 tablespoon almond flour
1 cup vegetable broth
½ teaspoon Dijon mustard

1. Begin by preheating the air fryer to 360°F (182°C). 2. Spread a generous layer of Dijon mustard over the pork tenderloin, then wrap it with strips of bacon, ensuring it is fully covered. 3. Place the bacon-wrapped tenderloin in the air fryer and cook for 12 minutes. Use a meat thermometer to check for doneness, ensuring it reaches the desired internal temperature. 4. To prepare the sauce, heat 1 tablespoon of ghee in a pan and sauté the shallots for 1 minute until fragrant. 5. Add the apples to the pan and cook for 4 minutes, or until they soften. 6. Stir in the flour and 2 tablespoons of ghee to create a roux. Gradually add the broth and mustard, stirring continuously to combine. 7. Once the sauce begins to bubble, mix in 1 cup of the sautéed apples and cook until the sauce thickens to your preferred consistency. 8. After the pork tenderloin is cooked, let it rest for 8 minutes before slicing to allow the juices to redistribute. 9. Serve the sliced tenderloin topped with the warm apple gravy for a delicious and flavorful dish.

Roast Beef with Horseradish Cream

Prep time: 5 minutes | Cook time: 35 to 45 minutes | Serves 6

2 pounds (907 g) beef roast top round or eye of round
1 tablespoon salt
2 teaspoons garlic powder
Horseradish Cream:
⅓ cup heavy cream
⅓ cup sour cream
⅓ cup prepared horseradish
2 teaspoons fresh lemon
1 teaspoon freshly ground black pepper
1 teaspoon dried thyme

juice
Salt and freshly ground black pepper, to taste

1. Begin by preheating the air fryer to 400°F (204°C). 2. Season the beef generously with salt, garlic powder, black pepper, and thyme. Place the beef fat-side down in the air fryer basket and lightly coat it with olive oil. Air fry for 35 to 45 minutes, pausing halfway through to turn the meat, until a thermometer inserted into the thickest part reaches your desired level of doneness: 125°F (52°C) for rare, 135°F (57°C) for medium-rare, or 150°F (66°C) for medium. Let the beef rest for 10 minutes before slicing to allow the juices to redistribute. 3. To prepare the horseradish cream: In a small bowl, whisk together the heavy cream, sour cream, horseradish, and lemon juice until smooth and well combined. Season with salt and freshly ground black pepper to taste. Serve the horseradish cream alongside the sliced beef for a flavorful accompaniment.

Spinach and Provolone Steak Rolls

Prep time: 10 minutes | Cook time: 12 minutes | Makes 8 rolls

1 (1 pound / 454 g) flank steak, butterflied
8 (1 ounce / 28 g, ¼-inch-thick) deli slices provolone cheese
1 cup fresh spinach leaves
½ teaspoon salt
¼ teaspoon ground black pepper

1. Begin by positioning the steak on a spacious plate. Arrange slices of provolone cheese over the steak, ensuring a 1-inch border around the edges remains uncovered. Distribute spinach leaves evenly atop the cheese. Carefully roll the steak into a tight bundle and secure it using kitchen twine or toothpicks. Proceed to slice the rolled steak into eight equal portions. Lightly season each piece with a sprinkle of salt and pepper. 2. Transfer the prepared rolls into the air fryer basket, ensuring the cut side faces upward. Set the air fryer to a temperature of 400°F (204°C) and allow the rolls to cook for approximately 12 minutes. The steak rolls should achieve a golden-brown exterior, with the cheese fully melted. For optimal doneness, verify the internal temperature reaches at least 150°F (66°C) for medium or 180°F (82°C) for well-done steak. Serve the dish while it is still warm.

Bacon, Cheese and Pear Stuffed Pork

Prep time: 10 minutes | Cook time: 24 minutes | Serves 3

4 slices bacon, chopped
1 tablespoon butter
½ cup finely diced onion
⅓ cup chicken stock
1½ cups seasoned stuffing cubes
1 egg, beaten
½ teaspoon dried thyme
½ teaspoon salt
⅛ teaspoon black pepper
1 pear, finely diced
⅓ cup crumbled blue cheese
3 boneless center-cut pork chops (2-inch thick)
Olive oil
Salt and freshly ground black pepper, to taste

1. Begin by preheating the air fryer to 400°F (204°C). 2. Arrange the bacon strips in the air fryer basket and cook for 6 minutes, ensuring to flip them halfway through the cooking process. Once done, transfer the bacon to a paper towel to drain and discard the grease collected at the bottom of the air fryer. 3. Prepare the stuffing: In a medium saucepan, melt butter over medium heat on the stovetop. Add the onion and cook until it begins to soften. Pour in the chicken stock and let it simmer for 1 minute. Remove the saucepan from the heat and mix in the stuffing cubes, stirring until the liquid is fully absorbed. Incorporate the egg, dried thyme, salt, and freshly ground black pepper, blending thoroughly. Gently fold in the diced pear and crumbled blue cheese. 4. Lay the pork chops on a cutting board. While holding each chop steady with your palm, carefully slice into the side to create a pocket, ensuring not to cut all the way through and leaving about an inch intact. Lightly brush both sides of the pork chops with olive oil and season with salt and freshly ground black pepper. Fill each chop with a third of the stuffing mixture, packing it firmly into the pocket. 5. Preheat the air fryer to 360°F (182°C). 6. Lightly coat the sides of the air fryer basket with oil. Position the pork chops in the basket with the stuffed side facing the outer edges. 7. Air fry the pork chops for 18 minutes, flipping them halfway through the cooking time. Once cooked, allow the chops to rest for 5 minutes before transferring them to a serving platter.

Caraway Crusted Beef Steaks

Prep time: 5 minutes | Cook time: 10 minutes | Serves 4

4 beef steaks	pepper, to taste
2 teaspoons caraway seeds	1 tablespoon melted butter
2 teaspoons garlic powder	⅓ cup almond flour
Sea salt and cayenne	2 eggs, beaten

1. Begin by preheating the air fryer to 355°F (179°C). 2. Place the beef steaks in a large bowl and toss them with caraway seeds, garlic powder, salt, and pepper until they are evenly coated with the seasoning mixture. 3. In a separate bowl, combine the melted butter and almond flour, stirring until well blended. In another bowl, whisk the eggs until smooth. 4. Dip each seasoned steak into the whisked eggs, ensuring full coverage, then press them into the almond and butter mixture to create a crust. 5. Arrange the coated steaks in the air fryer basket in a single layer. Cook for 10 minutes, flipping the steaks halfway through, until the internal temperature reaches at least 145°F (63°C) when measured with a meat thermometer. 6. Once cooked, transfer the steaks to serving plates. Allow them to rest for 5 minutes before serving hot.

Parmesan Herb Filet Mignon

Prep time: 20 minutes | Cook time: 13 minutes | Serves 4

1 pound (454 g) filet mignon	1 teaspoon dried thyme
Sea salt and ground black pepper, to taste	1 tablespoon sesame oil
	1 small-sized egg, well-whisked
½ teaspoon cayenne pepper	½ cup Parmesan cheese, grated
1 teaspoon dried basil	
1 teaspoon dried rosemary	

1. Generously season the filet mignon with salt, black pepper, cayenne pepper, basil, rosemary, and thyme, ensuring an even coating. Lightly brush the seasoned steak with sesame oil to enhance flavor and moisture. 2. Crack the egg into a shallow plate and beat it lightly. In a separate plate, spread out the Parmesan cheese evenly. 3. Dip the filet mignon into the beaten egg, ensuring it is fully coated, then press it into the Parmesan cheese to create a crust. Preheat the air fryer to 360°F (182°C). 4. Place the coated filet mignon in the air fryer and cook for 10 to 13 minutes, or until the exterior turns a golden brown and the desired doneness is achieved. Serve alongside a fresh mix of salad leaves for a complete and delightful meal.

Italian Sausage Links

Prep time: 10 minutes | Cook time: 24 minutes | Serves 4

1 bell pepper (any color), sliced	seasoning
	Sea salt and freshly ground black pepper, to taste
1 medium onion, sliced	
1 tablespoon avocado oil	1 pound (454 g) Italian sausage links
1 teaspoon Italian	

1. In a medium-sized bowl, combine the bell pepper and onion, then drizzle with avocado oil. Sprinkle with Italian seasoning, salt, and pepper according to your taste preferences, and toss thoroughly to coat the vegetables evenly. 2. Preheat the air fryer to 400°F (204°C). Transfer the seasoned vegetables into the air fryer basket and cook for 12 minutes. 3. After the initial cooking time, move the vegetables to the sides of the basket to create space. Arrange the sausage links in a single layer at the bottom of the basket, then redistribute the vegetables over the sausages. Continue cooking for another 12 minutes, tossing the ingredients halfway through, until the sausages reach an internal temperature of 160°F (71°C) when checked with an instant-read thermometer.

Ham Hock Mac and Cheese

Prep time: 20 minutes | Cook time: 25 minutes | Serves 4

2 large eggs, beaten	black pepper
2 cups cottage cheese, whole milk or 2%	2 cups uncooked elbow macaroni
2 cups grated sharp Cheddar cheese, divided	2 ham hocks (about 11 ounces / 312 g each), meat removed and diced
1 cup sour cream	
½ teaspoon salt	1 to 2 tablespoons oil
1 teaspoon freshly ground	

1. In a large bowl, combine the eggs, cottage cheese, 1 cup of the Cheddar cheese, sour cream, salt, and pepper, stirring until well mixed. 2. Add the macaroni and diced meat to the bowl, stirring to ensure they are evenly coated with the sauce. 3. Preheat the air fryer to 360°F (182°C) and lightly spray a baking pan with oil. 4. Pour the macaroni mixture into the prepared pan, making sure all the noodles are fully covered with the sauce. 5. Cook for 12 minutes, then stir in the remaining 1 cup of Cheddar cheese, ensuring the noodles are evenly coated. Continue cooking for an additional 13 minutes, or until the noodles are tender. Let the dish rest for 5 minutes before serving to allow the flavors to settle.

Beef, Pork, and Lamb

Greek Lamb Pita Pockets

Prep time: 15 minutes | Cook time: 6 minutes | Serves 4

Dressing:
- 1 cup plain yogurt
- 1 tablespoon lemon juice
- 1 teaspoon dried dill weed, crushed
- 1 teaspoon ground oregano
- ½ teaspoon salt

Meatballs:
- ½ pound (227 g) ground lamb
- 1 tablespoon diced onion
- 1 teaspoon dried parsley
- 1 teaspoon dried dill weed, crushed
- ¼ teaspoon oregano
- ¼ teaspoon coriander
- ¼ teaspoon ground cumin
- ¼ teaspoon salt
- 4 pita halves

Suggested Toppings:
- 1 red onion, slivered
- 1 medium cucumber, deseeded, thinly sliced
- Crumbled feta cheese
- Sliced black olives
- Chopped fresh peppers

1. Begin by preheating the air fryer to 390°F (199°C). 2. In a small bowl, mix the dressing ingredients thoroughly and place it in the refrigerator to chill while you prepare the lamb. 3. In a large bowl, combine all the meatball ingredients, stirring well to ensure the seasonings are evenly distributed throughout the mixture. 4. Shape the meat mixture into 12 small meatballs, forming them into either rounded shapes or slightly flattened discs, depending on your preference. 5. Place the meatballs in the preheated air fryer and cook for 6 minutes, or until they are fully cooked. Once done, remove the meatballs and let them drain on paper towels to absorb excess oil. 6. To serve, fill pita pockets with the meatballs and your choice of toppings, then drizzle generously with the chilled dressing.

Poblano Pepper Cheeseburgers

Prep time: 5 minutes | Cook time: 30 minutes | Serves 4

- 2 poblano chile peppers
- 1½ pounds (680 g) 85% lean ground beef
- 1 clove garlic, minced
- 1 teaspoon salt
- ½ teaspoon freshly ground black pepper
- 4 slices Cheddar cheese (about 3 ounces / 85 g)
- 4 large lettuce leaves

1. Start by preheating the air fryer to 400°F (204°C). 2. Place the poblano peppers in the air fryer basket, ensuring they are evenly spaced. Cook for 20 minutes, pausing halfway to turn the peppers, until they soften and develop a slight char. Once done, transfer the peppers to a large bowl and cover with a plate to steam. When cool enough to handle, peel off the skin, remove the seeds and stems, and slice them into strips. Set the strips aside for later use. 3. While the peppers are cooling, prepare the burger patties. In a large bowl, mix the ground beef with garlic, salt, and pepper. Shape the mixture into four evenly sized patties. 4. Reduce the air fryer temperature to 360°F (182°C). Arrange the patties in a single layer in the air fryer basket. Cook for 10 minutes, flipping the burgers halfway through, until a meat thermometer inserted into the thickest part reads 160°F (71°C). 5. Once the burgers are cooked, place a slice of cheese on top of each patty and air fry for an additional 1–2 minutes, or until the cheese is fully melted. Serve the burgers on a lettuce leaf, garnished with the roasted poblano pepper strips.

Greek Pork with Tzatziki Sauce

Prep time: 30 minutes | Cook time: 50 minutes | Serves 4

Greek Pork:
- 2 pounds (907 g) pork sirloin roast
- Salt and black pepper, to taste
- 1 teaspoon smoked paprika
- ½ teaspoon mustard seeds
- ½ teaspoon celery seeds
- 1 teaspoon fennel seeds
- 1 teaspoon Ancho chili powder
- 1 teaspoon turmeric powder
- ½ teaspoon ground ginger
- 2 tablespoons olive oil
- 2 cloves garlic, finely chopped

Tzatziki:
- ½ cucumber, finely chopped and squeezed
- 1 cup full-fat Greek yogurt
- 1 garlic clove, minced
- 1 tablespoon extra-virgin olive oil
- 1 teaspoon balsamic vinegar
- 1 teaspoon minced fresh dill
- A pinch of salt

1. In a large mixing bowl, combine all the ingredients for the Greek pork, tossing thoroughly until the meat is evenly coated. 2. Cook the pork in the preheated air fryer at 360°F (182°C) for 30 minutes, then turn it over and continue cooking for an additional 20 minutes. 3. While the pork is cooking, prepare the tzatziki by mixing all its ingredients together in a bowl. Refrigerate the tzatziki until it's ready to be served. 4. Once the pork sirloin roast is cooked, serve it with the chilled tzatziki on the side. Enjoy your flavorful meal!

Goat Cheese-Stuffed Flank Steak

Prep time: 10 minutes | Cook time: 14 minutes | Serves 6

1 pound (454 g) flank steak	black pepper
1 tablespoon avocado oil	2 ounces (57 g) goat cheese, crumbled
½ teaspoon sea salt	
½ teaspoon garlic powder	1 cup baby spinach, chopped
¼ teaspoon freshly ground	

1. Place the steak inside a large zip-top bag or between two sheets of plastic wrap. Using a meat mallet or the bottom of a heavy skillet, gently pound the steak until it reaches an even thickness of ¼ inch. 2. Lightly brush both sides of the flattened steak with avocado oil to ensure it stays moist during cooking. 3. In a small bowl, combine the salt, garlic powder, and pepper. Evenly sprinkle this seasoning mixture over both sides of the steak. 4. Spread a layer of goat cheese evenly over the steak, followed by a generous topping of spinach leaves. 5. Starting from one of the longer sides, tightly roll the steak into a log shape. Secure the roll by tying it with kitchen string at intervals of approximately 3 inches. 6. Preheat the air fryer to 400°F (204°C). Place the steak roll-up in the air fryer basket and cook for 7 minutes. Flip the steak and continue cooking for another 7 minutes, or until an instant-read thermometer inserted into the center reads 120°F (49°C) for medium-rare. Adjust the cooking time as needed to achieve your preferred level of doneness.

Hoisin BBQ Pork Chops

Prep time: 5 minutes | Cook time: 22 minutes | Serves 2 to 3

3 tablespoons hoisin sauce	1 to 2 teaspoons Sriracha sauce, to taste
¼ cup honey	
1 tablespoon soy sauce	2 to 3 bone-in center cut pork chops, 1-inch thick (about 1¼ pounds / 567 g)
3 tablespoons rice vinegar	
2 tablespoons brown sugar	
1½ teaspoons grated fresh ginger	Chopped scallions, for garnish

1. In a small saucepan, combine the hoisin sauce, honey, soy sauce, rice vinegar, brown sugar, ginger, and Sriracha sauce. Whisk the mixture thoroughly and bring it to a boil over medium-high heat on the stovetop. Once boiling, reduce the heat and let the sauce simmer for about 10 minutes, allowing it to reduce in volume and thicken slightly. 2. Preheat the air fryer to 400°F (204°C). 3. Place the pork chops in the air fryer basket and pour half of the prepared hoisin BBQ sauce over them. Air fry for 6 minutes, then flip the chops and pour the remaining sauce over the top. Continue air frying for an additional 5 to 6 minutes, adjusting the time based on the thickness of the pork chops. Ensure the internal temperature reaches 155°F (68°C) when checked with an instant-read thermometer. 4. Allow the pork chops to rest for 5 minutes before serving. If desired, spoon some of the sauce collected in the bottom of the air fryer over the chops. Garnish with chopped scallions and serve warm.

Sweet and Spicy Country-Style Ribs

Prep time: 10 minutes | Cook time: 25 minutes | Serves 4

2 tablespoons brown sugar	1 teaspoon black pepper
2 tablespoons smoked paprika	¼ to ½ teaspoon cayenne pepper
1 teaspoon garlic powder	1½ pounds (680 g) boneless country-style pork ribs
1 teaspoon onion powder	
1 teaspoon dry mustard	
1 teaspoon ground cumin	1 cup barbecue sauce
1 teaspoon kosher salt	

1. In a small bowl, thoroughly combine the brown sugar, paprika, garlic powder, onion powder, dry mustard, cumin, salt, black pepper, and cayenne, ensuring the mixture is evenly blended. 2. Use a paper towel to pat the ribs dry, then generously coat both sides with the prepared spice rub, pressing it into the meat with your fingers to ensure it adheres well. 3. Arrange the ribs in the air fryer basket and set the temperature to 350°F (177°C). Cook for 15 minutes, then flip the ribs and brush them with ½ cup of barbecue sauce. Continue cooking for another 10 minutes, or until a meat thermometer inserted into the thickest part of the ribs registers an internal temperature of 145°F (63°C). 4. Serve the ribs warm, accompanied by the remaining barbecue sauce for dipping or drizzling.

Chapter 7
Fish and Seafood

Herb-Infused Lemon Fish en Papillote

Prep time: 10 minutes | Cook time: 15 minutes | Serves 2

2 tablespoons salted butter, melted
1 tablespoon fresh lemon juice
½ teaspoon dried tarragon, crushed, or 2 sprigs fresh tarragon
1 teaspoon kosher salt
½ cup julienned carrots
½ cup julienned fennel, or ¼ cup julienned celery
½ cup thinly sliced red bell pepper
2 (6 ounces / 170 g) cod fillets, thawed if frozen
Vegetable oil spray
½ teaspoon black pepper

1. In a medium bowl, combine the butter, lemon juice, tarragon, and ½ teaspoon of the salt. Whisk well until you get a creamy sauce. Add the carrots, fennel, and bell pepper and toss to combine; set aside. 2. Cut two squares of parchment each large enough to hold one fillet and half the vegetables. Spray the fillets with vegetable oil spray. Season both sides with the remaining ½ teaspoon salt and the black pepper. 3. Lay one fillet down on each parchment square. Top each with half the vegetables. Pour any remaining sauce over the vegetables. 4. Fold over the parchment paper and crimp the sides in small, tight folds to hold the fish, vegetables, and sauce securely inside the packet. Place the packets in the air fryer basket. Set the air fryer to 350°F (177°C) for 15 minutes. 5. Transfer each packet to a plate. Cut open with scissors just before serving (be careful, as the steam inside will be hot).

Roasted Snapper with Shallots and Fresh Tomatoes

Prep time: 20 minutes | Cook time: 15 minutes | Serves 2

2 snapper fillets
1 shallot, peeled and sliced
2 garlic cloves, halved
1 bell pepper, sliced
1 small-sized serrano pepper, sliced
1 tomato, sliced
1 tablespoon olive oil
¼ teaspoon freshly ground black pepper
½ teaspoon paprika
Sea salt, to taste
2 bay leaves

1. Place two parchment sheets on a working surface. Place the fish in the center of one side of the parchment paper. 2. Top with the shallot, garlic, peppers, and tomato. Drizzle olive oil over the fish and vegetables. Season with black pepper, paprika, and salt. Add the bay leaves. 3. Fold over the other half of the parchment. Now, fold the paper around the edges tightly and create a half moon shape, sealing the fish inside. 4. Cook in the preheated air fryer at 390°F (199°C) for 15 minutes. Serve warm.

Zesty Lemon Pepper Grilled Shrimp

Prep time: 15 minutes | Cook time: 8 minutes | Serves 2

Oil, for spraying
12 ounces (340 g) medium raw shrimp, peeled and deveined
3 tablespoons lemon juice
1 tablespoon olive oil
1 teaspoon lemon pepper
¼ teaspoon paprika
¼ teaspoon granulated garlic

1. Preheat the air fryer to 400°F (204°C). Line the air fryer basket with parchment and spray lightly with oil. 2. In a medium bowl, toss together the shrimp, lemon juice, olive oil, lemon pepper, paprika, and garlic until evenly coated. 3. Place the shrimp in the prepared basket. 4. Cook for 6 to 8 minutes, or until pink and firm. Serve immediately.

Creamy Dijon Cod Fillets

Prep time: 10 minutes | Cook time: 10 minutes | Serves 4

Fish:
Oil, for spraying
1 pound (454 g) cod fillets
2 tablespoons olive oil
1 tablespoon lemon juice
1 teaspoon salt
½ teaspoon freshly ground black pepper

Mustard Sauce:
½ cup heavy cream
3 tablespoons Dijon mustard
1 tablespoon unsalted butter
1 teaspoon salt

Make the Fish: 1. Line the air fryer basket with parchment and spray lightly with oil. 2. Rub the cod with the olive oil and lemon juice. Season with the salt and black pepper. 3. Place the cod in the prepared basket. You may need to work in batches, depending on the size of your air fryer. 4. Roast at 350°F (177°C) for 5 minutes. Increase the temperature to 400°F (204°C) and cook for another 5 minutes, until flaky and the internal temperature reaches 145°F (63°C). Make the Mustard Sauce: 5. In a small saucepan, mix together the heavy cream, mustard, butter, and salt and bring to a simmer over low heat. Cook for 3 to 4 minutes, or until the sauce starts to thicken. 6. Transfer the cod to a serving plate and drizzle with the mustard sauce. Serve immediately.

Baked Scallops with Parmesan Crust

Prep time: 10 minutes | Cook time: 9 minutes | Serves 2

Scallops:
½ cup half-and-half
½ cup grated Parmesan cheese
¼ cup thinly sliced green onions
¼ cup chopped fresh parsley
3 cloves garlic, minced
½ teaspoon kosher salt
½ teaspoon black pepper
1 pound (454 g) sea scallops

Topping:
¼ cup crushed pork rinds or panko bread crumbs
¼ cup grated Parmesan cheese
Vegetable oil spray

For Serving:
Lemon wedges
Crusty French bread (optional)

1. For the scallops: In a baking pan, combine the half-and-half, cheese, green onions, parsley, garlic, salt, and pepper. Stir in the scallops. 2. For the topping: In a small bowl, combine the pork rinds or bread crumbs and cheese. Sprinkle evenly over the scallops. Spray the topping with vegetable oil spray. 3. Place the pan in the air fryer basket. Set the air fryer to 325ºF (163ºC) for 6 minutes. Set the air fryer to 400ºF (204ºC) for 3 minutes until the topping has browned. 4. To serve: Squeeze the lemon wedges over the gratin and serve with crusty French bread, if desired.

Chinese-Style Ginger-Scallion Fish Fillets

Prep time: 15 minutes | Cook time: 15 minutes | Serves 2

Bean Sauce:
2 tablespoons soy sauce
1 tablespoon rice wine
1 tablespoon doubanjiang (Chinese black bean paste)

Vegetables and Fish:
1 tablespoon peanut oil
¼ cup julienned green onions (white and green parts)
¼ cup chopped fresh cilantro
1 teaspoon minced fresh ginger
1 clove garlic, minced
2 tablespoons julienned fresh ginger
2 (6 ounces / 170 g) white fish fillets, such as tilapia

1. For the sauce: In a small bowl, combine all the ingredients and stir until well combined; set aside. 2. For the vegetables and fish: In a medium bowl, combine the peanut oil, green onions, cilantro, and ginger. Toss to combine. 3. Cut two squares of parchment large enough to hold one fillet and half of the vegetables. Place one fillet on each parchment square, top with the vegetables, and pour over the sauce. Fold over the parchment paper and crimp the sides in small, tight folds to hold the fish, vegetables, and sauce securely inside the packet. 4. Place the packets in a single layer in the air fryer basket. Set fryer to 350ºF (177ºC) for 15 minutes. 5. Transfer each packet to a dinner plate. Cut open with scissors just before serving.

Herb-Glazed Salmon with Cauliflower Florets

Prep time: 10 minutes | Cook time: 25 minutes | Serves 4

1 pound (454 g) salmon fillet, diced
1 cup cauliflower, shredded
1 tablespoon dried cilantro
1 tablespoon coconut oil, melted
1 teaspoon ground turmeric
¼ cup coconut cream

1. Mix salmon with cauliflower, dried cilantro, ground turmeric, coconut cream, and coconut oil. 2. Transfer the salmon mixture into the air fryer and cook the meal at 350ºF (177ºC) for 25 minutes. Stir the meal every 5 minutes to avoid the burning.

Spicy Cajun Lemon Cod Fillets

Prep time: 5 minutes | Cook time: 12 minutes | Makes 2 cod fillets

1 tablespoon Cajun seasoning
1 teaspoon salt
½ teaspoon lemon pepper
½ teaspoon freshly ground black pepper
2 (8 ounces / 227 g) cod fillets, cut to fit into the air fryer basket
Cooking spray
2 tablespoons unsalted butter, melted
1 lemon, cut into 4 wedges

1. Preheat the air fryer to 360ºF (182ºC). Spritz the air fryer basket with cooking spray. 2. Thoroughly combine the Cajun seasoning, salt, lemon pepper, and black pepper in a small bowl. Rub this mixture all over the cod fillets until completely coated. 3. Put the fillets in the air fryer basket and brush the melted butter over both sides of each fillet. 4. Bake in the preheated air fryer for 12 minutes, flipping the fillets halfway through, or until the fish flakes easily with a fork. 5. Remove the fillets from the basket and serve with fresh lemon wedges.

Grilled Shrimp with Smoky Tomato Vinaigrette

Prep time: 5 minutes | Cook time: 8 minutes | Serves 2

3 tablespoons mayonnaise
1 tablespoon ketchup
1 tablespoon minced garlic
1 teaspoon Sriracha
½ teaspoon smoked paprika
½ teaspoon kosher salt
1 pound (454 g) large raw shrimp (21 to 25 count), peeled (tails left on) and deveined
Vegetable oil spray
½ cup chopped scallions

1. In a large bowl, combine the mayonnaise, ketchup, garlic, Sriracha, paprika, and salt. Add the shrimp and toss to coat with the sauce. 2. Spray the air fryer basket with vegetable oil spray. Place the shrimp in the basket. Set the air fryer to 350°F (177°C) for 8 minutes, tossing and spraying the shrimp with vegetable oil spray halfway through the cooking time. 3. Sprinkle with the chopped scallions before serving.

Basil Pesto Fish Pot Pie

Prep time: 15 minutes | Cook time: 15 minutes | Serves 4

2 tablespoons prepared pesto
¼ cup half-and-half
¼ cup grated Parmesan cheese
1 teaspoon kosher salt
1 teaspoon black pepper
Vegetable oil spray
1 (10 ounces / 283 g) package frozen chopped spinach, thawed and squeezed dry
1 pound (454 g) firm white fish, cut into 2-inch chunks
½ cup cherry tomatoes, quartered
All-purpose flour
½ sheet frozen puff pastry (from a 17.3 ounces / 490 g package), thawed

1. In a small bowl, combine the pesto, half-and-half, Parmesan, salt, and pepper. Stir until well combined; set aside. 2. Spray a baking pan with vegetable oil spray. Arrange the spinach evenly across the bottom of the pan. Top with the fish and tomatoes. Pour the pesto mixture evenly over everything. 3. On a lightly floured surface, roll the puff pastry sheet into a circle. Place the pastry on top of the pan and tuck it in around the edges of the pan. (Or, do what I do and stretch it with your hands and then pat it into place.) 4. Place the pan in the air fryer basket. Set the air fryer to 400°F (204°C) for 15 minutes, or until the pastry is well browned. Let stand 5 minutes before serving.

Tandoori Salmon with Roasted Potatoes

Prep time: 10 minutes | Cook time: 28 minutes | Serves 2

1 pound (454 g) fingerling potatoes
2 tablespoons vegetable oil, divided
Kosher salt and freshly ground black pepper, to taste
1 teaspoon ground turmeric
1 teaspoon ground cumin
1 teaspoon ground ginger
½ teaspoon smoked paprika
¼ teaspoon cayenne pepper
2 (6 ounces / 170 g) skin-on salmon fillets

1. Preheat the air fryer to 375°F (191°C). 2. In a bowl, toss the potatoes with 1 tablespoon of the oil until evenly coated. Season with salt and pepper. Transfer the potatoes to the air fryer and air fry for 20 minutes. 3. Meanwhile, in a bowl, combine the remaining 1 tablespoon oil, the turmeric, cumin, ginger, paprika, and cayenne. Add the salmon fillets and turn in the spice mixture until fully coated all over. 4. After the potatoes have cooked for 20 minutes, place the salmon fillets, skin-side up, on top of the potatoes, and continue cooking until the potatoes are tender, the salmon is cooked, and the salmon skin is slightly crisp. 5. Transfer the salmon fillets to two plates and serve with the potatoes while both are warm.

Bell Pepper-Studded Crab Cakes

Prep time: 5 minutes | Cook time: 10 minutes | Serves 4

8 ounces (227 g) jumbo lump crab meat
1 egg, beaten
Juice of ½ lemon
⅓ cup bread crumbs
¼ cup diced green bell pepper
¼ cup diced red bell pepper
¼ cup mayonnaise
1 tablespoon Old Bay seasoning
1 teaspoon flour
Cooking spray

1. Preheat the air fryer to 375°F (190°C). 2. Make the crab cakes: Place all the ingredients except the flour and oil in a large bowl and stir until well incorporated. 3. Divide the crab mixture into four equal portions and shape each portion into a patty with your hands. Top each patty with a sprinkle of ¼ teaspoon of flour. 4. Arrange the crab cakes in the air fryer basket and spritz them with cooking spray. 5. Air fry for 10 minutes, flipping the crab cakes halfway through, or until they are cooked through. 6. Divide the crab cakes among four plates and serve.

Baked Flounder Fillets

Prep time: 10 minutes | Cook time: 5 to 8 minutes | Serves 4

1 egg white	4 (4-ounce / 113-g) flounder fillets
1 tablespoon water	
1 cup panko bread crumbs	Salt and pepper, to taste
2 tablespoons extra-light virgin olive oil	Oil for misting or cooking spray

1. Preheat the air fryer to 390ºF (199ºC). 2. Beat together egg white and water in shallow dish. 3. In another shallow dish, mix panko crumbs and oil until well combined and crumbly (best done by hand). 4. Season flounder fillets with salt and pepper to taste. Dip each fillet into egg mixture and then roll in panko crumbs, pressing in crumbs so that fish is nicely coated. 5. Spray the air fryer basket with nonstick cooking spray and add fillets. Air fry at 390ºF (199ºC) for 3 minutes. 6. Spray fish fillets but do not turn. Cook 2 to 5 minutes longer or until golden brown and crispy. Using a spatula, carefully remove fish from basket and serve.

Tropical Crab Cakes with Mango Aioli

Prep time: 25 minutes | Cook time: 15 minutes | Serves 4

Crab Cakes:

½ cup chopped red onion	2 teaspoons minced fresh ginger
½ cup fresh cilantro leaves	
1 small serrano chile or jalapeño, seeded and quartered	½ teaspoon ground cumin
	½ teaspoon ground coriander
½ pound (227 g) lump crab meat	¼ teaspoon kosher salt
	2 tablespoons fresh lemon juice
1 large egg	
1 tablespoon mayonnaise	1½ cups panko bread crumbs
1 tablespoon whole-grain mustard	
	Vegetable oil spray

Mango Mayo:

½ cup diced fresh mango	2 teaspoons fresh lime juice
½ cup mayonnaise	
½ teaspoon grated lime zest	Pinch of cayenne pepper

1. For the crab cakes: Combine the onion, cilantro, and serrano in a food processor. Pulse until minced. 2. In a large bowl, combine the minced vegetable mixture with the crab meat, egg, mayonnaise, mustard, ginger, cumin, coriander, and salt. Add the lemon juice and mix gently until thoroughly combined. Add 1 cup of the bread crumbs. Mix gently again until well blended. 3. Form into four evenly sized patties. Put the remaining ½ cup bread crumbs in a shallow bowl and press both sides of each patty into the bread crumbs. 4. Arrange the patties in the air fryer basket. Spray with vegetable oil spray. Set the air fryer to 375ºF (191ºC) for 15 minutes, turning and spraying other side of the patties with vegetable oil spray halfway through the cooking time, until the crab cakes are golden brown and crisp. 5. Meanwhile, for the mayonnaise: In a blender, combine the mango, mayonnaise, lime zest, lime juice, and cayenne. Blend until smooth. 6. Serve the crab cakes warm, with the mango mayo.

Spicy Fish Tacos with Lime Jalapeño Drizzle

Prep time: 25 minutes | Cook time: 7 to 10 minutes | Serves 4

Fish Tacos:

1 pound (454 g) fish fillets	¼ teaspoon smoked paprika
¼ teaspoon cumin	
¼ teaspoon coriander	1 teaspoon oil
⅛ teaspoon ground red pepper	Cooking spray
	6 to 8 corn or flour tortillas (6-inch size)
1 tablespoon lime zest	

Jalapeño-Lime Sauce:

½ cup sour cream	½ teaspoon minced jalapeño (flesh only)
1 tablespoon lime juice	
¼ teaspoon grated lime zest	¼ teaspoon cumin

Napa Cabbage Garnish:

1 cup shredded Napa cabbage	bell pepper
	¼ cup slivered onion
¼ cup slivered red or green	

1. Slice the fish fillets into strips approximately ½-inch thick. 2. Put the strips into a sealable plastic bag along with the cumin, coriander, red pepper, lime zest, smoked paprika, and oil. Massage seasonings into the fish until evenly distributed. 3. Spray the air fryer basket with nonstick cooking spray and place seasoned fish inside. 4. Air fry at 390ºF (199ºC) for approximately 5 minutes. Shake basket to distribute fish. Cook an additional 2 to 5 minutes, until fish flakes easily. 5. While the fish is cooking, prepare the Jalapeño-Lime Sauce by mixing the sour cream, lime juice, lime zest, jalapeño, and cumin together to make a smooth sauce. Set aside. 6. Mix the cabbage, bell pepper, and onion together and set aside. 7. To warm refrigerated tortillas, wrap in damp paper towels and microwave for 30 to 60 seconds. 8. To serve, spoon some of fish into a warm tortilla. Add one or two tablespoons Napa Cabbage Garnish and drizzle with Jalapeño-Lime Sauce.

Classic Fish Burger with Tartar Sauce

Prep time: 10 minutes | Cook time: 17 minutes | Serves 2

Tartar Sauce:
- ½ cup mayonnaise
- 2 tablespoons dried minced onion
- 1 dill pickle spear, finely chopped
- 2 teaspoons pickle juice
- ¼ teaspoon salt
- ⅛ teaspoon ground black pepper

Fish:
- 2 tablespoons all-purpose flour
- 1 egg, lightly beaten
- 1 cup panko
- 2 teaspoons lemon pepper
- 2 tilapia fillets
- Cooking spray
- 2 hoagie rolls

1. Preheat the air fryer to 400°F (204°C). 2. In a small bowl, combine the mayonnaise, dried minced onion, pickle, pickle juice, salt, and pepper. 3. Whisk to combine and chill in the refrigerator while you make the fish. 4. Place a parchment liner in the air fryer basket. 5. Scoop the flour out onto a plate; set aside. 6. Put the beaten egg in a medium shallow bowl. 7. On another plate, mix to combine the panko and lemon pepper. 8. Dredge the tilapia fillets in the flour, then dip in the egg, and then press into the panko mixture. 9. Place the prepared fillets on the liner in the air fryer in a single layer. 10. Spray lightly with cooking spray and air fry for 8 minutes. Carefully flip the fillets, spray with more cooking spray, and air fry for an additional 9 minutes, until golden and crispy. 11. Place each cooked fillet in a hoagie roll, top with a little bit of tartar sauce, and serve.

Savory Tex-Mex Salmon Bowl

Prep time: 15 minutes | Cook time: 9 to 14 minutes | Serves 4

- 12 ounces (340 g) salmon fillets, cut into 1½-inch cubes
- 1 red onion, chopped
- 1 jalapeño pepper, minced
- 1 red bell pepper, chopped
- ¼ cup low-sodium salsa
- 2 teaspoons peanut oil or safflower oil
- 2 tablespoons low-sodium tomato juice
- 1 teaspoon chili powder

1. Preheat the air fryer to 370°F (188°C). 2. Mix together the salmon cubes, red onion, jalapeño, red bell pepper, salsa, peanut oil, tomato juice, chili powder in a medium metal bowl and stir until well incorporated. 3. Transfer the bowl to the air fryer basket and bake for 9 to 14 minutes, stirring once, or until the salmon is cooked through and the veggies are fork-tender. 4. Serve warm.

Barbecued Shrimp with Spicy Butter Sauce

Prep time: 10 minutes | Cook time: 12 to 15 minutes | Serves 4

- 6 tablespoons unsalted butter
- ⅓ cup Worcestershire sauce
- 3 cloves garlic, minced
- Juice of 1 lemon
- 1 teaspoon paprika
- 1 teaspoon Creole seasoning
- 1½ pounds (680 g) large uncooked shrimp, peeled and deveined
- 2 tablespoons fresh parsley

1. Preheat the air fryer to 370°F (188°C). 2. In a large microwave-safe bowl, combine the butter, Worcestershire, and garlic. Microwave on high for 1 to 2 minutes until the butter is melted. Stir in the lemon juice, paprika, and Creole seasoning. Add the shrimp and toss until thoroughly coated. 3. Transfer the mixture to a casserole dish or pan that fits in your air fryer. Pausing halfway through the cooking time to turn the shrimp, air fry for 12 to 15 minutes, until the shrimp are cooked through. Top with the parsley just before serving.

Maple Balsamic Roasted Salmon

Prep time: 5 minutes | Cook time: 10 minutes | Serves 4

- 4 (6-ounce / 170-g) fillets of salmon
- Salt and freshly ground black pepper, to taste
- Vegetable oil
- ¼ cup pure maple syrup
- 3 tablespoons balsamic vinegar
- 1 teaspoon Dijon mustard

1. Preheat the air fryer to 400°F (204°C). 2. Season the salmon well with salt and freshly ground black pepper. Spray or brush the bottom of the air fryer basket with vegetable oil and place the salmon fillets inside. Air fry the salmon for 5 minutes. 3. While the salmon is air frying, combine the maple syrup, balsamic vinegar and Dijon mustard in a small saucepan over medium heat and stir to blend well. Let the mixture simmer while the fish is cooking. It should start to thicken slightly, but keep your eye on it so it doesn't burn. 4. Brush the glaze on the salmon fillets and air fry for an additional 5 minutes. The salmon should feel firm to the touch when finished and the glaze should be nicely browned on top. Brush a little more glaze on top before removing and serving with rice and vegetables, or a nice green salad.

Lemon Garlic Shrimp with Zucchini Ribbons

Prep time: 15 minutes | Cook time: 7 to 8 minutes | Serves 4

1¼ pounds (567 g) extra-large raw shrimp, peeled and deveined
2 medium zucchini (about 8 ounces / 227 g each), halved lengthwise and cut into ½-inch-thick slices
1½ tablespoons olive oil
½ teaspoon garlic salt
1½ teaspoons dried oregano
⅛ teaspoon crushed red pepper flakes (optional)
Juice of ½ lemon
1 tablespoon chopped fresh mint
1 tablespoon chopped fresh dill

1. Preheat the air fryer to 350ºF (177ºC). 2. In a large bowl, combine the shrimp, zucchini, oil, garlic salt, oregano, and pepper flakes (if using) and toss to coat. 3. Working in batches, arrange a single layer of the shrimp and zucchini in the air fryer basket. Air fry for 7 to 8 minutes, shaking the basket halfway, until the zucchini is golden and the shrimp are cooked through. 4. Transfer to a serving dish and tent with foil while you air fry the remaining shrimp and zucchini. 5. Top with the lemon juice, mint, and dill and serve.

Garlic Butter Shrimp

Prep time: 15 minutes | Cook time: 10 minutes | Serves 3

Shrimp:
Oil, for spraying
1 pound (454 g) medium raw shrimp, peeled and deveined
6 tablespoons unsalted butter, melted
Garlic Butter Sauce:
½ cup unsalted butter
2 teaspoons granulated garlic
1 cup panko bread crumbs
2 tablespoons granulated garlic
1 teaspoon salt
½ teaspoon freshly ground black pepper
¾ teaspoon salt (omit if using salted butter)

Make the Shrimp 1. Preheat the air fryer to 400ºF (204ºC). Line the air fryer basket with parchment and spray lightly with oil. 2. Place the shrimp and melted butter in a zip-top plastic bag, seal, and shake well, until evenly coated. 3. In a medium bowl, mix together the bread crumbs, garlic, salt, and black pepper. 4. Add the shrimp to the panko mixture and toss until evenly coated. Shake off any excess coating. 5. Place the shrimp in the prepared basket and spray lightly with oil. 6. Cook for 8 to 10 minutes, flipping and spraying with oil after 4 to 5 minutes, until golden brown and crispy. Make the Garlic Butter Sauce 7. In a microwave-safe bowl, combine the butter, garlic, and salt and microwave on 50% power for 30 to 60 seconds, stirring every 15 seconds, until completely melted. 8. Serve the shrimp immediately with the garlic butter sauce on the side for dipping.

Crispy Coconut Crusted Shrimp

Prep time: 5 minutes | Cook time: 6 minutes | Serves 2

8 ounces (227 g) medium shelled and deveined shrimp
2 tablespoons salted butter, melted
½ teaspoon Old Bay seasoning
¼ cup unsweetened shredded coconut

1. In a large bowl, toss the shrimp in butter and Old Bay seasoning. 2. Place shredded coconut in bowl. Coat each piece of shrimp in the coconut and place into the air fryer basket. 3. Adjust the temperature to 400ºF (204ºC) and air fry for 6 minutes. 4. Gently turn the shrimp halfway through the cooking time. Serve immediately.

Fresh Herb Salmon Burgers

Prep time: 10 minutes | Cook time: 8 minutes | Serves 4

2 (6 ounces / 170 g) fillets of salmon, finely chopped by hand or in a food processor
1 cup fine bread crumbs
1 teaspoon freshly grated lemon zest
2 tablespoons chopped fresh dill weed
1 teaspoon salt
Freshly ground black pepper, to taste
2 eggs, lightly beaten
4 brioche or hamburger buns
Lettuce, tomato, red onion, avocado, mayonnaise or mustard, for serving

1. Preheat the air fryer to 400ºF (204ºC). 2. Combine all the ingredients in a bowl. Mix together well and divide into four balls. Flatten the balls into patties, making an indentation in the center of each patty with your thumb (this will help the burger stay flat as it cooks) and flattening the sides of the burgers so that they fit nicely into the air fryer basket. 3. Transfer the burgers to the air fryer basket and air fry for 4 minutes. Flip the burgers over and air fry for another 3 to 4 minutes, until nicely browned and firm to the touch. 4. Serve on soft brioche buns with your choice of topping: lettuce, tomato, red onion, avocado, mayonnaise or mustard

Lemongrass-Infused Steamed Tuna

Prep time: 10 minutes | Cook time: 10 minutes | Serves 4

4 small tuna steaks
2 tablespoons low-sodium soy sauce
2 teaspoons sesame oil
2 teaspoons rice wine vinegar
1 teaspoon grated peeled fresh ginger
⅛ teaspoon freshly ground black pepper
1 stalk lemongrass, bent in half
3 tablespoons freshly squeezed lemon juice

1. Place the tuna steaks on a plate. 2. In a small bowl, whisk the soy sauce, sesame oil, vinegar, and ginger until combined. Pour this mixture over the tuna and gently rub it into both sides. Sprinkle the fish with the pepper. Let marinate for 10 minutes. 3. Insert the crisper plate into the basket and the basket into the unit. Preheat the unit by selecting BAKE, setting the temperature to 390°F (199°C), and setting the time to 3 minutes. Select START/STOP to begin. 4. Once the unit is preheated, place the lemongrass into the basket and top it with the tuna steaks. Drizzle the tuna with the lemon juice and 1 tablespoon of water. 5. Select BAKE, set the temperature to 390°F (199°C), and set the time to 10 minutes. Select START/STOP to begin. 6. When the cooking is complete, a food thermometer inserted into the tuna should register at least 145°F (63°C). Discard the lemongrass and serve the tuna.

Spicy Shrimp Tortilla Wraps

Prep time: 10 minutes | Cook time: 6 minutes | Serves 4

Spicy Mayo:
3 tablespoons mayonnaise
1 tablespoon Louisiana-style hot pepper sauce
Cilantro-Lime Slaw:
2 cups shredded green cabbage
½ small red onion, thinly sliced
1 small jalapeño, thinly sliced
2 tablespoons chopped fresh cilantro
Juice of 1 lime
¼ teaspoon kosher salt
Shrimp:
1 large egg, beaten
1 cup crushed tortilla chips
24 jumbo shrimp (about 1 pound / 454 g), peeled and deveined
⅛ teaspoon kosher salt
Cooking spray
8 corn tortillas, for serving

1. For the spicy mayo: In a small bowl, mix the mayonnaise and hot pepper sauce. 2. For the cilantro-lime slaw: In a large bowl, toss together the cabbage, onion, jalapeño, cilantro, lime juice, and salt to combine. Cover and refrigerate to chill. 3. For the shrimp: Place the egg in a shallow bowl and the crushed tortilla chips in another. Season the shrimp with the salt. Dip the shrimp in the egg, then in the crumbs, pressing gently to adhere. Place on a work surface and spray both sides with oil. 4. Preheat the air fryer to 360°F (182°C). 5. Working in batches, arrange a single layer of the shrimp in the air fryer basket. Air fry for 6 minutes, flipping halfway, until golden and cooked through in the center. 6. To serve, place 2 tortillas on each plate and top each with 3 shrimp. Top each taco with ¼ cup slaw, then drizzle with spicy mayo.

Crispy Mustard-Coated Fish

Prep time: 5 minutes | Cook time: 8 to 11 minutes | Serves 4

5 teaspoons low-sodium yellow mustard
1 tablespoon freshly squeezed lemon juice
4 (3½-ounce / 99-g) sole fillets
½ teaspoon dried thyme
½ teaspoon dried marjoram
⅛ teaspoon freshly ground black pepper
1 slice low-sodium whole-wheat bread, crumbled
2 teaspoons olive oil

1. In a small bowl, mix the mustard and lemon juice. Spread this evenly over the fillets. Place them in the air fryer basket. 2. In another small bowl, mix the thyme, marjoram, pepper, bread crumbs, and olive oil. Mix until combined. 3. Gently but firmly press the spice mixture onto the top of each fish fillet. 4. Bake at 320°F (160°C) for 8 to 11 minutes, or until the fish reaches an internal temperature of at least 145°F (63°C) on a meat thermometer and the topping is browned and crisp. Serve immediately.

Calamari with Fiery Sauce

Prep time: 10 minutes | Cook time: 6 minutes | Serves 2

10 ounces (283 g) calamari, trimmed
2 tablespoons keto hot sauce
1 tablespoon avocado oil

1. Slice the calamari and sprinkle with avocado oil. 2. Put the calamari in the air fryer and cook at 400°F (204°C) for 3 minutes per side. 3. Then transfer the calamari in the serving plate and sprinkle with hot sauce.

Fish and Seafood

Fresh Cucumber and Smoked Salmon Salad

Prep time: 10 minutes | Cook time: 8 to 10 minutes | Serves 2

1 pound (454 g) salmon fillet	1 seedless cucumber, thinly sliced
1½ tablespoons olive oil, divided	¼ Vidalia onion, thinly sliced
1 tablespoon sherry vinegar	2 tablespoons chopped fresh parsley
1 tablespoon capers, rinsed and drained	Salt and freshly ground black pepper, to taste

1. Preheat the air fryer to 400°F (204°C). 2. Lightly coat the salmon with ½ tablespoon of the olive oil. Place skin-side down in the air fryer basket and air fry for 8 to 10 minutes until the fish is opaque and flakes easily with a fork. Transfer the salmon to a plate and let cool to room temperature. Remove the skin and carefully flake the fish into bite-size chunks. 3. In a small bowl, whisk the remaining 1 tablespoon olive oil and the vinegar until thoroughly combined. Add the flaked fish, capers, cucumber, onion, and parsley. Season to taste with salt and freshly ground black pepper. Toss gently to coat. Serve immediately or cover and refrigerate for up to 4 hours.

Moroccan Halibut and Chickpea Bowl

Prep time: 15 minutes | Cook time: 12 minutes | Serves 2

¾ teaspoon ground coriander	1 (15-ounce / 425-g) can chickpeas, rinsed
½ teaspoon ground cumin	1 tablespoon lemon juice, plus lemon wedges for serving
¼ teaspoon ground ginger	
⅛ teaspoon ground cinnamon	1 teaspoon harissa
Salt and pepper, to taste	½ teaspoon honey
2 (8-ounce / 227-g) skinless halibut fillets, 1¼ inches thick	2 carrots, peeled and shredded
4 teaspoons extra-virgin olive oil, divided, plus extra for drizzling	2 tablespoons chopped fresh mint, divided
	Vegetable oil spray

1. Preheat the air fryer to 300°F (149°C). 2. Make foil sling for air fryer basket by folding 1 long sheet of aluminum foil so it is 4 inches wide. Lay sheet of foil widthwise across basket, pressing foil into and up sides of basket. Fold excess foil as needed so that edges of foil are flush with top of basket. Lightly spray foil and basket with vegetable oil spray. 3. Combine coriander, cumin, ginger, cinnamon, ⅛ teaspoon salt, and ⅛ teaspoon pepper in a small bowl. Pat halibut dry with paper towels, rub with 1 teaspoon oil, and sprinkle all over with spice mixture. Arrange fillets skinned side down on sling in prepared basket, spaced evenly apart. Bake until halibut flakes apart when gently prodded with a paring knife and registers 140°F (60°C), 12 to 16 minutes, using the sling to rotate fillets halfway through cooking. 4. Meanwhile, microwave chickpeas in medium bowl until heated through, about 2 minutes. Stir in remaining 1 tablespoon oil, lemon juice, harissa, honey, ⅛ teaspoon salt, and ⅛ teaspoon pepper. Add carrots and 1 tablespoon mint and toss to combine. Season with salt and pepper, to taste. 5. Using sling, carefully remove halibut from air fryer and transfer to individual plates. Sprinkle with remaining 1 tablespoon mint and drizzle with extra oil to taste. Serve with salad and lemon wedges.

Roasted Salmon with Fennel and Carrot

Prep time: 15 minutes | Cook time: 15 minutes | Serves 4

1 fennel bulb, thinly sliced	leaves
2 large carrots, sliced	4 (5-ounce / 142-g) salmon fillets
1 large onion, thinly sliced	
2 teaspoons extra-virgin olive oil	⅛ teaspoon salt
½ cup sour cream	¼ teaspoon coarsely ground black pepper
1 teaspoon dried tarragon	

1. Insert the crisper plate into the basket and the basket into the unit. Preheat the unit by selecting AIR ROAST, setting the temperature to 400°F (204°C), and setting the time to 3 minutes. Select START/STOP to begin. 2. In a medium bowl, toss together the fennel, carrots, and onion. Add the olive oil and toss again to coat the vegetables. Put the vegetables into a 6-inch round metal pan. 3. Once the unit is preheated, place the pan into the basket. 4. Select AIR ROAST, set the temperature to 400°F (204°C), and set the time to 15 minutes. Select START/STOP to begin. 5. After 5 minutes, the vegetables should be crisp-tender. Remove the pan and stir in the sour cream and tarragon. Top with the salmon fillets and sprinkle the fish with the salt and pepper. Reinsert the pan into the basket and resume cooking. 6. When the cooking is complete, the salmon should flake easily with a fork and a food thermometer should register at least 145°F (63°C). Serve the salmon on top of the vegetables.

Creamy Avocado and Tuna Snacks

Prep time: 10 minutes | Cook time: 7 minutes | Makes 12 bites

1 (10-ounce / 283-g) can tuna, drained	pitted, and mashed
¼ cup full-fat mayonnaise	½ cup blanched finely ground almond flour, divided
1 stalk celery, chopped	
1 medium avocado, peeled,	2 teaspoons coconut oil

1. In a large bowl, mix tuna, mayonnaise, celery, and mashed avocado. Form the mixture into balls. 2. Roll balls in almond flour and spritz with coconut oil. Place balls into the air fryer basket. 3. Adjust the temperature to 400°F (204°C) and set the timer for 7 minutes. 4. Gently turn tuna bites after 5 minutes. Serve warm.

Steamed Mussels in Apple Cider

Prep time: 10 minutes | Cook time: 2 minutes | Serves 5

2 pounds (907 g) mussels, cleaned, peeled	1 teaspoon ground cumin
1 teaspoon onion powder	1 tablespoon avocado oil
	¼ cup apple cider vinegar

1. Mix mussels with onion powder, ground cumin, avocado oil, and apple cider vinegar. 2. Put the mussels in the air fryer and cook at 395°F (202°C) for 2 minutes.

Cilantro-Lime Crispy Shrimp

Prep time: 40 minutes | Cook time: 10 minutes | Serves 4

1 pound (454 g) raw large shrimp, peeled and deveined with tails on or off	½ cup all-purpose flour
	1 egg
	¾ cup bread crumbs
½ cup chopped fresh cilantro	Salt and freshly ground black pepper, to taste
Juice of 1 lime	Cooking oil spray
	1 cup cocktail sauce

1. Place the shrimp in a resealable plastic bag and add the cilantro and lime juice. Seal the bag. Shake it to combine. Marinate the shrimp in the refrigerator for 30 minutes. 2. Place the flour in a small bowl. 3. In another small bowl, beat the egg. 4. Place the bread crumbs in a third small bowl, season with salt and pepper, and stir to combine. 5. Insert the crisper plate into the basket and the basket into the unit. Preheat the unit by selecting AIR FRY, setting the temperature to 400°F (204°C), and setting the time to 3 minutes. Select START/STOP to begin. 6. Remove the shrimp from the plastic bag. Dip each in the flour, the egg, and the bread crumbs to coat. Gently press the crumbs onto the shrimp. 7. Once the unit is preheated, spray the crisper plate and the basket with cooking oil. Place the shrimp in the basket. It is okay to stack them. Spray the shrimp with the cooking oil. 8. Select AIR FRY, set the temperature to 400°F (204°C), and set the time to 8 minutes. Select START/STOP to begin. 9. After 4 minutes, remove the basket and flip the shrimp one at a time. Reinsert the basket to resume cooking. 10. When the cooking is complete, the shrimp should be crisp. Let cool for 5 minutes. Serve with cocktail sauce.

Speedy Grilled Shrimp Skewers

Prep time: 10 minutes | Cook time: 5 minutes | Serves 5

4 pounds (1.8 kg) shrimp, peeled	1 tablespoon avocado oil
1 tablespoon dried rosemary	1 teaspoon apple cider vinegar

1. Mix the shrimps with dried rosemary, avocado oil, and apple cider vinegar. 2. Then sting the shrimps into skewers and put in the air fryer. 3. Cook the shrimps at 400°F (204°C) for 5 minutes.

Herb-Roasted Salmon Fillets

Prep time: 5 minutes | Cook time: 10 minutes | Serves 2

2 (8-ounce / 227 -g) skin-on salmon fillets, 1½ inches thick	1 teaspoon vegetable oil
	Salt and pepper, to taste
	Vegetable oil spray

1. Preheat the air fryer to 400°F (204°C). 2. Make foil sling for air fryer basket by folding 1 long sheet of aluminum foil so it is 4 inches wide. Lay sheet of foil widthwise across basket, pressing foil into and up sides of basket. Fold excess foil as needed so that edges of foil are flush with top of basket. Lightly spray foil and basket with vegetable oil spray. 3. Pat salmon dry with paper towels, rub with oil, and season with salt and pepper. Arrange fillets skin side down on sling in prepared basket, spaced evenly apart. Air fry salmon until center is still translucent when checked with the tip of a paring knife and registers 125°F (52°C) (for medium-rare), 10 to 14 minutes, using sling to rotate fillets halfway through cooking. 4. Using the sling, carefully remove salmon from air fryer. Slide fish spatula along underside of fillets and transfer to individual serving plates, leaving skin behind. Serve.

Crispy Cheesy Tuna Patties

Prep time: 5 minutes | Cook time: 17 to 18 minutes | Serves 4

Tuna Patties:
1 pound (454 g) canned tuna, drained
1 egg, whisked
2 tablespoons shallots, minced
1 garlic clove, minced
1 cup grated Romano cheese
Sea salt and ground black pepper, to taste
1 tablespoon sesame oil

Cheese Sauce:
1 tablespoon butter
1 cup beer
2 tablespoons grated Colby cheese

1. Mix together the canned tuna, whisked egg, shallots, garlic, cheese, salt, and pepper in a large bowl and stir to incorporate. 2. Divide the tuna mixture into four equal portions and form each portion into a patty with your hands. Refrigerate the patties for 2 hours. 3. When ready, brush both sides of each patty with sesame oil. 4. Preheat the air fryer to 360°F (182°C). 5. Place the patties in the air fryer basket and bake for 14 minutes, flipping the patties halfway through, or until lightly browned and cooked through. 6. Meanwhile, melt the butter in a pan over medium heat. 7. Pour in the beer and whisk constantly, or until it begins to bubble. 8. Add the grated Colby cheese and mix well. Continue cooking for 3 to 4 minutes, or until the cheese melts. Remove the patties from the basket to a plate. Drizzle them with the cheese sauce and serve immediately.

Sweet Honey-Glazed Baked Salmon

Prep time: 5 minutes | Cook time: 12 minutes | Serves 4

¼ cup raw honey
4 garlic cloves, minced
1 tablespoon olive oil
½ teaspoon salt
Olive oil cooking spray
4 (1½-inch-thick) salmon fillets

1. Preheat the air fryer to 380°F (193°C). 2. In a small bowl, mix together the honey, garlic, olive oil, and salt. 3. Spray the bottom of the air fryer basket with olive oil cooking spray, and place the salmon in a single layer on the bottom of the air fryer basket. 4. Brush the top of each fillet with the honey-garlic mixture, and roast for 10 to 12 minutes, or until the internal temperature reaches 145°F (63°C).

Cayenne Flounder Cutlets

Prep time: 15 minutes | Cook time: 10 minutes | Serves 2

1 egg
1 cup Pecorino Romano cheese, grated
Sea salt and white pepper, to taste
½ teaspoon cayenne pepper
1 teaspoon dried parsley flakes
2 flounder fillets

1. To make a breading station, whisk the egg until frothy. 2. In another bowl, mix Pecorino Romano cheese, and spices. 3. Dip the fish in the egg mixture and turn to coat evenly; then, dredge in the cracker crumb mixture, turning a couple of times to coat evenly. 4. Cook in the preheated air fryer at 390°F (199°C) for 5 minutes; turn them over and cook another 5 minutes. Enjoy!

Crispy South Indian-Style Fried Fish

Prep time: 20 minutes | Cook time: 8 minutes | Serves 4

2 tablespoons olive oil
2 tablespoons fresh lime or lemon juice
1 teaspoon minced fresh ginger
1 clove garlic, minced
1 teaspoon ground turmeric
½ teaspoon kosher salt
¼ to ½ teaspoon cayenne pepper
1 pound (454 g) tilapia fillets (2 to 3 fillets)
Olive oil spray
Lime or lemon wedges (optional)

1. In a large bowl, combine the oil, lime juice, ginger, garlic, turmeric, salt, and cayenne. Stir until well combined; set aside. 2. Cut each tilapia fillet into three or four equal-size pieces. Add the fish to the bowl and gently mix until all of the fish is coated in the marinade. Marinate for 10 to 15 minutes at room temperature. (Don't marinate any longer or the acid in the lime juice will "cook" the fish.) 3. Spray the air fryer basket with olive oil spray. Place the fish in the basket and spray the fish. Set the air fryer to 325°F (163°C) for 3 minutes to partially cook the fish. Set the air fryer to 400°F (204°C) for 5 minutes to finish cooking and crisp up the fish. (Thinner pieces of fish will cook faster so you may want to check at the 3-minute mark of the second cooking time and remove those that are cooked through, and then add them back toward the end of the second cooking time to crisp.) 4. Carefully remove the fish from the basket. Serve hot, with lemon wedges if desired.

Stuffed Tomatoes with Tuna Salad

Prep time: 5 minutes | Cook time: 5 minutes | Serves 2

2 medium beefsteak tomatoes, tops removed, seeded, membranes removed
2 (2.6-ounce / 74-g) pouches tuna packed in water, drained
1 medium stalk celery, trimmed and chopped
2 tablespoons mayonnaise
¼ teaspoon salt
¼ teaspoon ground black pepper
2 teaspoons coconut oil
¼ cup shredded mild Cheddar cheese

1. Scoop pulp out of each tomato, leaving ½-inch shell. 2. In a medium bowl, mix tuna, celery, mayonnaise, salt, and pepper. Drizzle with coconut oil. Spoon ½ mixture into each tomato and top each with 2 tablespoons Cheddar. 3. Place tomatoes into ungreased air fryer basket. Adjust the temperature to 320°F (160°C) and air fry for 5 minutes. Cheese will be melted when done. Serve warm.

Chapter 8
Vegetables and Sides

Cheesy Loaded Broccoli

Prep time: 10 minutes | Cook time: 10 minutes | Serves 2

3 cups fresh broccoli florets
1 tablespoon coconut oil
¼ teaspoon salt
½ cup shredded sharp Cheddar cheese
¼ cup sour cream
4 slices cooked sugar-free bacon, crumbled
1 medium scallion, trimmed and sliced on the bias

1. Begin by placing the broccoli into the air fryer basket without greasing it. Lightly drizzle coconut oil over the broccoli and season with a pinch of salt. Set the air fryer to 350°F (177°C) and let it roast for 8 minutes. To ensure even cooking and prevent any burnt areas, shake the basket three times throughout the process. 2. Once the initial cooking time is complete, evenly sprinkle the broccoli with Cheddar cheese. Return the basket to the air fryer and cook for an additional 2 minutes. The broccoli should be tender, and the cheese should be fully melted by the end of this step. 3. Transfer the cooked broccoli to a large serving dish while it's still warm. Finish by topping it with a dollop of sour cream, a generous amount of crumbled bacon, and a scattering of fresh scallion slices for added flavor and presentation.

Lemony Broccoli

Prep time: 10 minutes | Cook time: 9 to 14 minutes per batch | Serves 4

1 large head broccoli, rinsed and patted dry
2 teaspoons extra-virgin olive oil
1 tablespoon freshly squeezed lemon juice
Olive oil spray

1. Start by cutting the broccoli florets away from the main stem and separating them into smaller pieces. Don't discard the stems—peel them and chop into 1-inch chunks for added texture and flavor. 2. Assemble the air fryer by inserting the crisper plate into the basket and placing the basket into the unit. Preheat the appliance by selecting the AIR ROAST function, setting the temperature to 390°F (199°C), and adjusting the timer to 3 minutes. Press START/STOP to initiate the preheating process. 3. In a large mixing bowl, combine the broccoli florets and stems with olive oil and lemon juice, tossing thoroughly to ensure even coating. 4. Once the unit has preheated, lightly spray the crisper plate with olive oil to prevent sticking. Working in batches, arrange half of the broccoli mixture evenly in the basket. 5. Choose the AIR ROAST function again, maintaining the temperature at 390°F (199°C), and set the timer for 14 minutes. Press START/STOP to begin cooking. 6. After 5 minutes of cooking, carefully remove the basket and shake the broccoli to promote even browning. Return the basket to the unit to continue cooking. Check the broccoli after another 5 minutes. If it appears crisp-tender with lightly browned edges, it's ready. If not, allow it to cook further. 7. Once the broccoli is perfectly cooked, transfer it to a serving bowl. Repeat steps 5 and 6 with the remaining broccoli. Serve the dish immediately for the best flavor and texture.

Roasted Eggplant

Prep time: 15 minutes | Cook time: 15 minutes | Serves 4

1 large eggplant
2 tablespoons olive oil
¼ teaspoon salt
½ teaspoon garlic powder

1. Start by trimming off the top and bottom of the eggplant, then slice it into ¼-inch-thick rounds. 2. Lightly brush both sides of each eggplant slice with olive oil and sprinkle with salt and garlic powder for seasoning. Arrange the slices in a single layer in the air fryer basket. 3. Set the air fryer to 390°F (199°C) and cook for 15 minutes, or until the eggplant is tender and slightly golden. 4. Serve the eggplant slices immediately while they're warm and flavorful. Enjoy as a tasty side dish or appetizer!

Roasted Brussels Sprouts with Orange and Garlic

Prep time: 5 minutes | Cook time: 10 minutes | Serves 4

1 pound (454 g) Brussels sprouts, quartered
2 garlic cloves, minced
2 tablespoons olive oil
½ teaspoon salt
1 orange, cut into rings

1. Begin by preheating the air fryer to 360°F (182°C) to ensure it reaches the optimal temperature for cooking. 2. In a large mixing bowl, combine the quartered Brussels sprouts with minced garlic, olive oil, and salt, tossing thoroughly until the sprouts are evenly coated with the mixture. 3. Transfer the seasoned Brussels sprouts into the air fryer basket, then arrange the orange slices on top of them in a single layer. Roast for 10 minutes, allowing the flavors to meld together. 4. Once the cooking time is complete, carefully remove the Brussels sprouts from the air fryer and set the orange slices aside. Give the Brussels sprouts a final toss before serving to ensure they are well mixed and ready to enjoy.

Southwestern Roasted Corn

Prep time: 10 minutes | Cook time: 10 minutes | Serves 4

Corn:
- 1½ cups thawed frozen corn kernels
- 1 cup diced yellow onion
- 1 cup mixed diced bell peppers
- 1 jalapeño, diced
- 1 tablespoon fresh lemon juice
- 1 teaspoon ground cumin
- ½ teaspoon ancho chile powder
- ½ teaspoon kosher salt

For Serving:
- ¼ cup queso fresco or feta cheese
- ¼ cup chopped fresh cilantro
- 1 tablespoon fresh lemon juice

1. To prepare the corn mixture, combine the corn, onion, bell peppers, jalapeño, lemon juice, cumin, chile powder, and salt in a large mixing bowl. Stir thoroughly until all ingredients are evenly distributed and well blended. 2. Carefully pour the seasoned vegetable mixture into the air fryer basket. Set the air fryer to 375°F (191°C) and cook for 10 minutes, making sure to stir the mixture halfway through the cooking process to ensure even roasting. 3. Once cooked, transfer the corn mixture to a serving bowl. Add the cheese, cilantro, and an extra splash of lemon juice, then stir everything together until fully combined. Serve the dish immediately while it's warm and flavorful.

Brussels Sprouts with Pecans and Gorgonzola

Prep time: 10 minutes | Cook time: 25 minutes | Serves 4

- ½ cup pecans
- 1½ pounds (680 g) fresh Brussels sprouts, trimmed and quartered
- 2 tablespoons olive oil
- Salt and freshly ground black pepper, to taste
- ¼ cup crumbled Gorgonzola cheese

1. Start by spreading the pecans in a single layer across the air fryer basket. Set the temperature to 350°F (177°C) and air fry for 3 to 5 minutes, or until the pecans are lightly toasted and aromatic. Once done, transfer the pecans to a plate. Increase the air fryer temperature to 400°F (204°C) and allow it to continue preheating. 2. In a large mixing bowl, combine the Brussels sprouts with olive oil, ensuring they are evenly coated. Season generously with salt and black pepper according to your taste preferences. 3. If needed, cook the Brussels sprouts in batches to avoid overcrowding. Arrange them in a single layer in the air fryer basket. Air fry for 20 to 25 minutes, pausing halfway through to shake the basket for even cooking. The sprouts should become tender and develop a slight browning on the edges when ready. 4. Once cooked, transfer the Brussels sprouts to a serving bowl. Top them with the toasted pecans and crumbled Gorgonzola cheese. Serve the dish warm or allow it to cool to room temperature, depending on your preference.

Dill-and-Garlic Beets

Prep time: 10 minutes | Cook time: 30 minutes | Serves 4

- 4 beets, cleaned, peeled, and sliced
- 1 garlic clove, minced
- 2 tablespoons chopped fresh dill
- ¼ teaspoon salt
- ¼ teaspoon black pepper
- 3 tablespoons olive oil

1. Begin by preheating the air fryer to 380°F (193°C) to ensure it reaches the ideal temperature for roasting. 2. In a large mixing bowl, combine all the ingredients, making sure the beets are thoroughly coated with the oil and seasonings. 3. Transfer the beet mixture into the air fryer basket, spreading it evenly. Roast for 15 minutes, then give the mixture a good stir to promote even cooking. Continue roasting for an additional 15 minutes, or until the beets are tender and caramelized to your desired level.

Parmesan and Herb Sweet Potatoes

Prep time: 10 minutes | Cook time: 18 minutes | Serves 4

- 2 large sweet potatoes, peeled and cubed
- ¼ cup olive oil
- 1 teaspoon dried rosemary
- ½ teaspoon salt
- 2 tablespoons shredded Parmesan

1. Start by preheating the air fryer to 360°F (182°C) to ensure it reaches the optimal temperature for roasting. 2. In a large mixing bowl, combine the sweet potatoes with olive oil, rosemary, and salt, tossing thoroughly to coat the potatoes evenly with the mixture. 3. Transfer the seasoned sweet potatoes into the air fryer basket, spreading them out in an even layer. Roast for 10 minutes, then stir the potatoes to ensure even cooking. Sprinkle the Parmesan cheese over the top and continue roasting for an additional 8 minutes. 4. Once the sweet potatoes are tender and golden, serve them hot and savor the delicious flavors.

Mashed Sweet Potato Tots

Prep time: 10 minutes | Cook time: 12 to 13 minutes per batch | Makes 18 to 24 tots

1 cup cooked mashed sweet potatoes	pecans
1 egg white, beaten	1½ teaspoons honey
⅛ teaspoon ground cinnamon	Salt, to taste
1 dash nutmeg	½ cup panko bread crumbs
2 tablespoons chopped	Oil for misting or cooking spray

1. Start by preheating the air fryer to 390°F (199°C) to ensure it's ready for cooking. 2. In a large mixing bowl, combine the sweet potatoes, egg white, cinnamon, nutmeg, pecans, honey, and salt, stirring until the mixture is well blended and evenly seasoned. 3. Spread the panko crumbs evenly onto a sheet of wax paper for easy coating. 4. For each tot, scoop approximately 2 teaspoons of the sweet potato mixture. Gently drop the portion onto the panko crumbs, then press the crumbs around the edges to coat. Flip the tot to coat the other side thoroughly with crumbs, ensuring an even layer. 5. Lightly mist the tots with oil or cooking spray and arrange them in a single layer in the air fryer basket. 6. Air fry at 390°F (199°C) for 12 to 13 minutes, or until the tots are golden brown and crispy on the outside. 7. Repeat steps 5 and 6 to cook the remaining tots in batches, ensuring each batch is cooked to perfection.

Rosemary New Potatoes

Prep time: 10 minutes | Cook time: 5 to 6 minutes | Serves 4

3 large red potatoes (enough to make 3 cups sliced)	⅛ teaspoon salt
	⅛ teaspoon ground black pepper
¼ teaspoon ground rosemary	2 teaspoons extra-light olive oil
¼ teaspoon ground thyme	

1. Begin by preheating the air fryer to 330°F (166°C) to ensure it's ready for cooking. 2. Place the potatoes in a large bowl and generously sprinkle them with rosemary, thyme, salt, and pepper for seasoning. 3. Use a spoon to stir the potatoes, ensuring the herbs and spices are evenly distributed throughout. 4. Drizzle oil over the seasoned potatoes and stir again to coat them thoroughly, making sure each piece is well covered. 5. Transfer the potatoes to the air fryer basket and cook at 330°F (166°C) for 4 minutes. After this time, stir the potatoes and gently separate any pieces that may have stuck together. 6. Continue cooking for an additional 1 to 2 minutes, or until the potatoes are fork-tender and perfectly cooked. Serve immediately for the best texture and flavor.

Tingly Chili-Roasted Broccoli

Prep time: 5 minutes | Cook time: 10 minutes | Serves 2

12 ounces (340 g) broccoli florets	chopped
2 tablespoons Asian hot chili oil	1 (2-inch) piece fresh ginger, peeled and finely chopped
1 teaspoon ground Sichuan peppercorns (or black pepper)	Kosher salt and freshly ground black pepper, to taste
2 garlic cloves, finely	

1. In a large mixing bowl, combine the broccoli with chili oil, Sichuan peppercorns, minced garlic, grated ginger, and a generous seasoning of salt and black pepper. Toss everything together until the broccoli is evenly coated with the flavorful mixture. 2. Transfer the seasoned broccoli to the air fryer basket and roast at 375°F (191°C). Shake the basket halfway through the cooking time to ensure even roasting. Cook for about 10 minutes, or until the broccoli is tender and lightly charred around the edges. 3. Remove the broccoli from the air fryer and serve it warm, allowing the bold and aromatic flavors to shine.

Simple Zucchini Crisps

Prep time: 5 minutes | Cook time: 14 minutes | Serves 4

2 zucchini, sliced into ¼ to ½-inch-thick rounds (about 2 cups)	⅛ teaspoon sea salt
	Freshly ground black pepper, to taste (optional)
¼ teaspoon garlic granules	Cooking spray

1. Begin by preheating the air fryer to 392°F (200°C). Lightly spray the air fryer basket with cooking spray to prevent sticking. 2. Arrange the zucchini rounds in the air fryer basket, spreading them out in a single layer as much as possible. Sprinkle garlic granules, sea salt, and black pepper (if desired) over the zucchini for added flavor. Lightly spritz the rounds with cooking spray to help them crisp up. 3. Roast the zucchini for 14 minutes, flipping the rounds halfway through the cooking time to ensure even browning. The zucchini should be crisp-tender when done. 4. Allow the zucchini rounds to rest for 5 minutes before serving, giving them time to cool slightly and develop their texture. Serve warm and enjoy!

Lemon-Garlic Mushrooms

Prep time: 10 minutes | Cook time: 10 to 15 minutes | Serves 6

12 ounces (340 g) sliced mushrooms
1 tablespoon avocado oil
Sea salt and freshly ground black pepper, to taste
3 tablespoons unsalted butter
1 teaspoon minced garlic
1 teaspoon freshly squeezed lemon juice
½ teaspoon red pepper flakes
2 tablespoons chopped fresh parsley

1. In a medium-sized bowl, combine the mushrooms with oil, tossing them until evenly coated. Season generously with salt and pepper according to your taste preferences. 2. Arrange the mushrooms in a single layer in the air fryer basket. Set the air fryer to 375°F (191°C) and roast for 10 to 15 minutes, or until the mushrooms are tender and slightly golden. 3. While the mushrooms are cooking, melt the butter in a small pot or skillet over medium-low heat. Add the garlic and cook for 30 seconds, stirring constantly to release its aroma. Remove the pot from the heat and mix in the lemon juice and red pepper flakes, creating a flavorful lemon-garlic butter. 4. Once the mushrooms are done, toss them in the lemon-garlic butter until well coated. Garnish with fresh parsley before serving, adding a vibrant touch to the dish. Enjoy warm!

Golden Pickles

Prep time: 10 minutes | Cook time: 15 minutes | Serves 4

14 dill pickles, sliced
¼ cup flour
⅛ teaspoon baking powder
Pinch of salt
2 tablespoons cornstarch
plus 3 tablespoons water
6 tablespoons panko bread crumbs
½ teaspoon paprika
Cooking spray

1. Begin by preheating the air fryer to 400°F (204°C) to ensure it's ready for cooking. 2. Pat the dill pickles dry with a paper towel to remove any excess moisture, which helps the coating adhere better. 3. In a medium bowl, mix together the flour, baking powder, and salt until well combined. 4. Add the cornstarch and water mixture to the dry ingredients, whisking thoroughly until a smooth batter forms. 5. In a separate shallow dish, combine the panko bread crumbs and paprika, mixing them evenly to create a seasoned coating. 6. Dip each pickle into the flour batter, ensuring it's fully coated, then roll it in the bread crumb mixture to cover completely. Lightly spritz all the coated pickles with cooking spray to help them crisp up. 7. Place the pickles in the air fryer basket in a single layer and air fry for 15 minutes, or until they turn golden brown and crispy. 8. Serve the pickles immediately while they're hot and crunchy for the best flavor and texture. Enjoy!

Tamarind Sweet Potatoes

Prep time: 5 minutes | Cook time: 20 to 25 minutes | Serves 4

5 garnet sweet potatoes, peeled and diced
1½ tablespoons fresh lime juice
1 tablespoon butter, melted
2 teaspoons tamarind paste
1½ teaspoon ground allspice
⅓ teaspoon white pepper
½ teaspoon turmeric powder
A few drops liquid stevia

1. Start by preheating the air fryer to 400°F (204°C) to ensure it reaches the ideal temperature for cooking. 2. In a large mixing bowl, combine all the ingredients, tossing thoroughly until the sweet potatoes are evenly coated with the seasonings and oil. 3. Transfer the sweet potatoes to the air fryer basket, spreading them out in a single layer. Air fry for 20 to 25 minutes, shaking the basket twice during the cooking process to promote even browning. The sweet potatoes should be crispy on the outside and tender on the inside when done. 4. Allow the sweet potatoes to cool for 5 minutes before serving, giving them time to set and develop their texture. Serve warm and enjoy!

Tofu Bites

Prep time: 15 minutes | Cook time: 30 minutes | Serves 4

1 packaged firm tofu, cubed and pressed to remove excess water
1 tablespoon soy sauce
1 tablespoon ketchup
1 tablespoon maple syrup
½ teaspoon vinegar
1 teaspoon liquid smoke
1 teaspoon hot sauce
2 tablespoons sesame seeds
1 teaspoon garlic powder
Salt and ground black pepper, to taste
Cooking spray

1. Begin by preheating the air fryer to 375°F (191°C) to ensure it's ready for cooking. 2. Lightly spritz a baking dish with cooking spray to prevent the tofu from sticking. 3. In a large bowl, combine all the ingredients, ensuring the tofu is fully coated with the marinade. Let it sit for 30 minutes to allow the flavors to absorb. 4. Transfer the marinated tofu to the prepared baking dish and place it in the air fryer. Cook for 15 minutes, then flip the tofu pieces over and air fry for an additional 15 minutes on the other side, or until golden and crispy. 5. Serve the tofu immediately while it's hot and flavorful, making for a delicious and satisfying dish. Enjoy!

Cauliflower with Lime Juice

Prep time: 10 minutes | Cook time: 7 minutes | Serves 4

2 cups chopped cauliflower florets
2 tablespoons coconut oil, melted
2 teaspoons chili powder
½ teaspoon garlic powder
1 medium lime
2 tablespoons chopped cilantro

1. In a large mixing bowl, toss the cauliflower florets with coconut oil until evenly coated. Sprinkle with chili powder and garlic powder, then transfer the seasoned cauliflower to the air fryer basket. 2. Set the air fryer temperature to 350°F (177°C) and cook for 7 minutes, allowing the cauliflower to become tender and slightly golden at the edges. 3. Once cooked, transfer the cauliflower to a serving bowl. 4. Cut the lime into quarters and squeeze fresh lime juice over the cauliflower for a zesty flavor. Garnish with chopped cilantro for a fresh, aromatic finish. Serve immediately and enjoy!

Chermoula-Roasted Beets

Prep time: 15 minutes | Cook time: 25 minutes | Serves 4

Chermoula:
1 cup packed fresh cilantro leaves
½ cup packed fresh parsley leaves
6 cloves garlic, peeled
2 teaspoons smoked paprika
2 teaspoons ground cumin
1 teaspoon ground coriander
½ to 1 teaspoon cayenne pepper
Pinch crushed saffron (optional)
½ cup extra-virgin olive oil
Kosher salt, to taste
Beets:
3 medium beets, trimmed, peeled, and cut into 1-inch chunks
2 tablespoons chopped fresh cilantro
2 tablespoons chopped fresh parsley

1. To prepare the chermoula, combine cilantro, parsley, garlic, paprika, cumin, coriander, and cayenne in a food processor. Pulse until the mixture is coarsely chopped. Add saffron (if using) and process until fully incorporated. While the food processor is running, slowly drizzle in the olive oil in a steady stream, blending until the sauce is smooth and uniform. Season with salt to taste. 2. For the beets, place them in a large bowl and drizzle with ½ cup of the prepared chermoula, or enough to coat them evenly. Arrange the coated beets in the air fryer basket. Set the air fryer to 375°F (191°C) and cook for 25 minutes, or until the beets are tender and caramelized. 3. Transfer the cooked beets to a serving platter. Garnish with freshly chopped cilantro and parsley for added freshness and flavor. Serve warm and enjoy this vibrant and aromatic dish!

Easy Rosemary Green Beans

Prep time: 5 minutes | Cook time: 5 minutes | Serves 1

1 tablespoon butter, melted
2 tablespoons rosemary
½ teaspoon salt
3 cloves garlic, minced
¾ cup chopped green beans

1. Start by preheating the air fryer to 390°F (199°C) to ensure it reaches the optimal temperature for cooking. 2. In a large bowl, mix the melted butter with rosemary, salt, and minced garlic until well combined. Add the green beans to the mixture and toss thoroughly, ensuring they are evenly coated with the seasoned butter. 3. Transfer the green beans to the air fryer basket and cook for 5 minutes, allowing them to become tender and slightly crisp. 4. Serve the green beans immediately while they are hot and flavorful, making for a perfect side dish.

Dinner Rolls

Prep time: 10 minutes | Cook time: 12 minutes | Serves 6

1 cup shredded Mozzarella cheese
1 ounce (28 g) full-fat cream cheese
1 cup blanched finely ground almond flour
¼ cup ground flaxseed
½ teaspoon baking powder
1 large egg

1. In a large microwave-safe bowl, combine the Mozzarella, cream cheese, and almond flour. Microwave the mixture for 1 minute, then stir until it becomes smooth and well blended. 2. Add the flaxseed, baking powder, and egg to the mixture, stirring thoroughly until fully incorporated and the dough is smooth. If the dough becomes too firm, microwave it for an additional 15 seconds to soften. 3. Divide the dough into six equal portions and roll each piece into a ball. Place the dough balls into the air fryer basket, ensuring they are spaced apart for even cooking. 4. Set the air fryer temperature to 320°F (160°C) and cook for 12 minutes, or until the rolls are golden and cooked through. 5. Let the rolls cool completely before serving to allow them to set and achieve the perfect texture. Enjoy as a delicious low-carb treat!

Vegetables and Sides

Crispy Garlic Sliced Eggplant

Prep time: 5 minutes | Cook time: 25 minutes | Serves 4

1 egg
1 tablespoon water
½ cup whole wheat bread crumbs
1 teaspoon garlic powder
½ teaspoon dried oregano
½ teaspoon salt
½ teaspoon paprika
1 medium eggplant, sliced into ¼-inch-thick rounds
1 tablespoon olive oil

1. Begin by preheating the air fryer to 360°F (182°C) to ensure it reaches the optimal temperature for cooking. 2. In a medium shallow bowl, whisk together the egg and water until the mixture becomes frothy and well combined. 3. In another medium shallow bowl, combine the bread crumbs, garlic powder, oregano, salt, and paprika, mixing thoroughly to create a seasoned coating. 4. Dip each eggplant slice first into the egg mixture, ensuring it's fully coated, then into the bread crumb mixture, pressing gently to adhere the crumbs to the surface. Arrange the coated slices in a single layer in the air fryer basket. 5. Lightly drizzle the tops of the eggplant slices with olive oil. Air fry for 15 minutes, then flip each slice and cook for an additional 10 minutes, or until golden brown and crispy. Serve warm and enjoy!

Fig, Chickpea, and Arugula Salad

Prep time: 15 minutes | Cook time: 20 minutes | Serves 4

8 fresh figs, halved
1½ cups cooked chickpeas
1 teaspoon crushed roasted cumin seeds
4 tablespoons balsamic vinegar
2 tablespoons extra-virgin olive oil, plus more for greasing
Salt and ground black pepper, to taste
3 cups arugula rocket, washed and dried

1. Begin by preheating the air fryer to 375°F (191°C) to ensure it's ready for cooking. 2. Line the air fryer basket with aluminum foil and lightly grease it with oil. Arrange the figs in the basket and air fry for 10 minutes until they soften and develop a slight caramelization. 3. In a medium bowl, toss the chickpeas with cumin seeds until evenly coated. 4. Remove the figs from the air fryer and set them aside. Place the seasoned chickpeas in the basket and air fry for 10 minutes, or until crispy. Allow the chickpeas to cool completely. 5. While the chickpeas cool, prepare the dressing by whisking together balsamic vinegar, olive oil, salt, and pepper in a small bowl until smooth and well combined. 6. In a large salad bowl, combine the arugula rocket with the cooled figs and chickpeas. 7. Drizzle the dressing over the salad and toss gently to ensure all ingredients are evenly coated. Serve immediately and enjoy this vibrant and flavorful dish!

Cauliflower Rice Balls

Prep time: 10 minutes | Cook time: 8 minutes | Serves 4

1 (10 ounces / 283 g) steamer bag cauliflower rice, cooked according to package instructions
½ cup shredded Mozzarella cheese
1 large egg
2 ounces (57 g) plain pork rinds, finely crushed
¼ teaspoon salt
½ teaspoon Italian seasoning

1. In a large bowl, combine the cauliflower and Mozzarella, mixing until well incorporated. 2. In a separate medium bowl, whisk the egg until smooth. In another large bowl, combine the crushed pork rinds with salt and Italian seasoning. 3. Divide the cauliflower mixture into four equal portions and shape each into a ball. Dip each ball into the whisked egg, ensuring it's fully coated, then roll it in the seasoned pork rind mixture to cover evenly. Repeat with the remaining balls. 4. Place the coated cauliflower balls in the air fryer basket without greasing it. Set the air fryer to 400°F (204°C) and cook for 8 minutes, or until the balls are golden and crispy. 5. Use a spatula to carefully transfer the cauliflower balls to a serving dish. Serve warm and enjoy this delicious and creative dish!

Golden Garlicky Mushrooms

Prep time: 10 minutes | Cook time: 10 minutes | Serves 4

6 small mushrooms
1 tablespoon bread crumbs
1 tablespoon olive oil
1 ounce (28 g) onion, peeled and diced
1 teaspoon parsley
1 teaspoon garlic purée
Salt and ground black pepper, to taste

1. Start by preheating the air fryer to 350°F (177°C) to ensure it's ready for cooking. 2. In a medium bowl, mix together the bread crumbs, oil, finely chopped onion, parsley, salt, pepper, and minced garlic until well combined. Remove the stalks from the mushrooms and generously stuff each cap with the prepared crumb mixture. 3. Place the stuffed mushrooms in the air fryer basket and cook for 10 minutes, or until the filling is golden and the mushrooms are tender. 4. Serve the mushrooms hot, making for a delicious and savory appetizer or side dish. Enjoy!

Asparagus Fries

Prep time: 15 minutes | Cook time: 5 to 7 minutes per batch | Serves 4

- 12 ounces (340 g) fresh asparagus spears with tough ends trimmed off
- 2 egg whites
- ¼ cup water
- ¾ cup panko bread crumbs
- ¼ cup grated Parmesan cheese, plus 2 tablespoons
- ¼ teaspoon salt
- Oil for misting or cooking spray

1. Start by preheating the air fryer to 390°F (199°C) to ensure it's ready for cooking. 2. In a shallow dish, whisk together the egg whites and water until the mixture becomes slightly foamy. 3. In another shallow dish, combine the panko breadcrumbs, grated Parmesan, and salt, mixing thoroughly to create a seasoned coating. 4. Dip each asparagus spear into the egg mixture, ensuring it's fully coated, then roll it in the breadcrumb mixture to cover evenly. Lightly spray the coated spears with oil or cooking spray. 5. Arrange a layer of asparagus in the air fryer basket, leaving a little space between each spear. Stack another layer on top, placing them crosswise to allow even airflow. Air fry at 390°F (199°C) for 5 to 7 minutes, or until the asparagus is crispy and golden brown. 6. Repeat the process to cook the remaining asparagus spears. Serve warm and enjoy this crispy, flavorful dish!

Asian-Inspired Roasted Broccoli

Prep time: 10 minutes | Cook time: 15 minutes | Serves 4

Broccoli:
- Oil, for spraying
- 1 pound (454 g) broccoli florets
- 2 teaspoons peanut oil
- 1 tablespoon minced garlic
- ½ teaspoon salt

Sauce:
- 2 tablespoons soy sauce
- 2 teaspoons honey
- 2 teaspoons Sriracha
- 1 teaspoon rice vinegar

1. Begin by lining the air fryer basket with parchment paper and lightly spraying it with oil to prevent sticking. 2. In a large mixing bowl, toss the broccoli florets with peanut oil, minced garlic, and salt until they are evenly coated. 3. Spread the broccoli in a single, even layer in the prepared air fryer basket. 4. Air fry at 400°F (204°C) for 15 minutes, stirring halfway through to ensure even cooking and browning. 5. While the broccoli cooks, prepare the sauce by combining soy sauce, honey, Sriracha, and rice vinegar in a small microwave-safe bowl. Microwave on high for about 15 seconds, then stir until the ingredients are well blended. 6. Transfer the cooked broccoli to a serving bowl and pour the sauce over it. Gently toss until the broccoli is evenly coated with the sauce. Serve immediately for a flavorful and vibrant dish!

Curry Roasted Cauliflower

Prep time: 10 minutes | Cook time: 20 minutes | Serves 4

- ¼ cup olive oil
- 2 teaspoons curry powder
- ½ teaspoon salt
- ¼ teaspoon freshly ground black pepper
- 1 head cauliflower, cut into bite-size florets
- ½ red onion, sliced
- 2 tablespoons freshly chopped parsley, for garnish (optional)

1. Start by preheating the air fryer to 400°F (204°C) to ensure it's ready for cooking. 2. In a large mixing bowl, whisk together the olive oil, curry powder, salt, and pepper. Add the cauliflower florets and onion, tossing gently until the vegetables are evenly coated with the seasoned oil mixture. Transfer the coated vegetables to the air fryer basket. 3. Air fry for 20 minutes, pausing halfway through to shake the basket for even cooking. The cauliflower should be tender and lightly browned when done. Garnish with fresh parsley, if desired, before serving. Enjoy this aromatic and flavorful dish!

Sweet and Crispy Roasted Pearl Onions

Prep time: 5 minutes | Cook time: 18 minutes | Serves 3

- 1 (14½ ounces / 411 g) package frozen pearl onions (do not thaw)
- 2 tablespoons extra-virgin olive oil
- 2 tablespoons balsamic vinegar
- 2 teaspoons finely chopped fresh rosemary
- ½ teaspoon kosher salt
- ¼ teaspoon black pepper

1. In a medium mixing bowl, combine the onions with olive oil, vinegar, rosemary, salt, and pepper, tossing until the onions are evenly coated with the mixture. 2. Transfer the onions to the air fryer basket, spreading them out in a single layer. Set the air fryer to 400°F (204°C) and cook for 18 minutes, or until the onions are tender and lightly charred. Stir the onions once or twice during the cooking time to ensure even browning. Serve warm and enjoy this flavorful and aromatic dish!

Mushrooms with Goat Cheese

Prep time: 10 minutes | Cook time: 10 minutes | Serves 4

3 tablespoons vegetable oil
1 pound (454 g) mixed mushrooms, trimmed and sliced
1 clove garlic, minced
¼ teaspoon dried thyme
½ teaspoon black pepper
4 ounces (113 g) goat cheese, diced
2 teaspoons chopped fresh thyme leaves (optional)

1. In a baking pan, mix together the oil, mushrooms, minced garlic, dried thyme, and pepper until well combined. Stir in the goat cheese, ensuring it's evenly distributed. Place the pan in the air fryer basket and set the air fryer to 400°F (204°C). Cook for 10 minutes, stirring halfway through to ensure even cooking. 2. Once done, sprinkle with fresh thyme for an extra burst of flavor, if desired. Serve warm and enjoy this rich and savory dish!

Chili Fingerling Potatoes

Prep time: 10 minutes | Cook time: 16 minutes | Serves 4

1 pound (454 g) fingerling potatoes, rinsed and cut into wedges
1 teaspoon olive oil
1 teaspoon salt
1 teaspoon black pepper
1 teaspoon cayenne pepper
1 teaspoon nutritional yeast
½ teaspoon garlic powder

1. Begin by preheating the air fryer to 400°F (204°C) to ensure it's ready for cooking. 2. In a large bowl, coat the potatoes evenly with the remaining ingredients, ensuring they are well seasoned and covered. 3. Transfer the coated potatoes to the air fryer basket, spreading them out in a single layer. Air fry for 16 minutes, shaking the basket halfway through to promote even cooking and browning. 4. Serve the potatoes immediately while they're hot and crispy for the best flavor and texture. Enjoy!

Dijon Roast Cabbage

Prep time: 10 minutes | Cook time: 10 minutes | Serves 4

1 small head cabbage, cored and sliced into 1-inch-thick slices
2 tablespoons olive oil, divided
½ teaspoon salt
1 tablespoon Dijon mustard
1 teaspoon apple cider vinegar
1 teaspoon granular erythritol

1. Lightly drizzle each cabbage slice with 1 tablespoon of olive oil and sprinkle with salt. Arrange the slices in the air fryer basket without greasing it, working in batches if necessary. Set the air fryer to 350°F (177°C) and cook for 10 minutes, or until the cabbage is tender and the edges start to brown. 2. In a small bowl, whisk together the remaining olive oil, mustard, vinegar, and erythritol until well combined. Transfer the cooked cabbage to a large serving dish and drizzle the dressing over the top. Serve warm and enjoy this simple yet flavorful dish!

Spiced Honey-Walnut Carrots

Prep time: 5 minutes | Cook time: 12 minutes | Serves 6

1 pound (454 g) baby carrots
2 tablespoons olive oil
¼ cup raw honey
¼ teaspoon ground cinnamon
¼ cup black walnuts, chopped

1. Start by preheating the air fryer to 360°F (182°C) to ensure it's ready for cooking. 2. In a large mixing bowl, toss the baby carrots with olive oil, honey, and cinnamon until they are evenly coated with the mixture. 3. Transfer the carrots to the air fryer basket and roast for 6 minutes. Shake the basket to ensure even cooking, then sprinkle the walnuts over the carrots and roast for an additional 6 minutes. 4. Remove the carrots from the air fryer and serve warm, enjoying the sweet and nutty flavors of this delightful dish!

Sesame-Ginger Broccoli

Prep time: 10 minutes | Cook time: 15 minutes | Serves 4

3 tablespoons toasted sesame oil
2 teaspoons sesame seeds
1 tablespoon chili-garlic sauce
2 teaspoons minced fresh ginger
½ teaspoon kosher salt
½ teaspoon black pepper
1 (16-ounce / 454-g) package frozen broccoli florets (do not thaw)

1. In a large mixing bowl, whisk together the sesame oil, sesame seeds, chili-garlic sauce, grated ginger, salt, and pepper until well combined. Add the broccoli florets and toss until they are evenly coated with the flavorful mixture. 2. Arrange the broccoli in a single layer in the air fryer basket. Set the air fryer to 325°F (163°C) and cook for 15 minutes, or until the broccoli is crisp-tender and the edges are lightly browned. Gently toss the broccoli halfway through the cooking time to ensure even roasting. Serve warm and enjoy this aromatic and slightly spicy dish!

Vegetables and Sides

Ratatouille

Prep time: 15 minutes | Cook time: 20 minutes | Serves 2 to 3

2 cups ¾-inch cubed peeled eggplant
1 small red, yellow, or orange bell pepper, stemmed, seeded, and diced
1 cup cherry tomatoes
6 to 8 cloves garlic, peeled and halved lengthwise
3 tablespoons olive oil
1 teaspoon dried oregano
½ teaspoon dried thyme
1 teaspoon kosher salt
½ teaspoon black pepper

1. In a medium mixing bowl, combine the diced eggplant, bell pepper, tomatoes, minced garlic, olive oil, oregano, thyme, salt, and pepper. Toss everything together until the vegetables are evenly coated with the seasonings and oil. 2. Transfer the vegetable mixture to the air fryer basket, spreading it out in an even layer. Set the air fryer to 400°F (204°C) and cook for 20 minutes, or until the vegetables are crisp-tender and slightly caramelized. Serve warm and enjoy this flavorful and healthy dish!

Citrus Sweet Potatoes and Carrots

Prep time: 5 minutes | Cook time: 20 to 25 minutes | Serves 4

2 large carrots, cut into 1-inch chunks
1 medium sweet potato, peeled and cut into 1-inch cubes
½ cup chopped onion
2 garlic cloves, minced
2 tablespoons honey
1 tablespoon freshly squeezed orange juice
2 teaspoons butter, melted

1. Insert the crisper plate into the basket and place the basket into the air fryer unit. Preheat the unit by selecting the AIR ROAST function, setting the temperature to 400°F (204°C), and setting the timer to 3 minutes. Press START/STOP to begin preheating. 2. In a 6-by-2-inch round pan, combine the carrots, sweet potato, onion, garlic, honey, orange juice, and melted butter, tossing until the vegetables are evenly coated. 3. Once the unit is preheated, place the pan into the air fryer basket. 4. Select the AIR ROAST function again, set the temperature to 400°F (204°C), and set the timer to 25 minutes. Press START/STOP to begin cooking. 5. After 15 minutes, remove the basket and shake the vegetables to ensure even cooking. Reinsert the basket to continue cooking. Check the vegetables after 5 more minutes; if they are tender and glazed, they are done. If not, resume cooking until they reach the desired texture. 6. Once the cooking is complete, serve the vegetables immediately while they're warm and flavorful. Enjoy this sweet and savory dish!

Parmesan-Thyme Butternut Squash

Prep time: 15 minutes | Cook time: 20 minutes | Serves 4

2½ cups butternut squash, cubed into 1-inch pieces (approximately 1 medium)
2 tablespoons olive oil
¼ teaspoon salt
¼ teaspoon garlic powder
¼ teaspoon black pepper
1 tablespoon fresh thyme
¼ cup grated Parmesan

1. Begin by preheating the air fryer to 360°F (182°C) to ensure it reaches the ideal temperature for roasting. 2. In a large mixing bowl, toss the cubed squash with olive oil, salt, garlic powder, pepper, and thyme until the squash is evenly coated with the seasonings. 3. Transfer the seasoned squash to the air fryer basket and roast for 10 minutes. Stir the squash to ensure even cooking, then continue roasting for an additional 8 to 10 minutes, or until tender and slightly caramelized. 4. Remove the squash from the air fryer and toss it with freshly grated Parmesan cheese for a rich, savory finish. Serve warm and enjoy this flavorful side dish!

Zesty Fried Asparagus

Prep time: 3 minutes | Cook time: 10 minutes | Serves 4

Oil, for spraying
10 to 12 spears asparagus, trimmed
2 tablespoons olive oil
1 tablespoon granulated garlic
1 teaspoon chili powder
½ teaspoon ground cumin
¼ teaspoon salt

1. Begin by lining the air fryer basket with parchment paper and lightly spraying it with oil to prevent sticking. 2. If the asparagus spears are too long to fit comfortably in the air fryer, cut them in half for easier cooking. 3. Place the asparagus, olive oil, minced garlic, chili powder, cumin, and salt in a zip-top plastic bag. Seal the bag and shake or toss until the asparagus is evenly coated with the seasoning mixture. 4. Arrange the asparagus in a single layer in the prepared air fryer basket. 5. Roast at 390°F (199°C) for 5 minutes, then flip the asparagus and cook for an additional 5 minutes, or until they are bright green and tender yet still firm. Serve warm and enjoy this flavorful and vibrant side dish!

Rosemary-Roasted Red Potatoes

Prep time: 5 minutes | Cook time: 20 minutes | Serves 6

1 pound (454 g) red potatoes, quartered
¼ cup olive oil
½ teaspoon kosher salt
¼ teaspoon black pepper
1 garlic clove, minced
4 rosemary sprigs

1. Begin by preheating the air fryer to 360°F (182°C) to ensure it's ready for cooking. 2. In a large mixing bowl, toss the potatoes with olive oil, salt, pepper, and minced garlic until they are evenly coated with the seasoning mixture. 3. Transfer the potatoes to the air fryer basket and place the rosemary sprigs on top for added flavor. 4. Roast the potatoes for 10 minutes, then stir or toss them to ensure even cooking. Continue roasting for an additional 10 minutes, or until the potatoes are golden and tender. 5. Remove the rosemary sprigs before serving. Season the potatoes with additional salt and pepper, if desired, and serve warm. Enjoy this aromatic and satisfying side dish!

Buttery Green Beans

Prep time: 5 minutes | Cook time: 8 to 10 minutes | Serves 6

1 pound (454 g) green beans, trimmed
1 tablespoon avocado oil
1 teaspoon garlic powder
Sea salt and freshly ground black pepper, to taste
¼ cup (4 tablespoons) unsalted butter, melted
¼ cup freshly grated Parmesan cheese

1. In a large mixing bowl, toss the green beans with avocado oil and garlic powder, seasoning generously with salt and pepper to taste. 2. Preheat the air fryer to 400°F (204°C). Arrange the green beans in a single layer in the air fryer basket. Air fry for 8 to 10 minutes, shaking the basket halfway through to ensure even cooking. 3. Transfer the cooked green beans to a large bowl and toss them with melted butter until evenly coated. Sprinkle with Parmesan cheese and serve warm for a delicious and savory side dish. Enjoy!

Chapter 9: Vegetarian Mains

Creamy Basmati Rice Risotto

Prep time: 10 minutes | Cook time: 30 minutes | Serves 2

1 onion, diced	1 clove garlic, minced
1 small carrot, diced	¾ cup long-grain basmati rice
2 cups vegetable broth, boiling	1 tablespoon olive oil
½ cup grated Cheddar cheese	1 tablespoon unsalted butter

1. Preheat the air fryer to 390ºF (199ºC). 2. Grease a baking tin with oil and stir in the butter, garlic, carrot, and onion. 3. Put the tin in the air fryer and bake for 4 minutes. 4. Pour in the rice and bake for a further 4 minutes, stirring three times throughout the baking time. 5. Turn the temperature down to 320ºF (160ºC). 6. Add the vegetable broth and give the dish a gentle stir. Bake for 22 minutes, leaving the air fryer uncovered. 7. Pour in the cheese, stir once more and serve.

Sweet Pepper Nachos with Melted Cheese

Prep time: 10 minutes | Cook time: 5 minutes | Serves 2

6 mini sweet peppers, seeded and sliced in half	jalapeños
¾ cup shredded Colby jack cheese	½ medium avocado, peeled, pitted, and diced
¼ cup sliced pickled	2 tablespoons sour cream

1. Place peppers into an ungreased round nonstick baking dish. Sprinkle with Colby and top with jalapeños. 2. Place dish into air fryer basket. Adjust the temperature to 350ºF (177ºC) and bake for 5 minutes. Cheese will be melted and bubbly when done. 3. Remove dish from air fryer and top with avocado. Drizzle with sour cream. Serve warm.

Mediterranean-Style Olive Pan Pizza

Prep time: 5 minutes | Cook time: 8 minutes | Serves 2

1 cup shredded Mozzarella cheese	spinach leaves
¼ medium red bell pepper, seeded and chopped	2 tablespoons chopped black olives
½ cup chopped fresh	2 tablespoons crumbled feta cheese

1. Sprinkle Mozzarella into an ungreased round nonstick baking dish in an even layer. Add remaining ingredients on top. 2. Place dish into air fryer basket. Adjust the temperature to 350ºF (177ºC) and bake for 8 minutes, checking halfway through to avoid burning. Top of pizza will be golden brown and the cheese melted when done. 3. Remove dish from fryer and let cool 5 minutes before slicing and serving.

Oven-Roasted Zucchini Slices

Prep time: 10 minutes | Cook time: 8 minutes | Serves 4

2 tablespoons salted butter	cream cheese
¼ cup diced white onion	1 cup shredded sharp Cheddar cheese
½ teaspoon minced garlic	2 medium zucchini, spiralized
½ cup heavy whipping cream	
2 ounces (57 g) full-fat	

1. In a large saucepan over medium heat, melt butter. Add onion and sauté until it begins to soften, 1 to 3 minutes. Add garlic and sauté for 30 seconds, then pour in cream and add cream cheese. 2. Remove the pan from heat and stir in Cheddar. Add the zucchini and toss in the sauce, then put into a round baking dish. Cover the dish with foil and place into the air fryer basket. 3. Adjust the temperature to 370ºF (188ºC) and set the timer for 8 minutes. 4. After 6 minutes remove the foil and let the top brown for remaining cooking time. Stir and serve.

Fresh Summer Veggie Rolls

Prep time: 15 minutes | Cook time: 15 minutes | Serves 4

1 cup shiitake mushroom, sliced thinly	1 teaspoon sugar
1 celery stalk, chopped	1 tablespoon soy sauce
1 medium carrot, shredded	1 teaspoon nutritional yeast
½ teaspoon finely chopped ginger	8 spring roll sheets
	1 teaspoon corn starch
	2 tablespoons water

1. In a bowl, combine the ginger, soy sauce, nutritional yeast, carrots, celery, mushroom, and sugar. 2. Mix the cornstarch and water to create an adhesive for the spring rolls. 3. Scoop a tablespoonful of the vegetable mixture into the middle of the spring roll sheets. Brush the edges of the sheets with the cornstarch adhesive and enclose around the filling to make spring rolls. 4. Preheat the air fryer to 400ºF (204ºC). When warm, place the rolls inside and air fry for 15 minutes or until crisp. 5. Serve hot.

Herb-Roasted Mixed Vegetables

Prep time: 10 minutes | Cook time: 14 to 18 minutes | Serves 4

1 (8-ounce / 227-g) package sliced mushrooms	3 cloves garlic, sliced
1 yellow summer squash, sliced	1 tablespoon olive oil
	½ teaspoon dried basil
1 red bell pepper, sliced	½ teaspoon dried thyme
	½ teaspoon dried tarragon

1. Preheat the air fryer to 350ºF (177ºC). 2. Toss the mushrooms, squash, and bell pepper with the garlic and olive oil in a large bowl until well coated. Mix in the basil, thyme, and tarragon and toss again. 3. Spread the vegetables evenly in the air fryer basket and roast for 14 to 18 minutes, or until the vegetables are fork-tender. 4. Cool for 5 minutes before serving.

Creamy Russet Potato Au Gratin

Prep time: 10 minutes | Cook time: 35 minutes | Serves 6

½ cup milk	½ cup heavy whipping cream
7 medium russet potatoes, peeled	
	½ cup grated semi-mature cheese
Salt, to taste	
1 teaspoon black pepper	½ teaspoon nutmeg

1. Preheat the air fryer to 390ºF (199ºC). 2. Cut the potatoes into wafer-thin slices. 3. In a bowl, combine the milk and cream and sprinkle with salt, pepper, and nutmeg. 4. Use the milk mixture to coat the slices of potatoes. Put in a baking dish. Top the potatoes with the rest of the milk mixture. 5. Put the baking dish into the air fryer basket and bake for 25 minutes. 6. Pour the cheese over the potatoes. 7. Bake for an additional 10 minutes, ensuring the top is nicely browned before serving.

Sweet Teriyaki Glazed Cauliflower

Prep time: 5 minutes | Cook time: 14 minutes | Serves 4

½ cup soy sauce	2 cloves garlic, chopped
⅓ cup water	½ teaspoon chili powder
1 tablespoon brown sugar	1 big cauliflower head, cut into florets
1 teaspoon sesame oil	
1 teaspoon cornstarch	

1. Preheat the air fryer to 340ºF (171ºC). 2. Make the teriyaki sauce: In a small bowl, whisk together the soy sauce, water, brown sugar, sesame oil, cornstarch, garlic, and chili powder until well combined. 3. Place the cauliflower florets in a large bowl and drizzle the top with the prepared teriyaki sauce and toss to coat well. 4. Put the cauliflower florets in the air fryer basket and air fry for 14 minutes, shaking the basket halfway through, or until the cauliflower is crisp-tender. 5. Let the cauliflower cool for 5 minutes before serving.

Baked Cabbage Wedges with Cheese

Prep time: 5 minutes | Cook time: 20 minutes | Serves 4

4 tablespoons melted butter	Salt and black pepper, to taste
1 head cabbage, cut into wedges	
	½ cup shredded Mozzarella cheese
1 cup shredded Parmesan cheese	

1. Preheat the air fryer to 380ºF (193ºC). 2. Brush the melted butter over the cut sides of cabbage wedges and sprinkle both sides with the Parmesan cheese. Season with salt and pepper to taste. 3. Place the cabbage wedges in the air fryer basket and air fry for 20 minutes, flipping the cabbage halfway through, or until the cabbage wedges are lightly browned. 4. Transfer the cabbage wedges to a plate and serve with the Mozzarella cheese sprinkled on top.

Cheddar Cauliflower Pizza Base

Prep time: 15 minutes | Cook time: 11 minutes | Serves 2

1 (12 ounces / 340 g) steamer bag cauliflower	2 tablespoons blanched finely ground almond flour
½ cup shredded sharp Cheddar cheese	1 teaspoon Italian blend seasoning
1 large egg	

1. Cook cauliflower according to package instructions. Remove from bag and place into cheesecloth or paper towel to remove excess water. Place cauliflower into a large bowl. 2. Add cheese, egg, almond flour, and Italian seasoning to the bowl and mix well. 3. Cut a piece of parchment to fit your air fryer basket. Press cauliflower into 6-inch round circle. Place into the air fryer basket. 4. Adjust the temperature to 360ºF (182ºC) and air fry for 11 minutes. 5. After 7 minutes, flip the pizza crust. 6. Add preferred toppings to pizza. Place back into air fryer basket and cook an additional 4 minutes or until fully cooked and golden. Serve immediately.

Air-Fried Mediterranean Vegetable Medley

Prep time: 10 minutes | Cook time: 6 minutes | Serves 4

1 large zucchini, sliced	1 teaspoon mixed herbs
1 cup cherry tomatoes, halved	1 teaspoon mustard
	1 teaspoon garlic purée
1 parsnip, sliced	6 tablespoons olive oil
1 green pepper, sliced	Salt and ground black pepper, to taste
1 carrot, sliced	

1. Preheat the air fryer to 400°F (204°C). 2. Combine all the ingredients in a bowl, making sure to coat the vegetables well. 3. Transfer to the air fryer and air fry for 6 minutes, ensuring the vegetables are tender and browned. 4. Serve immediately.

Spicy Black Bean Tomato Chili

Prep time: 15 minutes | Cook time: 23 minutes | Serves 6

1 tablespoon olive oil	2 chipotle peppers, chopped
1 medium onion, diced	
3 garlic cloves, minced	2 teaspoons cumin
1 cup vegetable broth	2 teaspoons chili powder
3 cans black beans, drained and rinsed	1 teaspoon dried oregano
	½ teaspoon salt
2 cans diced tomatoes	

1. Over a medium heat, fry the garlic and onions in the olive oil for 3 minutes. 2. Add the remaining ingredients, stirring constantly and scraping the bottom to prevent sticking. 3. Preheat the air fryer to 400°F (204°C). 4. Take a dish and place the mixture inside. Put a sheet of aluminum foil on top. 5. Transfer to the air fryer and bake for 20 minutes. 6. When ready, plate up and serve immediately.

Garlic-Infused Sesame Roasted Carrots

Prep time: 5 minutes | Cook time: 16 minutes | Serves 4 to 6

1 pound (454 g) baby carrots	Freshly ground black pepper, to taste
1 tablespoon sesame oil	6 cloves garlic, peeled
½ teaspoon dried dill	3 tablespoons sesame seeds
Pinch salt	

1. Preheat the air fryer to 380°F (193°C). 2. In a medium bowl, drizzle the baby carrots with the sesame oil. Sprinkle with the dill, salt, and pepper and toss to coat well. 3. Place the baby carrots in the air fryer basket and roast for 8 minutes. 4. Remove the basket and stir in the garlic. Return the basket to the air fryer and roast for another 8 minutes, or until the carrots are lightly browned. 5. Serve sprinkled with the sesame seeds.

Greek-Style Eggplant Boats

Prep time: 15 minutes | Cook time: 20 minutes | Serves 2

1 large eggplant	hearts
2 tablespoons unsalted butter	1 cup fresh spinach
	2 tablespoons diced red bell pepper
¼ medium yellow onion, diced	½ cup crumbled feta
¼ cup chopped artichoke	

1. Slice eggplant in half lengthwise and scoop out flesh, leaving enough inside for shell to remain intact. Take eggplant that was scooped out, chop it, and set aside. 2. In a medium skillet over medium heat, add butter and onion. Sauté until onions begin to soften, about 3 to 5 minutes. Add chopped eggplant, artichokes, spinach, and bell pepper. Continue cooking 5 minutes until peppers soften and spinach wilts. Remove from the heat and gently fold in the feta. 3. Place filling into each eggplant shell and place into the air fryer basket. 4. Adjust the temperature to 320°F (160°C) and air fry for 20 minutes. 5. Eggplant will be tender when done. Serve warm.

Scrambled Tofu with Potato and Broccoli

Prep time: 15 minutes | Cook time: 30 minutes | Serves 3

2½ cups chopped red potato	2 tablespoons tamari
	1 teaspoon turmeric powder
2 tablespoons olive oil, divided	½ teaspoon onion powder
	½ teaspoon garlic powder
1 block tofu, chopped finely	½ cup chopped onion
	4 cups broccoli florets

1. Preheat the air fryer to 400°F (204°C). 2. Toss together the potatoes and 1 tablespoon of the olive oil. 3. Air fry the potatoes in a baking dish for 15 minutes, shaking once during the cooking time to ensure they fry evenly. 4. Combine the tofu, the remaining 1 tablespoon of the olive oil, turmeric, onion powder, tamari, and garlic powder together, stirring in the onions, followed by the broccoli. 5. Top the potatoes with the tofu mixture and air fry for an additional 15 minutes. Serve warm.

Classic Baked Eggplant Parmesan

Prep time: 15 minutes | Cook time: 17 minutes | Serves 4

1 medium eggplant, ends trimmed, sliced into ½-inch rounds	1 ounce (28 g) 100% cheese crisps, finely crushed
¼ teaspoon salt	½ cup low-carb marinara sauce
2 tablespoons coconut oil	
½ cup grated Parmesan cheese	½ cup shredded Mozzarella cheese

1. Sprinkle eggplant rounds with salt on both sides and wrap in a kitchen towel for 30 minutes. Press to remove excess water, then drizzle rounds with coconut oil on both sides. 2. In a medium bowl, mix Parmesan and cheese crisps. Press each eggplant slice into mixture to coat both sides. 3. Place rounds into ungreased air fryer basket. Adjust the temperature to 350°F (177°C) and air fry for 15 minutes, turning rounds halfway through cooking. They will be crispy around the edges when done. 4. Spoon marinara over rounds and sprinkle with Mozzarella. Continue cooking an additional 2 minutes at 350°F (177°C) until cheese is melted. Serve warm.

Fully Loaded Cauliflower Steak

Prep time: 5 minutes | Cook time: 7 minutes | Serves 4

1 medium head cauliflower	¼ cup blue cheese crumbles
¼ cup hot sauce	
2 tablespoons salted butter, melted	¼ cup full-fat ranch dressing

1. Remove cauliflower leaves. Slice the head in ½-inch-thick slices. 2. In a small bowl, mix hot sauce and butter. Brush the mixture over the cauliflower. 3. Place each cauliflower steak into the air fryer, working in batches if necessary. 4. Adjust the temperature to 400°F (204°C) and air fry for 7 minutes. 5. When cooked, edges will begin turning dark and caramelized. 6. To serve, sprinkle steaks with crumbled blue cheese. Drizzle with ranch dressing.

Oven-Baked Spaghetti Squash

Prep time: 10 minutes | Cook time: 45 minutes | Serves 6

1 (4 pounds / 1.8 kg) spaghetti squash, halved and seeded	4 tablespoons salted butter, melted
2 tablespoons coconut oil	1 teaspoon garlic powder
	2 teaspoons dried parsley

1. Brush shell of spaghetti squash with coconut oil. Brush inside with butter. Sprinkle inside with garlic powder and parsley. 2. Place squash skin side down into ungreased air fryer basket, working in batches if needed. Adjust the temperature to 350°F (177°C) and set the timer for 30 minutes. When the timer beeps, flip squash and cook an additional 15 minutes until fork-tender. 3. Use a fork to remove spaghetti strands from shell and serve warm.

Spicy Crispy Fried Okra

Prep time: 5 minutes | Cook time: 10 minutes | Serves 4

3 tablespoons sour cream	Salt and black pepper, to taste
2 tablespoons flour	
2 tablespoons semolina	1 pound (454 g) okra, halved
½ teaspoon red chili powder	Cooking spray

1. Preheat the air fryer to 400°F (204°C). Spray the air fryer basket with cooking spray. 2. In a shallow bowl, place the sour cream. In another shallow bowl, thoroughly combine the flour, semolina, red chili powder, salt, and pepper. 3. Dredge the okra in the sour cream, then roll in the flour mixture until evenly coated. 4. Arrange the okra in the air fryer basket and air fry for 10 minutes, flipping the okra halfway through, or until golden brown and crispy. 5. Cool for 5 minutes before serving.

Zucchini Boats Stuffed with Cheese

Prep time: 20 minutes | Cook time: 8 minutes | Serves 4

1 large zucchini, cut into four pieces	1 heaping tablespoon coriander, minced
2 tablespoons olive oil	2 ounces (57 g) Cheddar cheese, preferably freshly grated
1 cup Ricotta cheese, room temperature	
2 tablespoons scallions, chopped	1 teaspoon celery seeds
	½ teaspoon salt
1 heaping tablespoon fresh parsley, roughly chopped	½ teaspoon garlic pepper

1. Cook your zucchini in the air fryer basket for approximately 10 minutes at 350°F (177°C). Check for doneness and cook for 2-3 minutes longer if needed. 2. Meanwhile, make the stuffing by mixing the other items. 3. When your zucchini is thoroughly cooked, open them up. Divide the stuffing among all zucchini pieces and bake an additional 5 minutes.

Vegetarian Mains

Chapter 10

Desserts

Lime Bars

Prep time: 10 minutes | Cook time: 33 minutes | Makes 12 bars

1½ cups blanched finely ground almond flour, divided
¾ cup confectioners' erythritol, divided
4 tablespoons salted butter, melted
½ cup fresh lime juice
2 large eggs, whisked

1. In a medium bowl, combine 1 cup of flour, ¼ cup of erythritol, and butter. Mix until crumbly, then press the mixture firmly into the bottom of an ungreased round nonstick cake pan to form the crust. 2. Place the pan into the air fryer basket. Set the temperature to 300°F (149°C) and bake for 13 minutes, or until the crust is golden brown and set in the center. 3. Remove the pan from the air fryer and let the crust cool in the pan for 10 minutes. 4. In another medium bowl, whisk together the remaining flour, remaining erythritol, lime juice, and eggs until smooth. Pour this mixture over the cooled crust and return the pan to the air fryer. Bake at 300°F (149°C) for 20 minutes, or until the top is browned and firm. 5. Allow the dessert to cool completely in the pan for about 30 minutes, then cover and refrigerate for at least 1 hour to chill. Serve cold and enjoy this refreshing and tangy treat!

Pumpkin Pudding with Vanilla Wafers

Prep time: 10 minutes | Cook time: 12 to 17 minutes | Serves 4

1 cup canned no-salt-added pumpkin purée (not pumpkin pie filling)
¼ cup packed brown sugar
3 tablespoons all-purpose flour
1 egg, whisked
2 tablespoons milk
1 tablespoon unsalted butter, melted
1 teaspoon pure vanilla extract
4 low-fat vanilla wafers, crumbled
Nonstick cooking spray

1. Begin by preheating the air fryer to 350°F (177°C). Lightly coat a baking pan with nonstick cooking spray and set it aside. 2. In a medium bowl, combine the pumpkin purée, brown sugar, flour, whisked egg, milk, melted butter, and vanilla extract. Whisk until the mixture is smooth and well combined. Pour the mixture into the prepared baking pan. 3. Place the baking pan in the air fryer basket and bake for 12 to 17 minutes, or until the pudding is set and firm. 4. Carefully remove the pudding from the air fryer and place it on a wire rack to cool slightly. 5. Divide the pudding into four serving bowls and sprinkle vanilla wafers on top for added crunch and flavor. Serve warm and enjoy this comforting dessert!

Maple-Pecan Tart with Sea Salt

Prep time: 15 minutes | Cook time: 25 minutes | Serves 8

Tart Crust:
Vegetable oil spray
⅓ cup (⅔ stick) butter, softened
¼ cup firmly packed brown sugar
1 cup all-purpose flour
¼ teaspoon kosher salt

Filling:
4 tablespoons (½ stick) butter, diced
½ cup packed brown sugar
¼ cup pure maple syrup
¼ cup whole milk
¼ teaspoon pure vanilla extract
1½ cups finely chopped pecans
¼ teaspoon flaked sea salt

1. For the crust: Line a baking pan with foil, leaving a couple of inches of overhang on the sides. Lightly spray the foil with vegetable oil spray. 2. In a medium bowl, combine the butter and brown sugar. Using an electric mixer on medium-low speed, beat until the mixture is light and fluffy. Add the flour and kosher salt, and continue beating until well blended. Transfer the crumbly mixture to the prepared pan and press it evenly into the bottom to form the crust. 3. Place the pan in the air fryer basket. Set the air fryer to 350°F (177°C) and cook for 13 minutes. When the crust has 5 minutes left to cook, begin preparing the filling. 4. For the filling: In a medium saucepan, combine the butter, brown sugar, maple syrup, and milk. Bring the mixture to a simmer over medium heat, stirring occasionally. Once it begins simmering, cook for 1 minute. Remove from the heat and stir in the vanilla extract and pecans. 5. Carefully pour the filling evenly over the crust, using a rubber spatula to gently spread it so the nuts and liquid are distributed evenly. Set the air fryer to 350°F (177°C) and cook for 12 minutes, or until the filling is bubbling. (The center should still be slightly jiggly, as it will thicken as it cools.) 6. Remove the pan from the air fryer and sprinkle the tart with sea salt. Allow it to cool completely on a wire rack until it reaches room temperature. 7. Transfer the pan to the refrigerator to chill. Once cold (this will make the tart easier to cut), use the foil overhang to lift the tart out of the pan. Cut it into 8 wedges and serve at room temperature. Enjoy this decadent and flavorful dessert!

Almond-Roasted Pears

Prep time: 10 minutes | Cook time: 15 to 20 minutes | Serves 4

Yogurt Topping:

1 container vanilla Greek yogurt (5 to 6 ounces / 142 to 170 g)
¼ teaspoon almond flavoring
2 whole pears
¼ cup crushed Biscoff cookies (approx. 4 cookies)
1 tablespoon sliced almonds
1 tablespoon butter

1. Mix the almond flavoring into the yogurt and set it aside to allow the flavors to meld while you prepare the pears. 2. Cut each pear in half and use a spoon to carefully remove the core from each half. 3. Arrange the pear halves in the air fryer basket, cut side up. 4. In a small bowl, combine the cookie crumbs and almonds. Spoon a quarter of this mixture into the hollow of each pear half. 5. Cut the butter into four equal pieces and place one piece on top of the crumb mixture in each pear half. 6. Roast the pears at 360°F (182°C) for 15 to 20 minutes, or until they are tender but still slightly firm. 7. Serve the warm pear halves with a dollop of the almond-flavored yogurt on top. Enjoy this delightful and elegant dessert!

Lemon Curd Pavlova

Prep time: 10 minutes | Cook time: 1 hour | Serves 4

Shell:

3 large egg whites
¼ teaspoon cream of tartar
¾ cup Swerve confectioners'-style sweetener or equivalent
amount of powdered sweetener
1 teaspoon grated lemon zest
1 teaspoon lemon extract

Lemon Curd:

1 cup Swerve confectioners'-style sweetener or equivalent amount of liquid or
powdered sweetener
½ cup lemon juice
4 large eggs
½ cup coconut oil

For Garnish (optional):

Blueberries
Swerve confectioners'-style sweetener or
equivalent amount of powdered sweetener

1. Preheat the air fryer to 275°F (135°C). Generously grease a pie pan with butter or coconut oil to prevent sticking. 2. To make the shell: In a small bowl, use a hand mixer to beat the egg whites and cream of tartar until soft peaks form. With the mixer on low speed, gradually sprinkle in the sweetener and continue mixing until it's fully incorporated. 3. Add the lemon zest and lemon extract to the mixture, then continue beating with the hand mixer until stiff peaks form. 4. Spoon the mixture into the greased pie pan, spreading it evenly across the bottom, up the sides, and onto the rim to form a shell. Bake in the air fryer for 1 hour. Once done, turn off the air fryer and let the shell sit inside for 20 minutes to set. (The shell can be prepared up to 3 days in advance and stored in an airtight container in the refrigerator, if desired.) 5. While the shell bakes, prepare the lemon curd: In a medium-sized heavy-bottomed saucepan, whisk together the sweetener, lemon juice, and eggs. Add the coconut oil and place the saucepan over medium heat. Once the oil has melted, whisk constantly until the mixture thickens and coats the back of a spoon, about 10 minutes. Be careful not to let the mixture boil. 6. Strain the lemon curd through a fine-mesh sieve into a medium-sized bowl. Place this bowl inside a larger bowl filled with ice water, whisking occasionally until the curd is completely cool, about 15 minutes. 7. Pour the cooled lemon curd into the prepared shell. Garnish with fresh blueberries and a dusting of powdered sweetener, if desired. Store any leftovers in the refrigerator for up to 4 days. Enjoy this tangy and refreshing dessert!

White Chocolate Cookies

Prep time: 5 minutes | Cook time: 11 minutes | Serves 10

8 ounces (227 g) unsweetened white chocolate
2 eggs, well beaten
¾ cup butter, at room temperature
1⅔ cups almond flour
½ cup coconut flour
¾ cup granulated Swerve
2 tablespoons coconut oil
⅓ teaspoon grated nutmeg
⅓ teaspoon ground allspice
⅓ teaspoon ground anise star
¼ teaspoon fine sea salt

1. Begin by preheating the air fryer to 350°F (177°C) and lining the air fryer basket with parchment paper for easy removal. 2. In a mixing bowl, combine all the ingredients and knead the mixture for approximately 3 to 4 minutes, or until a soft and pliable dough forms. Once ready, transfer the dough to the refrigerator to chill for 20 minutes. 3. To shape the cookies, roll the chilled dough into 1-inch balls and place them onto the parchment-lined basket, ensuring they are spaced about 2 inches apart. Gently flatten each ball using the back of a spoon. 4. Bake the cookies for around 11 minutes, or until they turn golden and feel firm when touched. 5. Carefully transfer the baked cookies to a wire rack, allowing them to cool completely before serving. Enjoy them fresh and delicious!

Vanilla Scones

Prep time: 20 minutes | Cook time: 10 minutes | Serves 6

4 ounces (113 g) coconut flour	2 teaspoons mascarpone
½ teaspoon baking powder	¼ cup heavy cream
1 teaspoon apple cider vinegar	1 teaspoon vanilla extract
	1 tablespoon erythritol
	Cooking spray

1. In a mixing bowl, combine the coconut flour, baking powder, apple cider vinegar, mascarpone, heavy cream, vanilla extract, and erythritol. Mix thoroughly until a dough forms. 2. Knead the dough gently on a clean surface, then shape and cut it into scones. 3. Place the scones in the air fryer basket and lightly spray them with cooking spray to help them brown evenly. 4. Air fry the scones at 365°F (185°C) for 10 minutes, or until they are golden and cooked through. Serve warm and enjoy these delicious, tender scones!

Chocolate Soufflés

Prep time: 5 minutes | Cook time: 14 minutes | Serves 2

Butter and sugar for greasing the ramekins	½ teaspoon pure vanilla extract
3 ounces (85 g) semi-sweet chocolate, chopped	2 tablespoons all-purpose flour
¼ cup unsalted butter	Powdered sugar, for dusting the finished soufflés
2 eggs, yolks and white separated	
3 tablespoons sugar	Heavy cream, for serving

1. Prepare the ramekins by buttering them generously, then coating the butter with sugar. To do this, sprinkle sugar into each ramekin, shake it around to coat the buttered surface, and discard any excess sugar. 2. Melt the chocolate and butter together using a microwave or double boiler. In a separate bowl, vigorously beat the egg yolks. Add the sugar and vanilla extract, and beat again until well combined. Slowly drizzle in the melted chocolate and butter mixture, stirring continuously. Finally, mix in the flour until the batter is smooth and free of lumps. 3. Preheat the air fryer to 330°F (166°C). 4. In another bowl, whisk the egg whites until they reach the soft peak stage (where the peaks gently droop when the whisk is lifted). Gently fold the whipped egg whites into the chocolate mixture in stages to maintain the airy texture. 5. Carefully pour the batter into the prepared ramekins, leaving about ½-inch of space at the top. (You may have enough batter for a third ramekin, depending on how airy the mixture is.) Place the ramekins in the air fryer basket and air fry for 14 minutes. The soufflés should rise beautifully and develop a golden-brown top. (A slightly darker top is fine, as it will be dusted with powdered sugar.) 6. Dust the soufflés with powdered sugar and serve immediately. Accompany with heavy cream for pouring over the top at the table. Enjoy this decadent and impressive dessert!

Pecan Brownies

Prep time: 10 minutes | Cook time: 20 minutes | Serves 6

½ cup blanched finely ground almond flour	¼ cup unsalted butter, softened
½ cup powdered erythritol	1 large egg
2 tablespoons unsweetened cocoa powder	¼ cup chopped pecans
	¼ cup low-carb, sugar-free chocolate chips
½ teaspoon baking powder	

1. In a large mixing bowl, combine the almond flour, erythritol, cocoa powder, and baking powder. Stir in the melted butter and egg until the mixture is well combined. 2. Gently fold in the pecans and chocolate chips. Scoop the mixture into a round baking pan and place the pan into the air fryer basket. 3. Set the air fryer temperature to 300°F (149°C) and bake for 20 minutes. 4. To check if the dessert is fully cooked, insert a toothpick into the center—it should come out clean. Allow the dessert to cool in the pan for 20 minutes to firm up before serving. Enjoy this rich and decadent treat!

Zucchini Bread

Prep time: 10 minutes | Cook time: 40 minutes | Serves 12

2 cups coconut flour	1 teaspoon vanilla extract
2 teaspoons baking powder	3 eggs, beaten
¾ cup erythritol	1 zucchini, grated
½ cup coconut oil, melted	1 teaspoon ground cinnamon
1 teaspoon apple cider vinegar	

1. In a mixing bowl, thoroughly combine the coconut flour, baking powder, erythritol, coconut oil, apple cider vinegar, vanilla extract, eggs, zucchini, and ground cinnamon until a uniform mixture is achieved. 2. Carefully transfer the mixture into the air fryer basket, shaping and flattening it to resemble the form of a loaf of bread. 3. Bake the bread in the air fryer at 350°F (177°C) for 40 minutes, or until it is fully cooked and golden.

Pecan Clusters

Prep time: 10 minutes | Cook time: 8 minutes | Serves 8

3 ounces (85 g) whole shelled pecans
1 tablespoon salted butter, melted
2 teaspoons confectioners' erythritol
½ teaspoon ground cinnamon
½ cup low-carb chocolate chips

1. In a medium bowl, toss the pecans with melted butter until evenly coated. Sprinkle with erythritol and cinnamon, stirring to ensure the pecans are well seasoned. 2. Place the pecans in the air fryer basket without greasing it. Set the air fryer to 350°F (177°C) and cook for 8 minutes, shaking the basket twice during the cooking process to ensure even roasting. The pecans will feel soft at first but will become crunchy as they cool. 3. Line a large baking sheet with parchment paper and set it aside. 4. In a microwave-safe bowl, melt the chocolate in the microwave by heating it in 20-second increments, stirring after each interval until smooth. Place 1 teaspoon of melted chocolate in rounded mounds on the parchment-lined baking sheet. Press one pecan into the top of each chocolate mound, repeating until all the chocolate and pecans are used. 5. Place the baking sheet in the refrigerator to cool for at least 30 minutes, allowing the chocolate to set. Once cooled, store the clusters in a sealed container in the refrigerator for up to 5 days. Enjoy these sweet and crunchy treats!

Double Chocolate Brownies

Prep time: 5 minutes | Cook time: 15 to 20 minutes | Serves 8

1 cup almond flour
½ cup unsweetened cocoa powder
½ teaspoon baking powder
⅓ cup Swerve
¼ teaspoon salt
½ cup unsalted butter, melted and cooled
3 eggs
1 teaspoon vanilla extract
2 tablespoons mini semisweet chocolate chips

1. Preheat the air fryer to 350°F (177°C). Line a cake pan with parchment paper and lightly brush it with oil to prevent sticking. 2. In a large mixing bowl, combine the almond flour, cocoa powder, baking powder, Swerve, and salt. Add the melted butter, eggs, and vanilla extract, stirring until the batter is thick and well combined. Spread the batter evenly into the prepared pan and sprinkle the chocolate chips on top. 3. Air fry for 15 to 20 minutes, or until the edges are set but the center still appears slightly undercooked (this ensures fudgy brownies). Allow the brownies to cool completely in the pan before slicing. Store any leftovers in a covered container in the refrigerator for up to 3 days. Enjoy these rich and decadent brownies!

Olive Oil Cake

Prep time: 10 minutes | Cook time: 30 minutes | Serves 8

2 cups blanched finely ground almond flour
5 large eggs, whisked
¾ cup extra-virgin olive oil
⅓ cup granular erythritol
1 teaspoon vanilla extract
1 teaspoon baking powder

1. In a large mixing bowl, combine all the ingredients and stir until the batter is smooth and well blended. Pour the batter into an ungreased round nonstick baking dish. 2. Place the dish into the air fryer basket. Set the temperature to 300°F (149°C) and bake for 30 minutes, or until the cake is golden on top and firm in the center. 3. Allow the cake to cool in the dish for 30 minutes to set before slicing and serving. Enjoy this simple and delicious dessert!

Baked Apples and Walnuts

Prep time: 6 minutes | Cook time: 20 minutes | Serves 4

4 small Granny Smith apples
⅓ cup chopped walnuts
¼ cup light brown sugar
2 tablespoons butter, melted
1 teaspoon ground cinnamon
½ teaspoon ground nutmeg
½ cup water, or apple juice

1. Cut off the top third of each apple and use a spoon to remove the core and some of the flesh, discarding the scraps. Place the hollowed apples in a small air fryer baking pan. 2. Insert the crisper plate into the basket and place the basket into the air fryer unit. Preheat the unit by selecting the BAKE function, setting the temperature to 350°F (177°C), and setting the timer to 3 minutes. Press START/STOP to begin preheating. 3. In a small bowl, mix together the chopped walnuts, brown sugar, melted butter, cinnamon, and nutmeg. Spoon this mixture into the centers of the hollowed apples, filling them generously. 4. Once the unit is preheated, pour the water into the crisper plate to create steam. Place the baking pan with the apples into the basket. 5. Select the BAKE function again, set the temperature to 350°F (177°C), and set the timer to 20 minutes. Press START/STOP to begin cooking. 6. When the cooking is complete, the apples should be tender when pierced with a fork and the filling should be bubbly. Serve warm and enjoy this comforting and aromatic dessert!

Bourbon Bread Pudding

Prep time: 10 minutes | Cook time: 20 minutes | Serves 4

3 slices whole grain bread, cubed	¼ cup maple syrup, divided
1 large egg	½ teaspoons ground cinnamon
1 cup whole milk	2 teaspoons sparkling sugar
2 tablespoons bourbon	
½ teaspoons vanilla extract	

1. Preheat the air fryer to 270ºF (132ºC). 2. Lightly spray a baking pan with nonstick cooking spray, then arrange the bread cubes in the pan. 3. In a medium bowl, whisk together the egg, milk, bourbon, vanilla extract, 3 tablespoons of maple syrup, and cinnamon. Pour this mixture evenly over the bread cubes, pressing down with a spatula to ensure all the bread is coated. Sprinkle the sparkling sugar on top. Bake in the air fryer for 20 minutes. 4. Remove the pudding from the air fryer and let it cool in the pan on a wire rack for 10 minutes. Drizzle the remaining 1 tablespoon of maple syrup over the top. Slice and serve warm for a comforting and indulgent dessert. Enjoy!

Blackberry Peach Cobbler with Vanilla

Prep time: 10 minutes | Cook time: 20 minutes | Serves 4

Filling:

1 (6-ounce / 170-g) package blackberries	cornstarch
1½ cups chopped peaches, cut into ½-inch thick slices	2 tablespoons coconut sugar
2 teaspoons arrowroot or	1 teaspoon lemon juice

Topping:

2 tablespoons sunflower oil	⅓ cup whole-wheat pastry flour
1 tablespoon maple syrup	1 teaspoon cinnamon
1 teaspoon vanilla	¼ teaspoon nutmeg
3 tablespoons coconut sugar	⅛ teaspoon sea salt
½ cup rolled oats	

1. Begin by preparing the filling: In a baking pan, mix together the blackberries, peaches, arrowroot, coconut sugar, and lemon juice. 2. Use a rubber spatula to thoroughly blend the ingredients until they are evenly combined. Once done, set the mixture aside. 3. For the topping, start by preheating the air fryer to 320ºF (160ºC). 4. In a separate mixing bowl, combine the oil, maple syrup, and vanilla, stirring until well mixed. Gradually whisk in the remaining ingredients until a smooth consistency is achieved. Spread this topping mixture evenly over the prepared filling. 5. Carefully place the pan into the air fryer basket and bake for approximately 20 minutes, or until the topping turns crispy and achieves a golden brown color. Serve the dish warm for the best flavor.

Homemade Mint Pie

Prep time: 15 minutes | Cook time: 25 minutes | Serves 2

1 tablespoon instant coffee	3 eggs, beaten
2 tablespoons almond butter, softened	1 teaspoon spearmint, dried
2 tablespoons erythritol	4 teaspoons coconut flour
1 teaspoon dried mint	Cooking spray

1. Lightly coat the air fryer basket with cooking spray to prevent sticking. 2. Next, combine all the ingredients in a mixer bowl, ensuring they are thoroughly blended. 3. Once a smooth and consistent mixture is achieved, carefully transfer it into the prepared air fryer basket, gently flattening it to create an even layer. 4. Cook the pie at 365ºF (185ºC) for 25 minutes, or until it is fully baked and golden.

Butter Flax Cookies

Prep time: 25 minutes | Cook time: 20 minutes | Serves 4

8 ounces (227 g) almond meal	A pinch of coarse salt
2 tablespoons flaxseed meal	1 large egg, room temperature.
1 ounce (28 g) monk fruit	1 stick butter, room temperature
1 teaspoon baking powder	1 teaspoon vanilla extract
A pinch of grated nutmeg	

1. In a mixing bowl, combine the almond meal, flaxseed meal, monk fruit, baking powder, grated nutmeg, and salt, ensuring they are evenly distributed. 2. In another bowl, whisk together the egg, butter, and vanilla extract until smooth and well incorporated. 3. Gradually add the egg mixture to the dry ingredients, stirring until a soft and cohesive dough forms. 4. Roll out the dough and use a cookie cutter of your choice to cut out shapes. Place them in the preheated air fryer and bake at 350ºF (177ºC) for 10 minutes. Then, reduce the temperature to 330ºF (166ºC) and continue baking for an additional 10 minutes. Enjoy your delicious creation! Bon appétit!

Desserts

Gluten-Free Spice Cookies

Prep time: 10 minutes | Cook time: 12 minutes | Serves 4

4 tablespoons (½ stick) unsalted butter, at room temperature
2 tablespoons agave nectar
1 large egg
2 tablespoons water
2½ cups almond flour
½ cup sugar
2 teaspoons ground ginger
1 teaspoon ground cinnamon
½ teaspoon freshly grated nutmeg
1 teaspoon baking soda
¼ teaspoon kosher salt

1. Start by cutting a piece of parchment paper to fit the bottom of the air fryer basket and lining it neatly. 2. In a large bowl, use a hand mixer to beat the butter, agave, egg, and water on medium speed until the mixture becomes light and fluffy. 3. Gradually add the almond flour, sugar, ginger, cinnamon, nutmeg, baking soda, and salt to the mixture, then beat on low speed until all ingredients are thoroughly combined. 4. Shape the dough into 2-tablespoon-sized balls and place them onto the parchment-lined basket, leaving a small gap between each one as they won't spread much. Set the air fryer to 325°F (163°C) and bake for 12 minutes, or until the cookie tops are lightly browned. 5. Carefully transfer the cookies to a wire rack and allow them to cool completely. Store in an airtight container for up to one week to maintain freshness.

Cinnamon Cupcakes with Cream Cheese Frosting

Prep time: 10 minutes | Cook time: 20 to 25 minutes | Serves 6

½ cup plus 2 tablespoons almond flour
2 tablespoons low-carb vanilla protein powder
⅛ teaspoon salt
1 teaspoon baking powder
¼ teaspoon ground cinnamon
Cream Cheese Frosting:
4 ounces (113 g) cream cheese, softened
2 tablespoons unsalted butter, softened
½ teaspoon vanilla extract
¼ cup unsalted butter
¼ cup Swerve
2 eggs
½ teaspoon vanilla extract
2 tablespoons heavy cream

2 tablespoons powdered Swerve
1 to 2 tablespoons heavy cream

1. Begin by preheating the air fryer to 320°F (160°C). Lightly grease 6 silicone muffin cups with oil and set them aside for later use. 2. In a medium-sized bowl, mix together the almond flour, protein powder, salt, baking powder, and cinnamon, then set this dry mixture aside. 3. Using a stand mixer equipped with a paddle attachment, beat the butter and Swerve until the mixture becomes creamy. Add the eggs, vanilla, and heavy cream, and continue beating until everything is well combined. Gradually incorporate the dry flour mixture into the butter mixture in two parts, mixing after each addition, until a smooth and creamy batter forms. 4. Evenly distribute the batter among the prepared muffin cups, filling each about three-fourths full. Place the muffin cups in the air fryer and cook for 20 to 25 minutes, or until a toothpick inserted into the center of a cupcake comes out clean. Once baked, transfer the cupcakes to a cooling rack and allow them to cool completely. 5. For the cream cheese frosting, use the stand mixer with the paddle attachment to beat the cream cheese, butter, and vanilla until the mixture becomes fluffy. Add the Swerve and mix again until fully incorporated. 6. While the mixer is running, add the heavy cream one tablespoon at a time until the frosting reaches a smooth and creamy consistency. Frost the cooled cupcakes as desired and enjoy!

Appendix 1
Air Fryer Cooking Chart

Beef

Item	Temp (°F)	Time (mins)	Item	Temp (°F)	Time (mins)
Beef Eye Round Roast (4 lbs.)	400 °F	45 to 55	Meatballs (1-inch)	370 °F	7
Burger Patty (4 oz.)	370 °F	16 to 20	Meatballs (3-inch)	380 °F	10
Filet Mignon (8 oz.)	400 °F	18	Ribeye, bone-in (1-inch, 8 oz)	400 °F	10 to 15
Flank Steak (1.5 lbs.)	400 °F	12	Sirloin steaks (1-inch, 12 oz)	400 °F	9 to 14
Flank Steak (2 lbs.)	400 °F	20 to 28			

Chicken

Item	Temp (°F)	Time (mins)	Item	Temp (°F)	Time (mins)
Breasts, bone in (1 ¼ lb.)	370 °F	25	Legs, bone-in (1 ¾ lb.)	380 °F	30
Breasts, boneless (4 oz)	380 °F	12	Thighs, boneless (1 ½ lb.)	380 °F	18 to 20
Drumsticks (2 ½ lb.)	370 °F	20	Wings (2 lb.)	400 °F	12
Game Hen (halved 2 lb.)	390 °F	20	Whole Chicken	360 °F	75
Thighs, bone-in (2 lb.)	380 °F	22	Tenders	360 °F	8 to 10

Pork & Lamb

Item	Temp (°F)	Time (mins)	Item	Temp (°F)	Time (mins)
Bacon (regular)	400 °F	5 to 7	Pork Tenderloin	370 °F	15
Bacon (thick cut)	400 °F	6 to 10	Sausages	380 °F	15
Pork Loin (2 lb.)	360 °F	55	Lamb Loin Chops (1-inch thick)	400 °F	8 to 12
Pork Chops, bone in (1-inch, 6.5 oz)	400 °F	12	Rack of Lamb (1.5 – 2 lb.)	380 °F	22

Fish & Seafood

Item	Temp (°F)	Time (mins)	Item	Temp (°F)	Time (mins)
Calamari (8 oz)	400 °F	4	Tuna Steak	400 °F	7 to 10
Fish Fillet (1-inch, 8 oz)	400 °F	10	Scallops	400 °F	5 to 7
Salmon, fillet (6 oz)	380 °F	12	Shrimp	400 °F	5
Swordfish steak	400 °F	10			

Vegetables

INGREDIENT	AMOUNT	PREPARATION	OIL	TEMP	COOK TIME
Asparagus	2 bunches	Cut in half, trim stems	2 Tbsp	420°F	12-15 mins
Beets	1½ lbs	Peel, cut in ½-inch cubes	1Tbsp	390°F	28-30 mins
Bell peppers (for roasting)	4 peppers	Cut in quarters, remove seeds	1Tbsp	400°F	15-20 mins
Broccoli	1 large head	Cut in 1-2-inch florets	1Tbsp	400°F	15-20 mins
Brussels sprouts	1lb	Cut in half, remove stems	1Tbsp	425°F	15-20 mins
Carrots	1lb	Peel, cut in ¼-inch rounds	1 Tbsp	425°F	10-15 mins
Cauliflower	1 head	Cut in 1-2-inch florets	2 Tbsp	400°F	20-22 mins
Corn on the cob	7 ears	Whole ears, remove husks	1 Tbps	400°F	14-17 mins
Green beans	1 bag (12 oz)	Trim	1 Tbps	420°F	18-20 mins
Kale (for chips)	4 oz	Tear into pieces, remove stems	None	325°F	5-8 mins
Mushrooms	16 oz	Rinse, slice thinly	1 Tbps	390°F	25-30 mins
Potatoes, russet	1½ lbs	Cut in 1-inch wedges	1 Tbps	390°F	25-30 mins
Potatoes, russet	1lb	Hand-cut fries, soak 30 mins in cold water, then pat dry	½ -3 Tbps	400°F	25-28 mins
Potatoes, sweet	1lb	Hand-cut fries, soak 30 mins in cold water, then pat dry	1 Tbps	400°F	25-28 mins
Zucchini	1lb	Cut in eighths lengthwise, then cut in half	1 Tbps	400°F	15-20 mins

Appendix 2

Index

A

Air-Fried Mediterranean Vegetable Medley···92
Almond-Roasted Pears···96
Asian-Inspired Roasted Broccoli···85
Asparagus Fries···85
Authentic Scotch Eggs···34
Avocado and Egg Burrito···21

B

Bacon Egg Muffin Sandwiches···13
Bacon-Wrapped Hot Dogs···21
Bacon-Wrapped Pickle Spears···30
Bacon-Wrapped Stuffed Chicken Rolls·52
Bacon Wrapped Pork with Apple Gravy···61
Bacon, Cheese and Pear Stuffed Pork···62
Baked Apples and Walnuts···98
Baked Cabbage Wedges with Cheese···91
Baked Flounder Fillets···70
Baked Scallops with Parmesan Crust···68
Baked Spanakopita Dip···37
Barbecue Ribs···54
Barbecued Shrimp with Spicy Butter Sauce···71
Basil Pesto Fish Pot Pie···69
Beef and Goat Cheese Stuffed Peppers·58
Beef and Tomato Sauce Meatloaf···58
Bell Pepper Egg Bake with Cheese···14
Bell Pepper-Studded Crab Cakes···69
Berry Cheesecake···18
Black Bean Corn Dip···29
Blackberry Peach Cobbler with Vanilla·99
Blue Cheese Steak Salad···59
Bourbon Bread Pudding···99
Broccoli Bacon Cheese Bake···14
Brussels Sprouts with Pecans and Gorgonzola···80
Buffalo Bites···29
Buffalo-Style Crunchy Chicken Strips··49
Butter Flax Cookies···99
Buttery Green Beans···88
Buttery Pork Chops···55

C

Cajun Bacon Pork Loin Fillet···58
Cajun Shrimp···22
Cajun-Style Morning Sausage···12
Calamari with Fiery Sauce···73
Caraway Crusted Beef Steaks···63
Carrot Chips···35
Cauliflower Rice Balls···84
Cauliflower with Lime Juice···83
Cayenne Flounder Cutlets···76
Cheddar Cauliflower Pizza Base···91
Cheese Drops···38
Cheesy Jalapeño Egg Cups···6
Cheesy Loaded Broccoli···79
Cheesy Roasted Sweet Potatoes···18
Chermoula-Roasted Beets···83
Chili Fingerling Potatoes···86
Chinese-Inspired Spareribs···18
Chinese-Style Baby Back Ribs···54
Chinese-Style Ginger-Scallion Fish Fillets···68
Chocolate Soufflés···97
Churro Bites···20
Cilantro-Lime Crispy Shrimp···75
Cinnamon Cupcakes with Cream Cheese Frosting···100
Cinnamon-Apple Chips···35
Cinnamon-Beef Kofta···57
Citrus Sweet Potatoes and Carrots···87
Classic Baked Eggplant Parmesan···93
Classic Cobb Salad with Bacon and Avocado···44
Classic Custard Egg Tarts···16
Classic Fish Burger with Tartar Sauce··71
Classic Melted Queso Dip···25
Corn Dog Muffins···31
Cranberry Turkey Quesadilla Melts···48
Cream Cheese Wontons···29
Creamy Avocado and Tuna Snacks···75
Creamy Avocado Bacon Egg···7
Creamy Bacon Cheese Quiche···6
Creamy Baked Cheese Grits···26
Creamy Basmati Rice Risotto···90
Creamy Butter-Glazed Sweet Potatoes·25
Creamy Chicken Broccoli Bake···47
Creamy Dijon Cod Fillets···67
Creamy Russet Potato Au Gratin···91
Crispy Air-Fried Buffalo Wings···48
Crispy Breaded Beef Cubes···32
Crispy Cajun Dill Pickle Chips···36
Crispy Cheesy Tuna Patties···76
Crispy Chicken Chimichangas···42
Crispy Coconut Crusted Shrimp···72
Crispy Garlic Dill Wings···45
Crispy Garlic Sliced Eggplant···84
Crispy General Tso's Chicken···48
Crispy Israeli Chicken Schnitzel···51
Crispy Mustard-Coated Fish···73
Crispy Roasted Green Beans···27
Crispy South Indian-Style Fried Fish··76
Crispy Southern-Style Fried Okra···24
Crispy Spaghetti Squash Fritters···15
Crunchy Nut Granola···7
Curry Roasted Cauliflower···85

D

Dijon Chicken and Ham Meatballs···43
Dijon Roast Cabbage···86
Dill-and-Garlic Beets···80
Dinner Rolls···83
DIY Breakfast Toaster Pastrie···10
Double Chocolate Brownies···98

E

Easy Rosemary Green Beans···83
Easy Turkey Meatballs···49
Egg-in-Toast Breakfast Cup···15
Eggplant Fries···29

Elephant Ears · 22

F

Fajita Meatball Lettuce Wraps · · · · · · · · · · 61
Fajita-Style Stuffed Chicken · · · · · · · · · · · · 42
Feta and Quinoa Stuffed Mushrooms · · · 38
Fig, Chickpea, and Arugula Salad · · · · · · · 84
Fish and Vegetable Tacos · · · · · · · · · · · · · · · 19
Fresh Beet Salad with Lemon Dressing 26
Fresh Cucumber and Smoked Salmon Salad · 74
Fresh Herb Salmon Burgers · · · · · · · · · · · · 72
Fresh Summer Veggie Rolls · · · · · · · · · · · · · 90
Fried Artichoke Hearts · · · · · · · · · · · · · · · · · · 34
Fried Green Tomatoes · · · · · · · · · · · · · · · · · · 20
Full English Breakfast · · · · · · · · · · · · · · · · · · · 10
Fully Loaded Breakfast Toast · · · · · · · · · · · · 9
Fully Loaded Cauliflower Steak · · · · · · · · · 93

G

Garlic Balsamic London Broil · · · · · · · · · · · 55
Garlic Butter Shrimp · 72
Garlic-Butter French Chicken · · · · · · · · · · · 46
Garlic-Infused Sesame Roasted Carrots 92
Garlic-Infused Zucchini Noodles · · · · · · · · 25
Garlic-Parmesan Croutons · · · · · · · · · · · · · · 33
Garlic-Roasted Tomatoes and Olives · · · 36
Gluten-Free Spice Cookies · · · · · · · · · · · · 100
Goat Cheese-Stuffed Flank Steak · · · · · · · 65
Golden Crispy Fried Chicken Breasts · · 47
Golden Duck with Sweet Cherry Glaze 50
Golden Garlicky Mushrooms · · · · · · · · · · · · 84
Golden Pickles · 82
Greek Lamb Pita Pockets · · · · · · · · · · · · · · · 64
Greek Pork with Tzatziki Sauce · · · · · · · · · 64
Greek Potato Skins with Olives and Feta · 30
Greek Stuffed Tenderloin · · · · · · · · · · · · · · · 61
Greek-Style Eggplant Boats · · · · · · · · · · · · · 92
Grilled Mediterranean Chicken Skewers · 49
Grilled Shrimp with Smoky Tomato Vinaigrette · 69

H

Ham Hock Mac and Cheese · · · · · · · · · · · · 63
Healthy Oat Bran Muffins · · · · · · · · · · · · · · · 8

Herb-Glazed Salmon with Cauliflower Florets · 68
Herb-Infused Lemon Fish en Papillote · 67
Herb-Infused Turkey Sausage Patties · · · 12
Herb-Roasted Mixed Vegetables · · · · · · · · 91
Herb-Roasted Peruvian Chicken · · · · · · · · 51
Herb-Roasted Salmon Fillets · · · · · · · · · · · 75
Herb-Roasted Thanksgiving Turkey Breast · 50
Hoisin BBQ Pork Chops · · · · · · · · · · · · · · · · 65
Homemade Crunchy Croutons · · · · · · · · · 24
Homemade Mint Pie · · · · · · · · · · · · · · · · · · · 99
Individual Cauliflower Crust Pizzas · · · · · 43

I

Italian Herb Chicken with Roma Tomatoes · 50
Italian Lamb Chops with Avocado Mayo · 55
Italian Rice Balls · 33
Italian Sausage and Cheese Meatballs · · 56
Italian Sausage Links · · · · · · · · · · · · · · · · · · · 63

J

Juicy Grilled Beef Brats · · · · · · · · · · · · · · · · · 24

K

Kale and Potato Nuggets · · · · · · · · · · · · · · · 11
Kale Chips with Tex-Mex Dip · · · · · · · · · · 30

L

Lebanese Muhammara · · · · · · · · · · · · · · · · · 39
Lemon and Herb Roasted Chicken · · · · · 44
Lemon Curd Pavlova · · · · · · · · · · · · · · · · · · · 96
Lemon Garlic Shrimp with Zucchini Ribbons · 72
Lemon Shrimp with Garlic Olive Oil · · · 35
Lemon-Garlic Mushrooms · · · · · · · · · · · · · · 82
Lemon-Garlic Roasted Asparagus · · · · · · 26
Lemongrass-Infused Steamed Tuna · · · · 73
Lemony Broccoli · 79
Lemony Pear Chips · 35
Lettuce-Wrapped Savory Turkey Meatballs · 42
Lime Bars · 95
Maple Balsamic Roasted Salmon · · · · · · · 71
Maple Crunch Granola · · · · · · · · · · · · · · · · · · 7

Maple Glazed Doughnuts · · · · · · · · · · · · · · 10
Maple-Pecan Tart with Sea Salt · · · · · · · · 95
Mashed Sweet Potato Tots · · · · · · · · · · · · · 81
Meat and Rice Stuffed Bell Peppers · · · 59
Meatball Subs · 19
Mediterranean Breakfast Gyro Patties · · 15
Mediterranean-Style Olive Pan Pizza · · · 90
Meringue Cookies · 20
Mexican-Style Shredded Beef · · · · · · · · · · 56
Middle Eastern Chicken Shawarma · · 44
Mixed Berry Breakfast Muffin · · · · · · · · · · 13
Mixed Berry Crumble · · · · · · · · · · · · · · · · · · 21
Moroccan Halibut and Chickpea Bowl · 74
Mozzarella Arancini · 33
Mushroom Spinach Bite-Size Quiche · · · 14
Mushrooms with Goat Cheese · · · · · · · · · 86
Mustard Lamb Chops · · · · · · · · · · · · · · · · · · 58

O

Old Bay Chicken Wings · · · · · · · · · · · · · · · · 32
Olive Oil Cake · 98
Oven-Baked Spaghetti Squash · · · · · · · · · 93
Oven-Roasted Zucchini Slices · · · · · · · · · · 90
Paprika-Seasoned Crispy Drumsticks · · · 52

P

Parmesan and Herb Sweet Potatoes · · · · 80
Parmesan French Fries · · · · · · · · · · · · · · · · · 32
Parmesan Herb Filet Mignon · · · · · · · · · · · 63
Parmesan-Thyme Butternut Squash · · · · 87
Parsley Garlic Butter Knots · · · · · · · · · · · · · 25
Pecan Brownies · 97
Pecan Clusters · 98
Peppercorn-Crusted Beef Tenderloin · · · 56
Pepperoni Chicken Cheese Pizza · · · · · · · 52
Pepperoni Pizza Dip · 36
Peppery Chicken Meatballs · · · · · · · · · · · · 38
Phyllo Vegetable Triangles · · · · · · · · · · · · · 18
Poblano Pepper Cheeseburgers · · · · · · · · 64
Pork and Tricolor Vegetables Kebabs · · · 55
Pork Milanese · 60
Pork Stuffing Meatballs · · · · · · · · · · · · · · · · 22
Pork Tenderloin with Avocado Lime Sauce · 60
Poutine with Waffle Fries · · · · · · · · · · · · · · 31
Provolone Stuffed Beef and Pork Meatballs · 56
Puffed Egg Tarts · 19

Pumpkin Pudding with Vanilla Wafers··95

Q

Quick Air Fryer Edamame Snacks ······25

R

Rack of Lamb with Pistachio Crust ······59
Ranch Oyster Snack Crackers············31
Ratatouille ·································87
Red Pepper Tapenade ··················34
Roast Beef with Horseradish Cream ····62
Roasted Brussels Sprouts with Orange and Garlic ····································79
Rosemary New Potatoes ···············81
Roasted Cauliflower Avocado Toast······12
Roasted Cherry Tomatoes with Garlic ··24
Roasted Eggplant ······················79
Roasted Grape Dip·····················31
Roasted Red Pepper and Feta Egg Bake 12
Roasted Salmon with Fennel and Carrot 74
Roasted Snapper with Shallots and Fresh Tomatoes ·······························67
Rosemary-Garlic Shoestring Fries·······33
Rosemary-Roasted Red Potatoes ········88
Rumaki ·································36

S

Satay-Style Chicken Strips ············45
Sausage and Cauliflower Arancini·······57
Sausage and Eggs with Tangy Mustard Sauce ··································13
Savory Tex-Mex Salmon Bowl ·········71
Scallops with Green Vegetables ·······21
Scrambled Tofu with Potato and Broccoli·
···92
Sesame-Ginger Broccoli ···············86
Shrimp Bite-Sized Frittata ·············· 8
Shrimp Egg Rolls ······················37
Simple Herb-Roasted Asparagus ·······26
Simple Zucchini Crisps ···············81
Smoky BBQ Chicken Nuggets·········47

Smoky Chipotle Aioli Wings ············44
Southwestern Roasted Corn ············80
Southwestern Turkey Burgers··········46
Speedy Grilled Shrimp Skewers ·········75
Spiced Apple Cider Donut Holes ······· 9
Spiced Brown Rice Fritters ·············24
Spiced Fennel Chicken Curry ··········51
Spiced Honey-Walnut Carrots ··········86
Spiced Raisin Bagels ·················· 7
Spiced Turkish Chicken Skewers·······43
Spicy Bacon Breakfast Pizza············13
Spicy Black Bean Tomato Chili ········92
Spicy Cajun Lemon Cod Fillets ········68
Spicy Cheddar Jalapeño Cornbread ·····26
Spicy Chicken Bites ··················34
Spicy Crispy Fried Okra ···············93
Spicy Fish Tacos with Lime Jalapeño Drizzle··································70
Spicy Jalapeño Chicken Bites··········41
Spicy Merguez-Style Meatballs·········52
Spicy Shrimp Tortilla Wraps ···········73
Spicy Tortilla Chips ··················30
Spinach and Cheese-Stuffed Chicken ··46
Spinach and Crab Meat Cups ··········37
Spinach and Provolone Steak Rolls ·····62
Spinach Bacon Egg Bites ·············14
Spring Veggie Strata ·················11
Steak and Vegetable Kebabs ··········20
Steak Tips and Potatoes ···············19
Steakhouse Eggs and Strips ···········11
Steaks with Walnut-Blue Cheese Butter 57
Steamed Mussels in Apple Cider ·······75
Stuffed Fried Mushrooms··············32
Stuffed Hash Browns with Mushrooms and Tomatoes ························· 8
Stuffed Tomatoes with Tuna Salad ······77
Swedish Meatloaf······················54
Sweet and Crispy Roasted Pearl Onions 85
Sweet and Spicy Country-Style Ribs ··65
Sweet and Spicy Korean Wings·········41
Sweet and Tangy Pineapple Peach Chicken································41

Sweet Honey-Glazed Baked Salmon ····76
Sweet Pepper Nachos with Melted Cheese
···90
Sweet Potato Breakfast Hash············· 6
Sweet Squash Ricotta Frittata ··········15
Sweet Teriyaki Glazed Cauliflower ·····91

T

Tamarind Sweet Potatoes ···············82
Tandoori Salmon with Roasted Potatoes 69
Thai Peanut Chicken Tacos············45
Tingly Chili-Roasted Broccoli ··········81
Toasted Cheese and Chile Bites········24
Tofu Bites ·····························82
Traditional Canadian Poutine ··········27
Traditional Hungarian Goulash ········47
Triple-Berry Oven Pancake ············ 8
Tropical Crab Cakes with Mango Aioli ·70
Twice-Dipped Cinnamon Biscuits ······· 6

U

Ultimate Everything Bagels ············ 9

V

Vanilla Scones························97
Veggie Shrimp Toast ·················38
Veggie Spinach and Carrot Bites ·······27
Veggie Tuna Melts····················22
Veggie-Packed Broccoli Mushroom Frittata·································11
White Chocolate Cookies··············96
Zesty Fried Asparagus·················87
Zesty Lemon and Blueberry Muffins···10
Zesty Lemon Herb Chicken ············48
Zesty Lemon Pepper Grilled Shrimp····67
Zesty London Broil ··················60
Zesty Old Bay Air Fried Shrimp········27
Zucchini Boats Stuffed with Cheese ····93
Zucchini Bread························97

Printed in Great Britain
by Amazon